ARTIST'S PROJECTS YOU CAN PAINT

10 Secret Gardens in Watercolor

by Betty Ganley

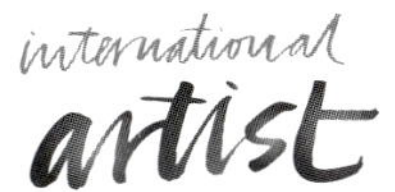

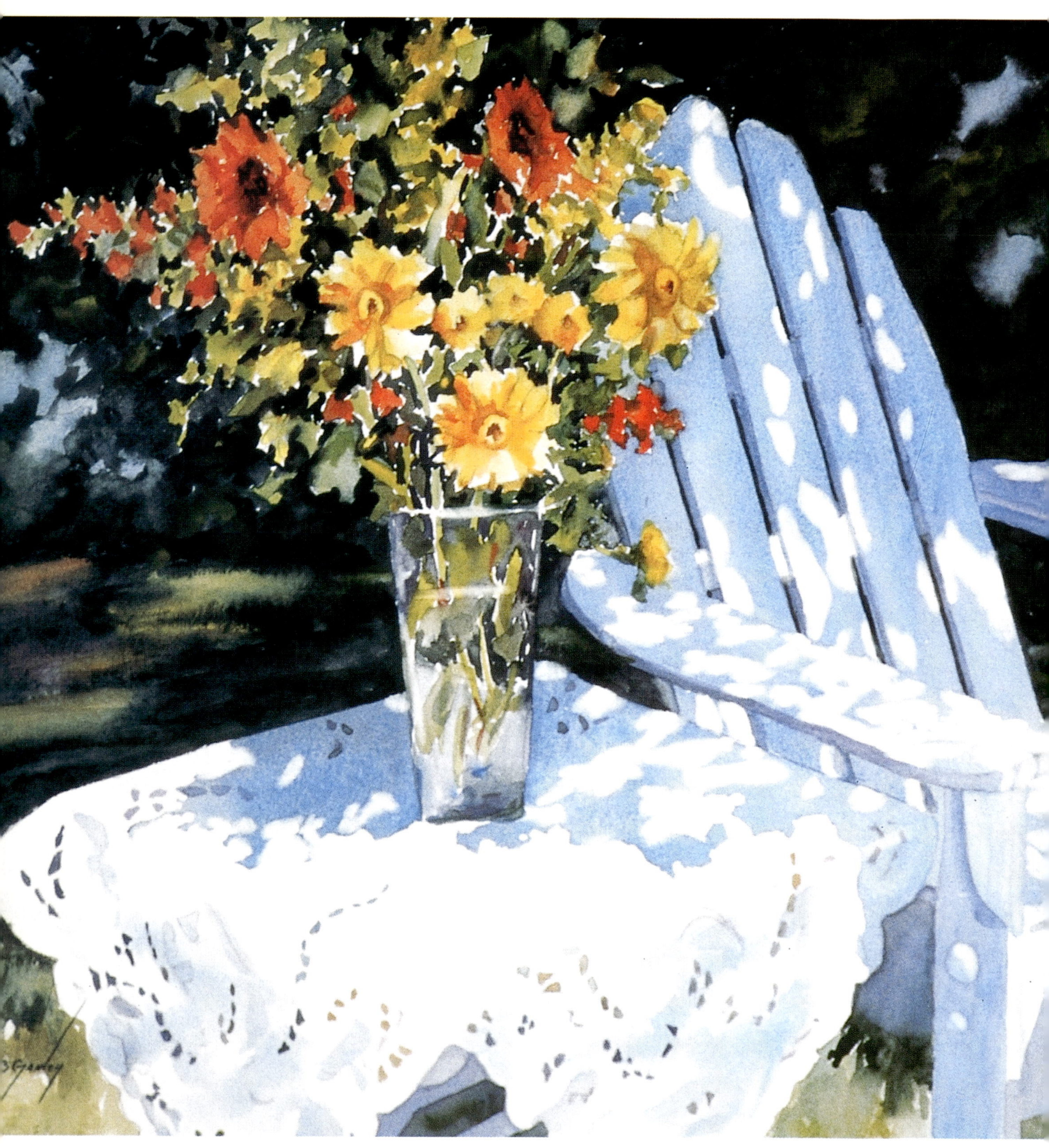

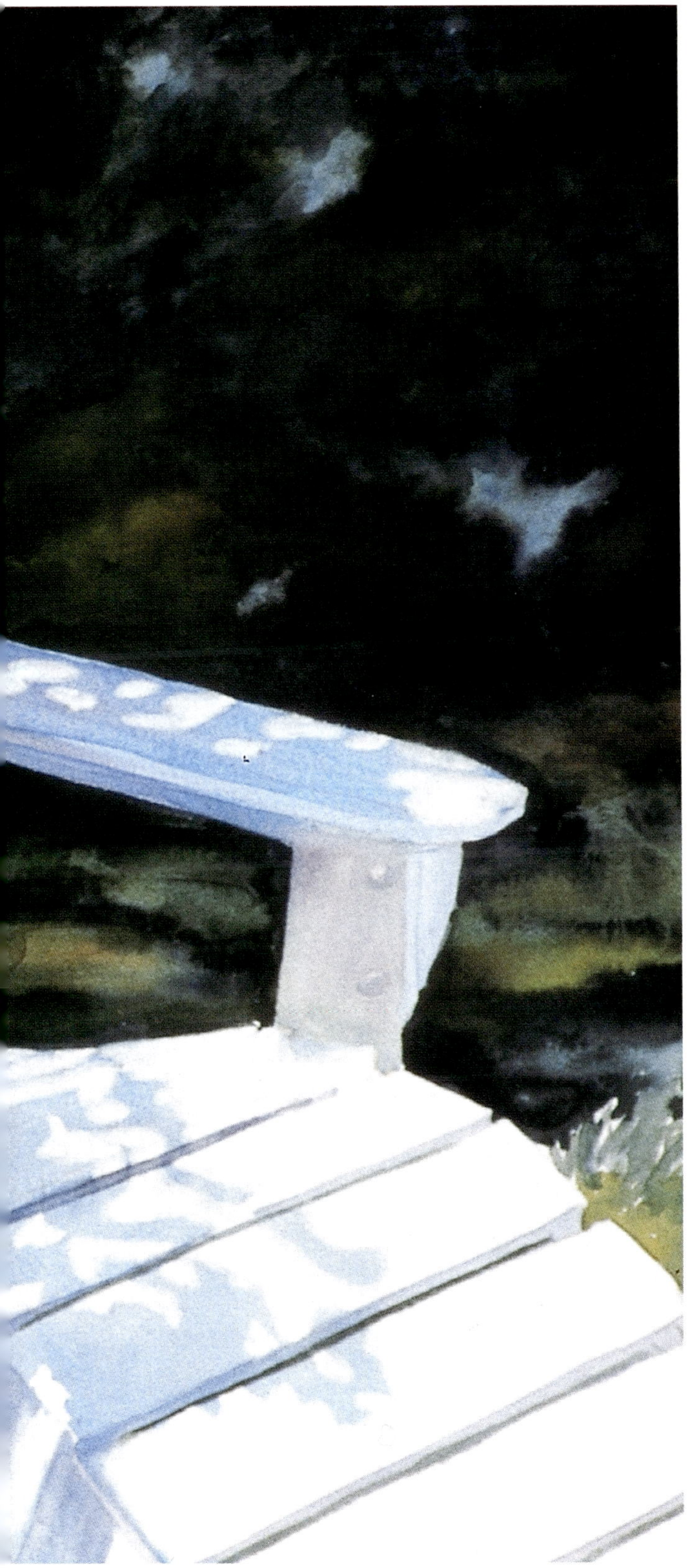

ARTIST'S PROJECTS YOU CAN PAINT

10 Secret Gardens in Watercolor

by Betty Ganley

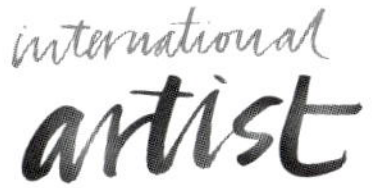

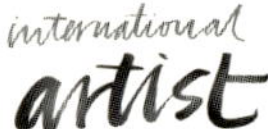

International Artist Publishing, Inc
2775 Old Highway 40
P.O. Box 1450
Verdi, Nevada 89439

Website: www.internationalartist.com

Edited by Terri Dodd
Designed by Vincent Miller
Typeset by Reid Helms and Lisa Rowsell

ISBN 1-929834-53-5

Printed in Hong Kong
First printed in 2005
08 07 06 05 6 5 4 3 2 1

Dedication

This book is dedicated to Marge and Walter Kenney, my parents. Dad, who can fix anything and who instilled in me his love of books, and Mom, who oohed and aahed over every stroke of my brushes as I learned to paint. To this day my very first paintings still hang in their home, and everyone should be so lucky to have the kind of love, praise and encouragement that they gave me.

This book is also dedicated to my darling granddaughters, Erin and Rachel Ganley, with the hope that they too may experience the pure joy of doing the work they love.

Acknowledgments

My sincerest thanks to all who have encouraged me over the years, and special thanks to Terri Dodd, who started me on the fascinating process that brought this book to fruition, and Vincent Miller, for believing in my abilities.

Raspberry Sorbet

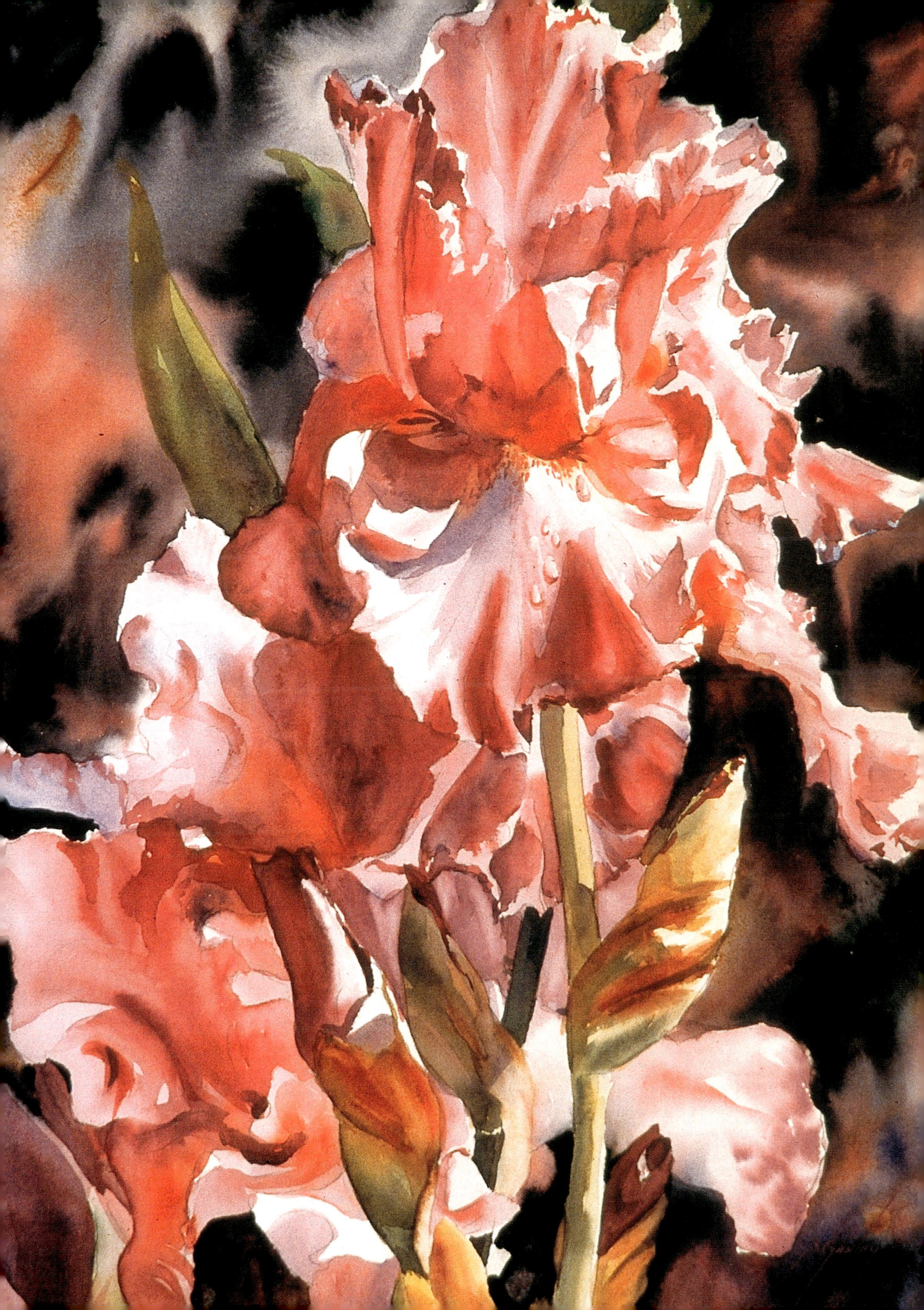

CONTENTS

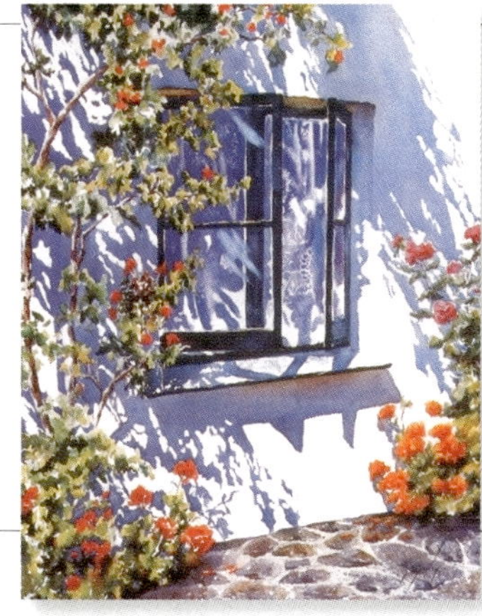

14 **PROJECT 1**
THE COURTYARD GARDEN
How to introduce colorful shadows for vitality and depth

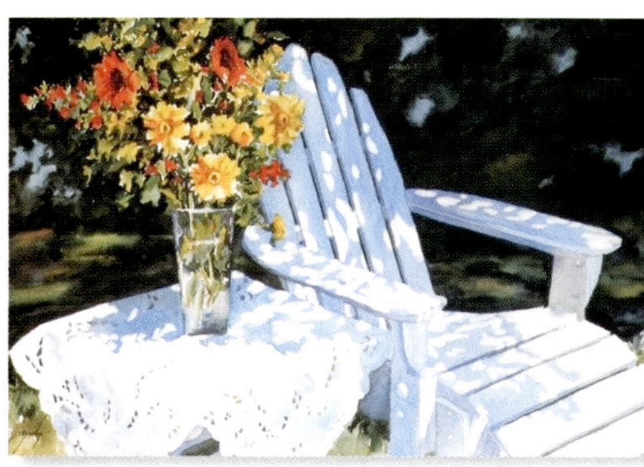

22 **PROJECT 2**
BACKYARD INVITATION
How to paint opaque backgrounds to intensify your subject

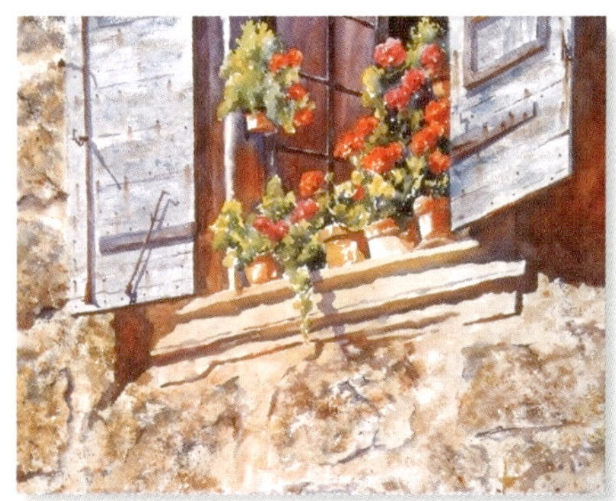

30 **PROJECT 3**
WINDOW GARDEN OF FRANCE
How to incorporate the rugged textures of old wood and stone in your garden scenes

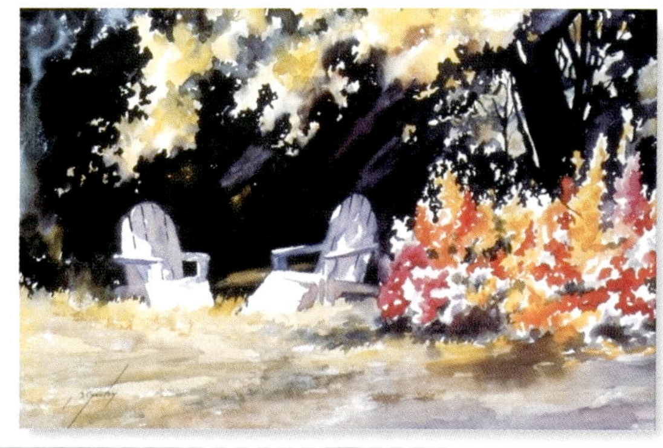

38 **PROJECT 4**
THE SECRET GARDEN
How to deal with competing centers of interest

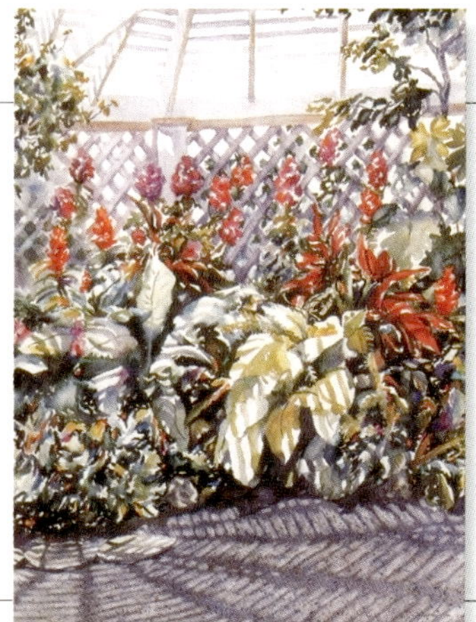

46 **PROJECT 5**
THE ORCHID GAZEBO
How to achieve balance in a painting

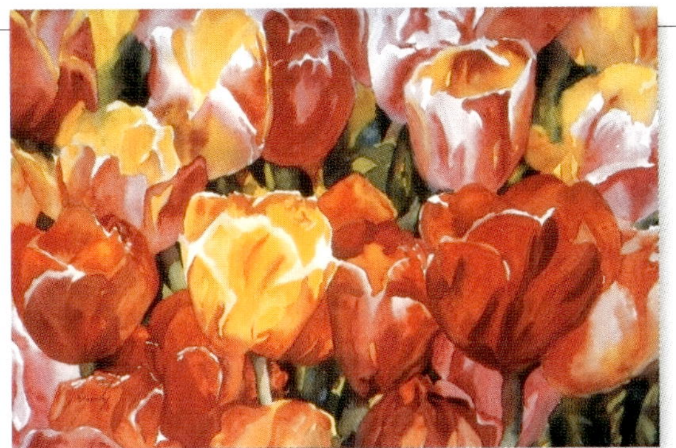

54 **PROJECT 6**
FESTIVAL OF COLOR
How to build up glazes to give color, form and substance

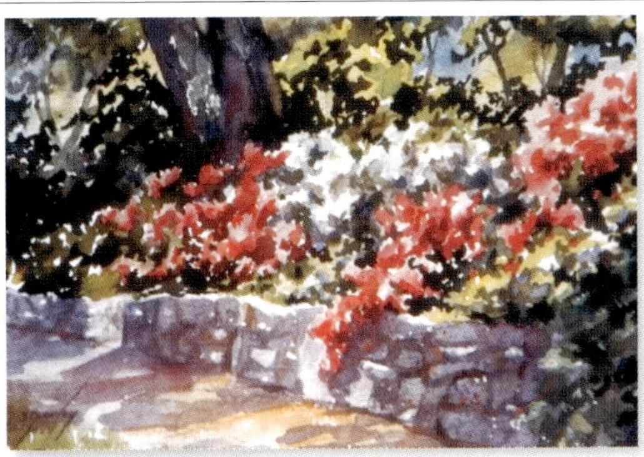

62 **PROJECT 7**
DAPPLED LIGHT IN ARLINGTON
How to create the look of dappled sunlight

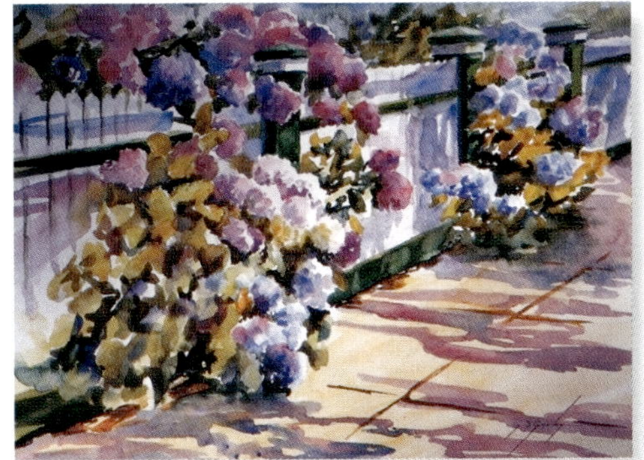

70 **PROJECT 8**
BURSTING OUT ALL OVER
How to repeat a main color combination for unity

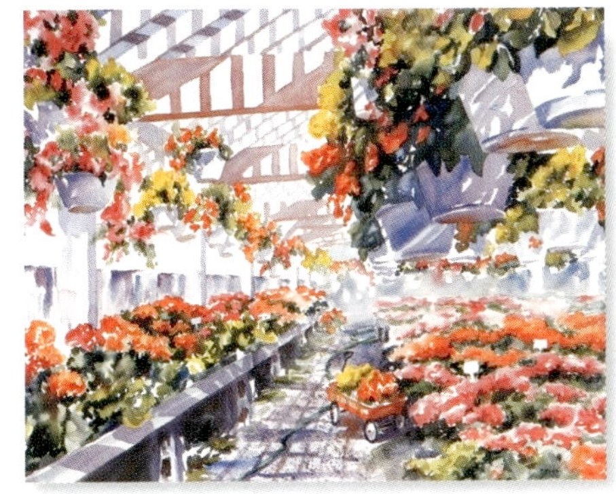

78 **PROJECT 9**
BURST OF SPRING
How to use tonal value to achieve depth

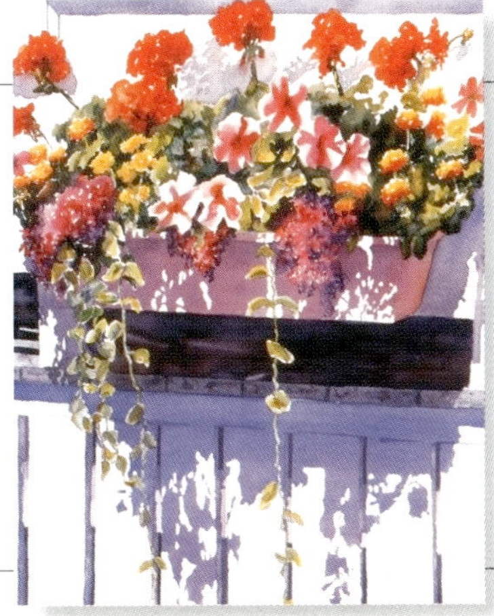

86 **PROJECT 10**
DIPPED IN COLOR
How to use strong color and tonal values to add drama

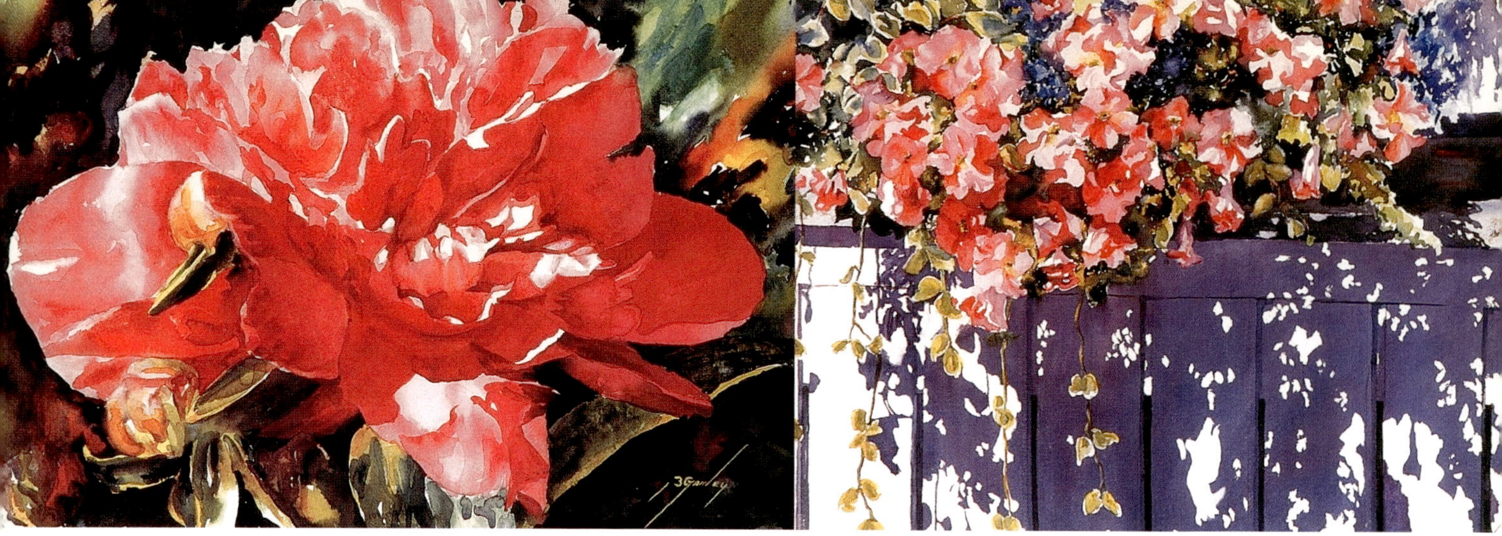

Rasperry Parfait

Sparkling Shadows

INTRODUCTION

Many years ago I turned to watercolor after painting in oils, mostly because I had no studio in which I could leave in-progress projects, but also because I had young children. A card table in a guest room was it. Watercolor was a great solution!

The ease of a fast set-up and break-down and the only medium being water made watercolor ideal. But to relearn techniques was a long process. My colors would always run together, and in those early days I turned out many a "brown mess." The trick turned out to be mastering the amount of **wetness in the paper** versus the amount of **water in the brush**.

There were also a few other breakthroughs for me. One was relearning and really understanding the basic rules of **composition**. Another breakthrough occurred when I purchased a 35-mm **camera** with a removable 27-210mm lens. I had no desire to become a professional photographer, I just wanted a record of things I happened to see. Any manipulation would be done with a brush. To this day my camera, set on automatic, goes with me everywhere. Project 7 in this book would not have happened if I hadn't had my camera and **sketchbook** when I saw that scene. The sun was moving fast. It was one of those "screech on the brakes" scenes. Within ten minutes I had my photos and a quick sketch. And there's another reason to have your camera and sketchbook with you wherever you go: Project 9 in this book was a garden center near my home, and I was very glad to have taken pictures because when the center was sold the new owners roofed the area, eliminating forever the magic of all the beam shadows.

Yet another great breakthrough for me as I became a watercolor painter was the world of **travel**. Up until that time my travel experience had been nil. But I kept hearing other artists talk about all the wonderful material to be found in places like Cape Anne in Massachusetts, and along the coast of Maine. So off I finally went! And after coastal Maine I signed up for **workshops** in France and England, where the fabulous flowers, gardens, countryside and small ancient fishing villages captured my heart. The sheer excitement of experiencing new places is a very powerful stimulation for your creativity, and without that travel most of the paintings in this book would not exist.

Garden painting secrets

Over the years I've found that my favorite subjects are flowers, gardens, and marine subjects of all kinds, and this book shares secrets I discovered. One of the secrets to capturing garden scenes is to paint **overlapping masses** of flowers rather than individual blooms. Another secret is to find your own **scale**. If you're intimidated by dealing with an entire garden bursting with colors, then there are always more intimate corners of the garden that will offer you virtually readymade compositions. And if a corner is still too big, you'll always find a single perfect flower that's shaded to perfection—or even a small abstract section of one flower.

The most spectacular gardens don't happen by accident. A great deal of planning and care go into their creation and perfection. The same is true with paintings, and in this book are all my most important secrets for how to plan and create spectacular watercolor paintings of gardens. But perhaps my single greatest secret is that the best gardens are themselves secret! The title of this book, 10 Secret Gardens in Watercolor, comes from the one pictured in Project 3, a small corner of my own backyard that no one but me can see. That's because while the setting and chairs do exist, the flowers exist only in my imagination.

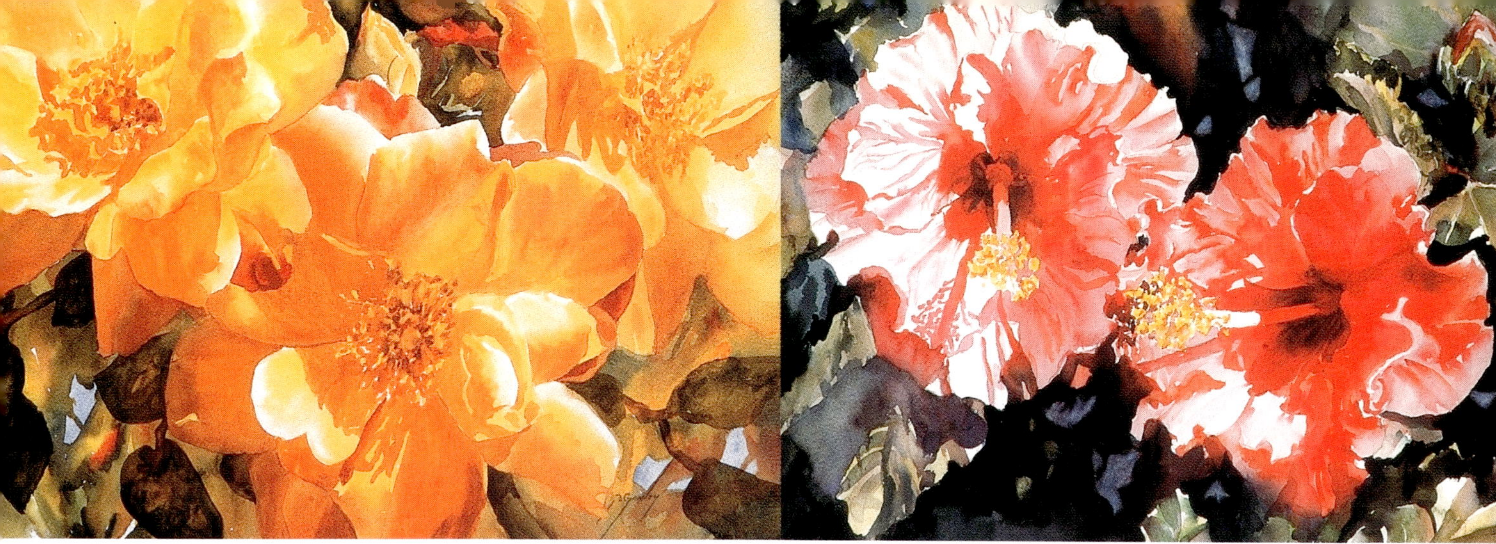

Sunbeams

Tropical Whispers

A Colorful Welcome

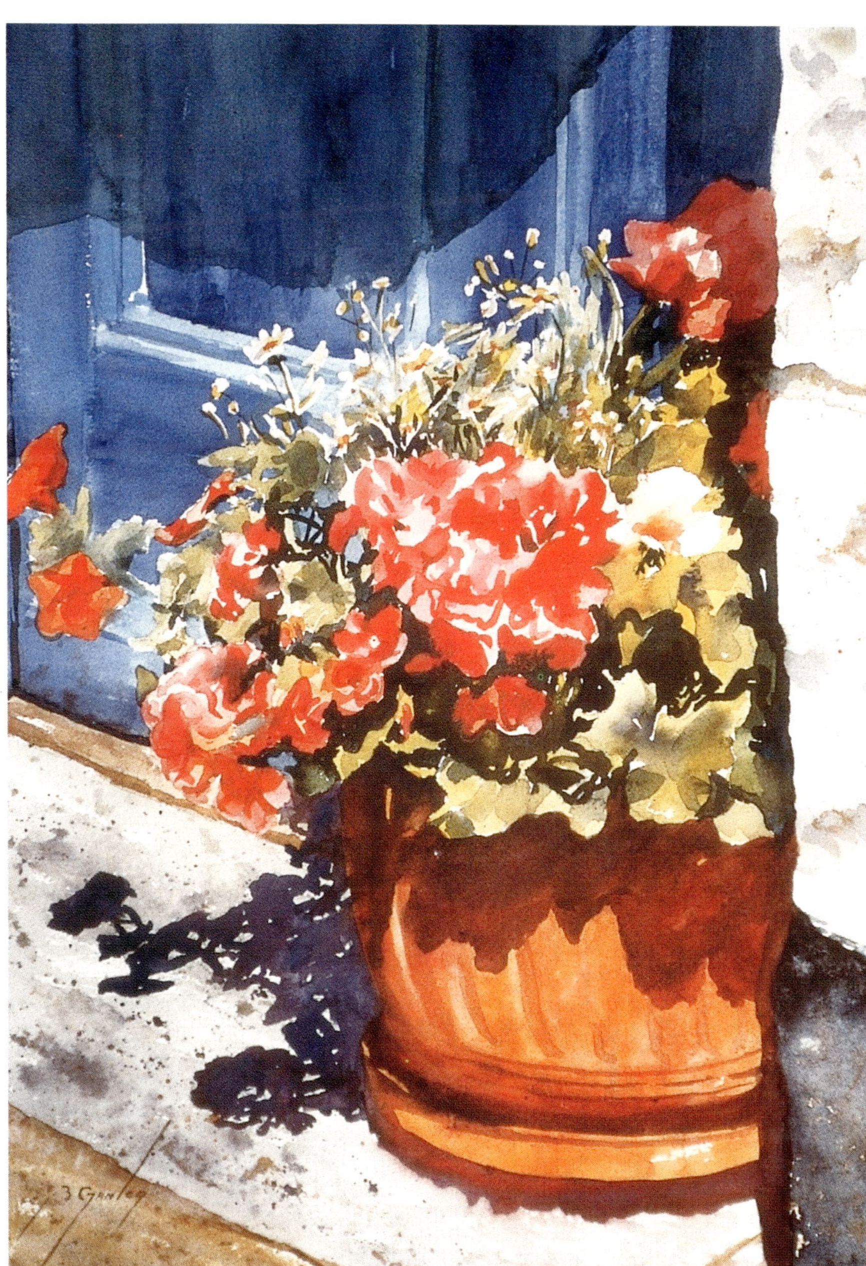

Copyright warning!

Artist Betty Ganley has generously supplied some exceptional paintings for you to copy. She knows that it is only through practice that skill is built. However, when you copy these paintings, please respect the artist's copyright. Other than for educational purposes, it is against the law to make copies of another artist's work and pass it off as your own. So, by all means show your finished versions of the projects to your family and friends, but please do not sign them as your own, exhibit them, or attempt to sell them as your own work.

Materials you will need to paint every project in this book

It is important to use artist quality materials because they will give you the best results. You may save a few dollars at first by using student grade supplies, but your painting will suffer. The colors will be weaker and duller, and you won't be able to control them as well. Paint won't lift or flow as well on poor-quality paper, and cheap brushes will shed bristles while making it difficult to manipulate your paint. Artist quality materials will work with you, not against you. The beauty of using artist quality colors is that because they are pure pigment not mixed with extenders they will last a long time.

When you reach a level of comfort and familiarity with artist quality materials, you will be able to focus all your energy on creating a beautiful painting, rather than the mechanics of manipulating paint on paper.

All the colors you need are listed. I have mostly given their generic names making it easier for you to match them. You may have most of these colors already, but they may be called by different brand names. Simply compare the colors shown here with what you have, then go shopping for the others.

PAPER

I advise you to buy artist quality watercolor paper from an art shop because it has been manufactured so that watercolor pigment will stick to it and not run off. The paper will work for you, not against you. Using cheap paper will rob you of some of the beautiful effects that are so important in watercolor painting. For the projects you will need.

- 140lb cold press watercolor paper
- 140lb rough watercolor paper
- 140lb hot pressed watercolor paper

What you should know about paper preparation for the projects in this book

I will give you three alternatives, so choose the method that suits you best. Ideally, and to build your knowledge of the medium, you should eventually try all three methods.

1. Paint on paper blocks

You can buy top quality watercolor paper padded in blocks that are gummed on all sides. These are perfect for taking along for on-site painting because the pad backing supports the paper and the gum prevents the paper from buckling. Work on this blocks dry, and if you want to work wet-in-wet, all you have to do is use a big clean brush and wet the paper with clean water, roll off excess water with a clean towel then start your initial washes. These blocks come in a variety of sizes. Start small first.

2. Paint on stretched sheets

Most professional artists stretch their paper to prevent it from buckling when it is wet — especially when they are working on a large scale.

- To stretch paper, soak it in the bath for about 5-10 minutes.
- To make sure both sides of the paper get wet, flip the paper over, but don't soak for too long because the important surface size that helps the pigment cling to the paper will release.
- Be careful when you handle it, because the paper could tear. Hold the paper up by the very edges and very gently remove it from the bath.
- Lay the paper face down on a piece of Gator board.
- Use a rolled-up towel to remove the excess water, leaving the paper still quite damp.
- Turn the paper face-up and roll that side.
- Then use masking tape or staple the edges to your Gator board, spacing the staples about an inch apart. (Gator board "absorbs" staple holes, so you can keep on using the same board over again for a long time.)

3. Paint on unstretched paper

Simply tape or staple your paper to your Gator board making sure it is completely flat and taut. Paint on the dry paper, or if you want to apply wet-in-wet washes, first use a big clean brush and wet the paper with clean water. Roll excess moisture off with your towel and begin applying your washes. Some initial washes can be applied on dry paper.

BRUSHES

- Daniel Smith 22-50 Series, Size #8 and #10
- Pro Arte Series 100, Size #12
- Fritch Scrubber (a stiff white nylon bristle brush with very short bristles,
- sold through Cheap Joe's catalog)
- Stiff round brush for mask application
- ¼", ½" and 1" flat brushes
- 2" hake

PALETTE

You will need a palette with many decent sized wells and sufficient mixing area.

WATER

- Use one jar to clean your brush and one jar of clean water for mixing paint.
- Atomizer

TOWEL

Have an old towel handy to wipe excess moisture from your brush as required, and another clean towel to roll off excess water from your paper.

OTHER MATERIALS

- No. 2 Pencils
- Tracing paper
- Tinted masking fluid
- Mask remover (optional)
- Mild shampoo (for protecting mask brush)
- Sponge
- Palette knife

artist quality watercolors

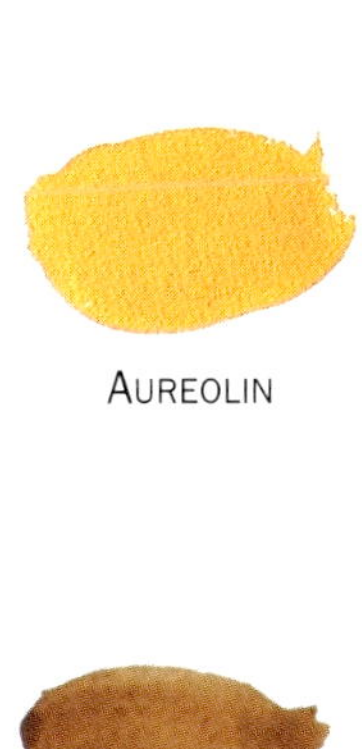

Aureolin

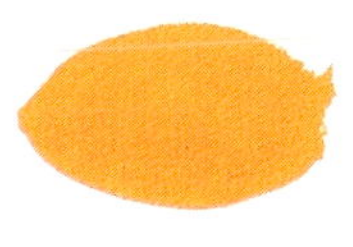

New Gamboge

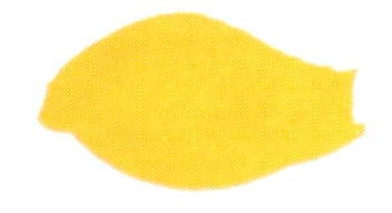

Cadmium Yellow Light

Cadmium Yellow

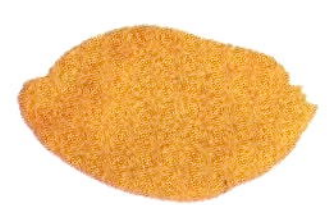

Raw Sienna

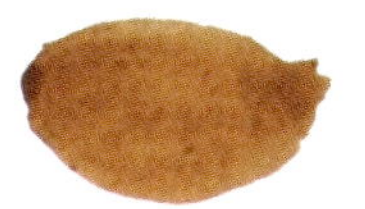

Raw Umber

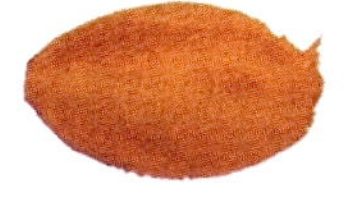

Burnt Sienna

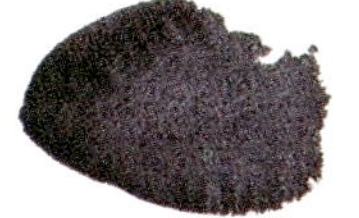

Payne's Grey

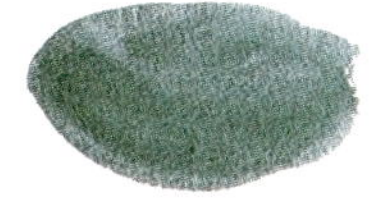

Viridian

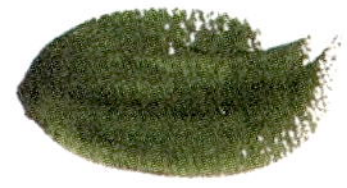

Sap Green

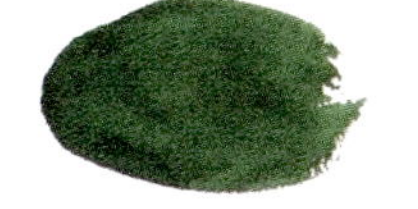

Hooker's Green Dark

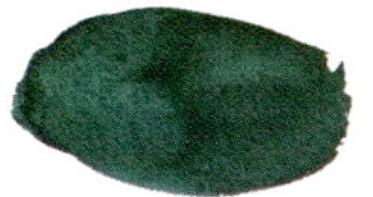

Phthalo Green

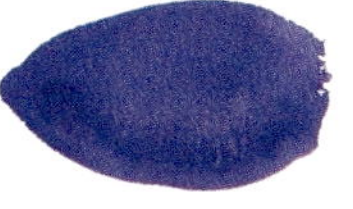

Cobalt Blue

Cerulean Blue

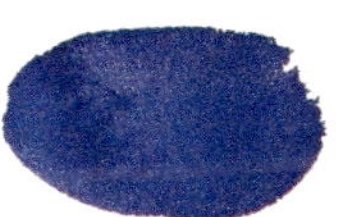

Phthalo Blue

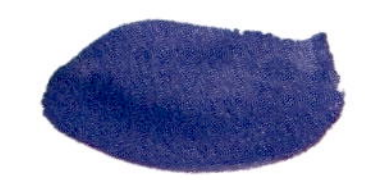

Ultramarine Blue

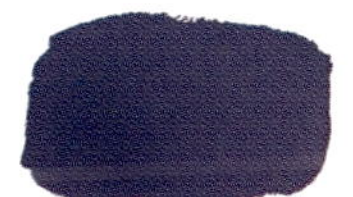

Prussian Blue

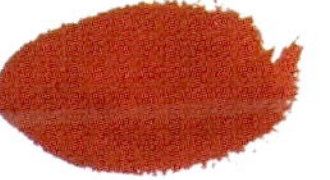

Permanent Rose

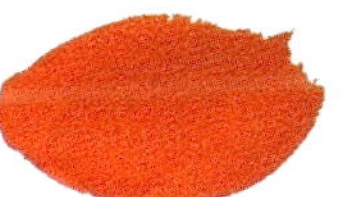

Cadmium Scarlet

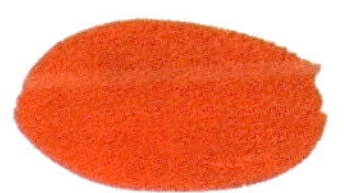

Cadmium Red

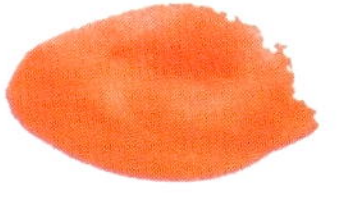

Scarlet Lake

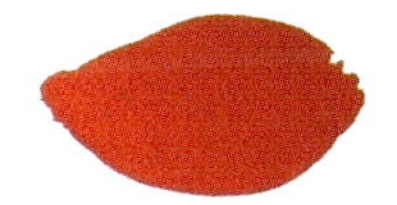

Permanent Red Deep

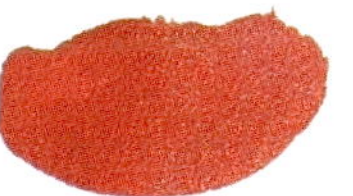

Quinacridone Red

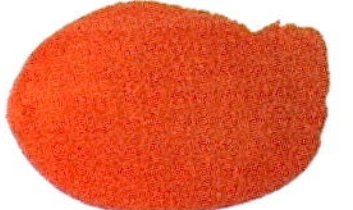

Windsor Red

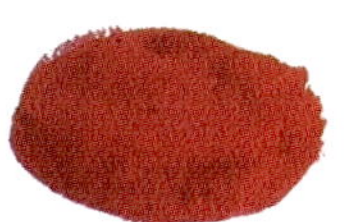

Quinacridone Rose

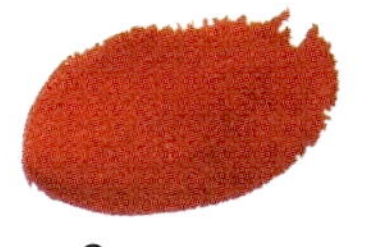

Quinacridone (Alizarin Crimson)

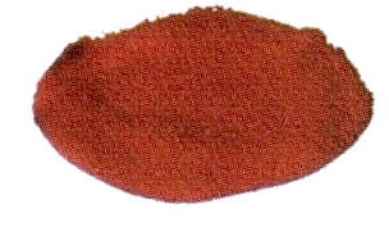

Carmine

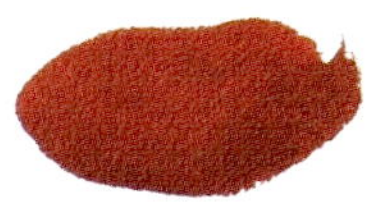

Quinacridone Magenta

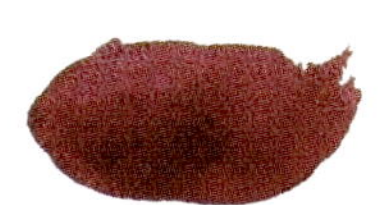

Permanent Magenta

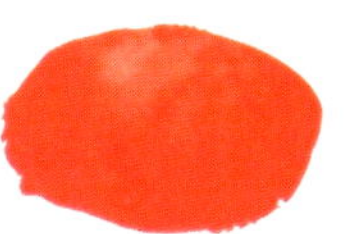

Cadmium Orange

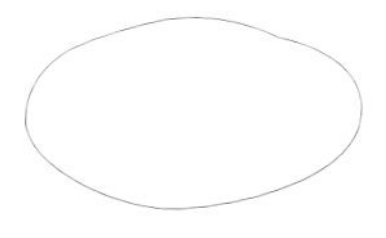

Permanent White Gouache

Techniques

Painting WET, MOIST, DAMP or DRY

Learning when to paint on wet, moist, damp paper or dry paper is one of the important lessons in watercolor painting.

Dry paper

This is the easiest stage to work on because it lasts forever, so you can take your time.

- For hard edged shapes and for dry brushing.
- Drawing, scraping and making lines.
- For creating sharp effects and details,
- If you move your brush quickly over dry paper you can create broken edges and textured effects.

Damp paper

On this nearly dry paper it is too easy to create unwanted "cauliflowers" or explosions, particularly if there is already a wash on the surface. When working on damp paper, use thicker consistency paint and fewer brushstrokes.

- For broken edges and shapes.
- A good time to lift pigment and to scratch out.

Moist paper

You can recognize this by its sheen. But work quickly.

- For soft, controlled edge shapes.
- Best for misty effects, shaping and blending.

Wet paper

This allows you to mix colors on the paper by letting them run into each other. You can made gradated washes, achieve granulation, create soft, lost edge shapes and generally play with washes using thinner mixtures.

- For soft, "lost" or uncontrolled edges.

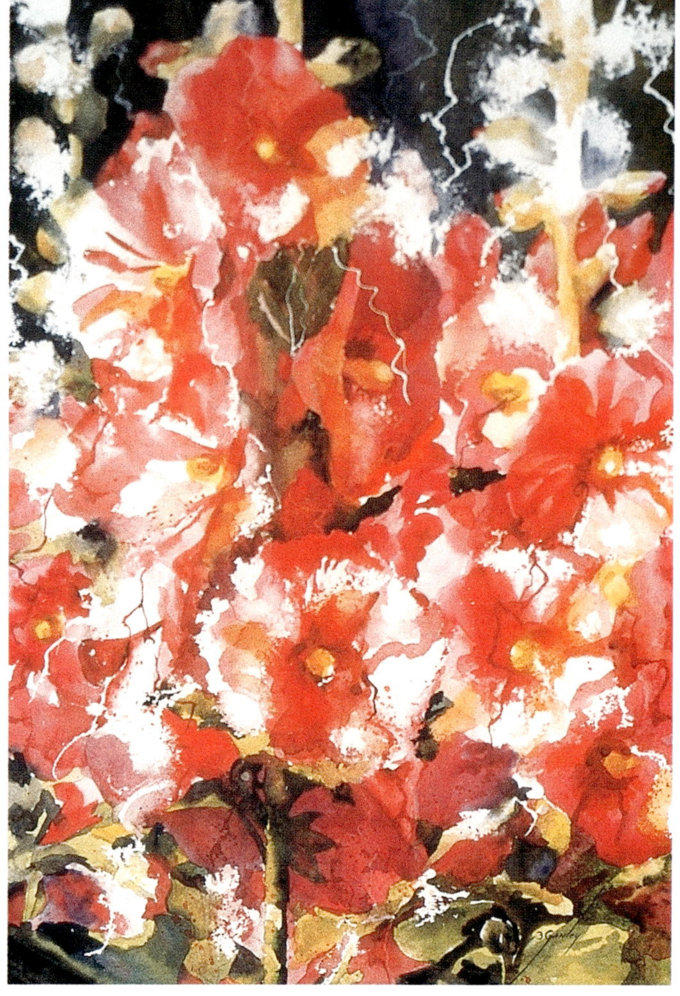

Hollyhock Festival

Amount of pigment compared to water

Your initial washes should be very watery (like tea), then use less water as you build up the painting through milky consistency to full cream — more pigment than water — which is perfect for making powerful, strong color notes. Eventually you will finish the painting by applying details and accents using full tone pigment and no water.

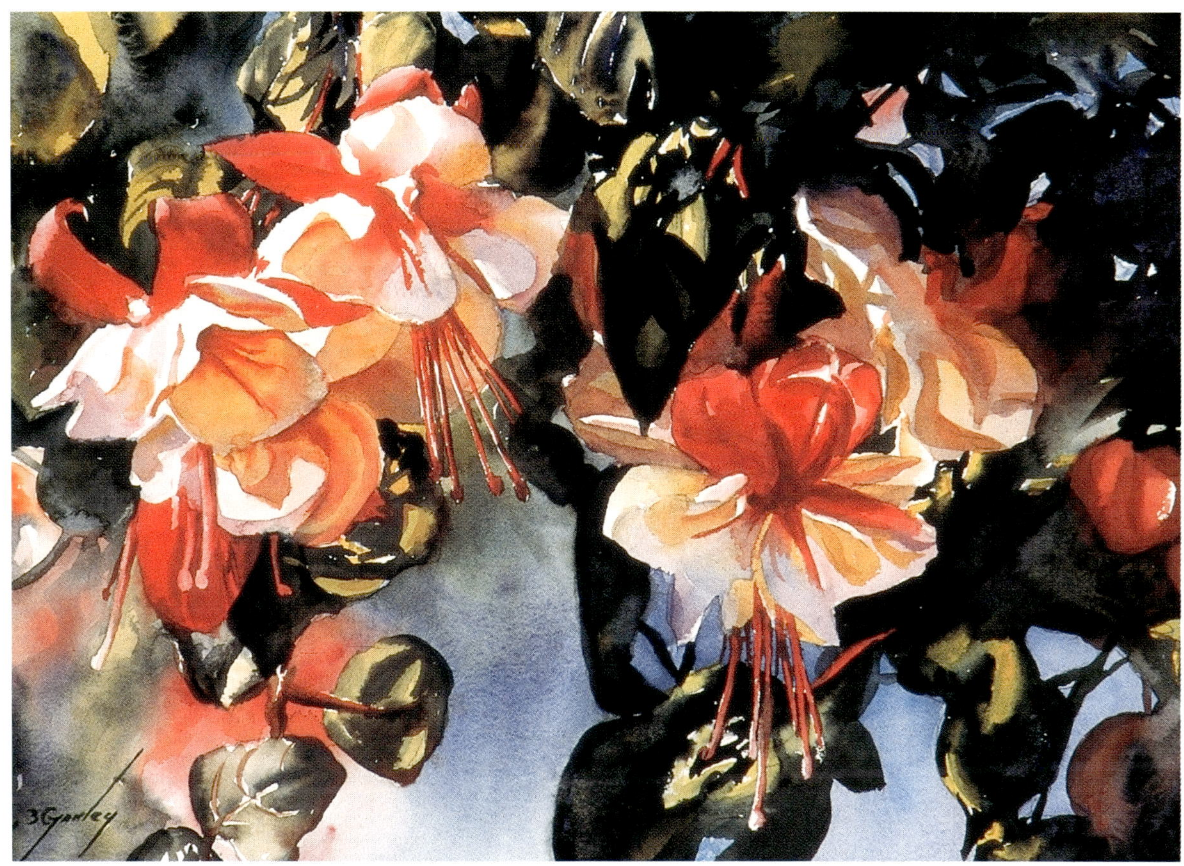

The Glow of Fuschia

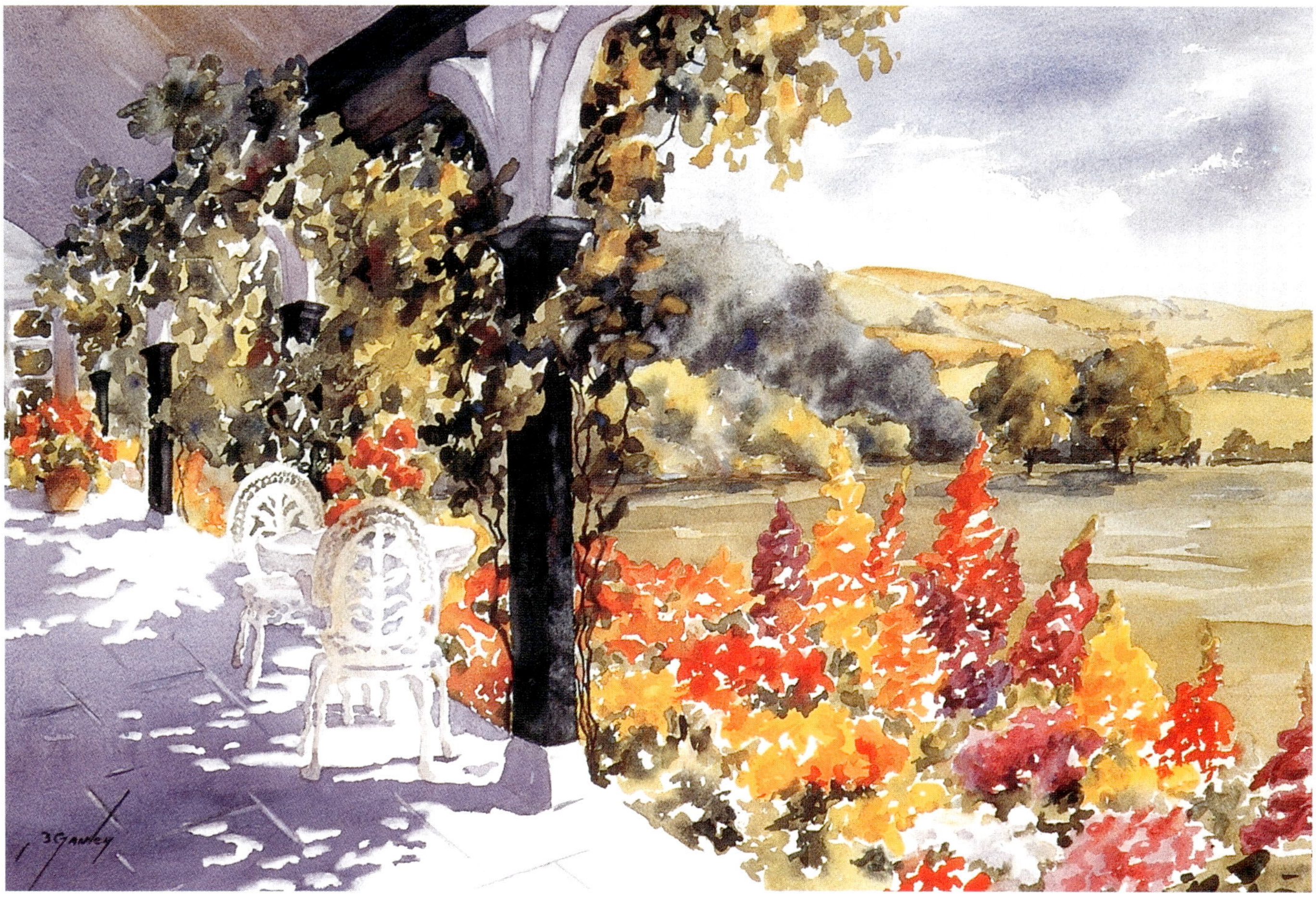

PROJECT 1 THE COURTYARD GARDEN

How to introduce colorful shadows for vitality and depth

In the drama of your painting, shadows are not supporting characters waiting in the wings but main actors with vital roles to play center-stage. They hold a painting together and their presence commands interest by conveying volume, three-dimensional form, and depth. By also exaggerating the design and colors of the shadows in your painting you can often make an ordinary scene spectacular. The secret is that shadows are not black but an entire palette of blues, greens and even reds. So a great way to make your painting more lively is to introduce color into the shadows. We will also work on rough paper, which will emphasize the texture.

The challenges

- To create smooth, even washes for shadow areas that are very intricate.
- To keep the shadows translucent and colorful.
- To create realistic lace curtains without going into a great deal of detail.

What you'll learn

- How to make colorful shadows a cohesive part of your composition.
- How to plan your design.
- How to make large washes easier.
- How to paint realistic stonework.
- How to paint lace.
- How to make the most of negative shapes.

Techniques you'll use

- Wet-into-wet blending.
- Creating texture through splattering masking fluid and paint, spritzing water, and dry-brushing.
- Handling large washes.

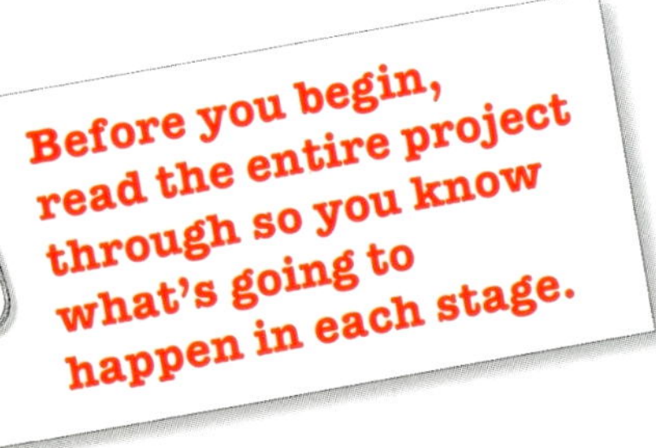

***The Courtyard Garden*, watercolor, 25 x 19¾" (64 x 50cm)**

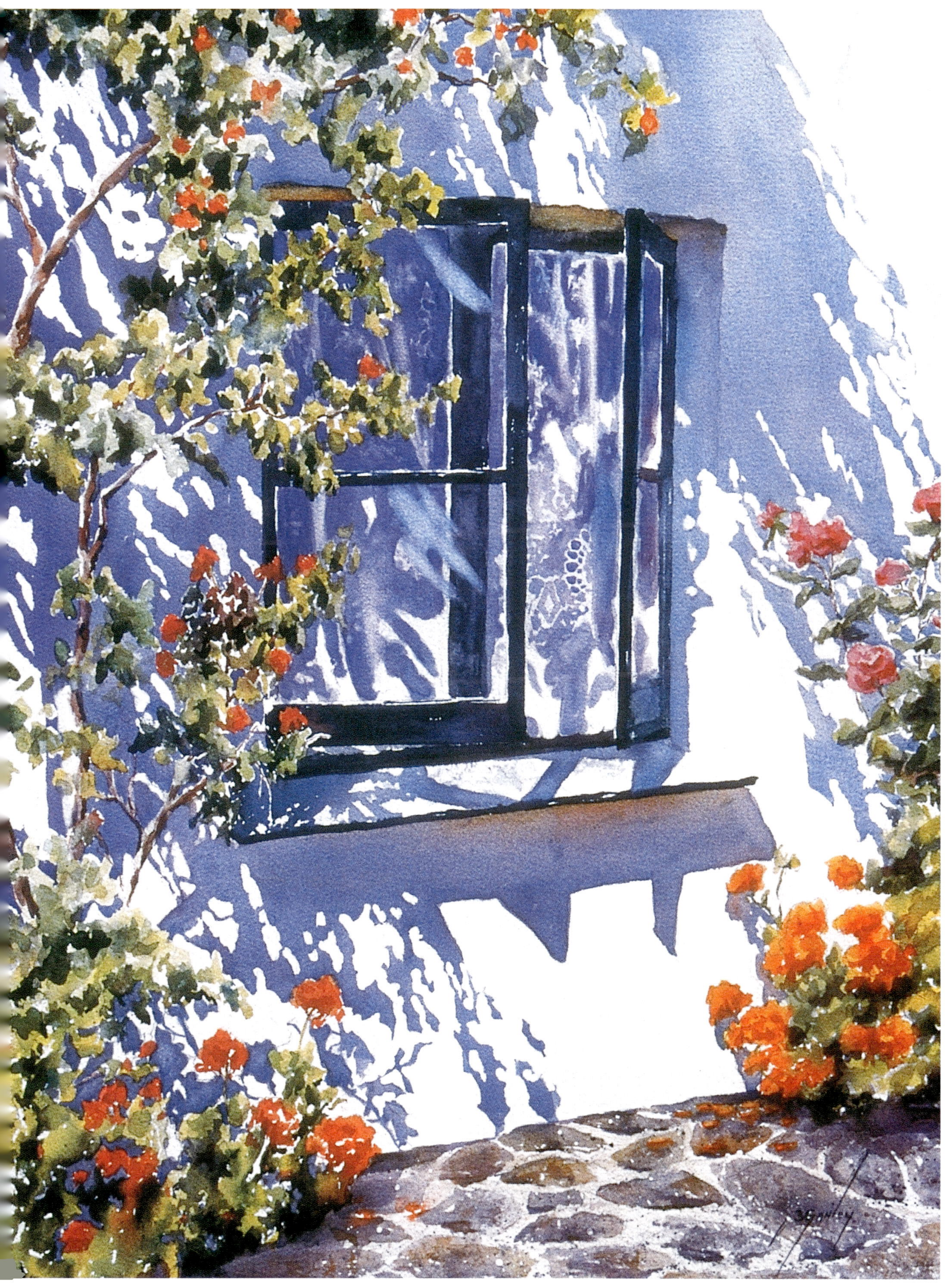

The materials you'll need for this project

Paper and board

- Gator board as a support for the paper
- 140lb (300gsm) rough watercolor paper

Brushes

- Daniel Smith 22-50 Series, Size #8 and #10
- Pro Arte Series 100, Size #12
- Fritch Scrubber (a stiff white nylon bristle brush with very short bristles, sold through Cheap Joe's catalog)
- Stiff round brush for mask application
- ¼", ½" and 1" flat brushes
- 2" hake

Tinted masking fluid

I've tried many masking products but I much prefer the type that covers well, peels off in long strips very easily without taking any paper, and is very slightly tinted so that you can see areas you may have missed. Despite the tint, it leaves no color on your paper.

Artist quality watercolors

I know that the rule of thumb is the fewer the colors the better, but when I paint flowers I sometimes use two palettes! Using pure colors, instead of trying to mix many colors to get the color you want, keeps the painting looking fresh and transparent — which is the beauty of the watercolor medium. Here are the colors you will need for this project.

Odds and ends

- No. 2 pencil for the initial drawing
- Stapler and staples
- Large natural sponge
- Small bottle of mild shampoo
- Paper towels
- Waxed paper
- Atomizer
- Mask remover (optional)

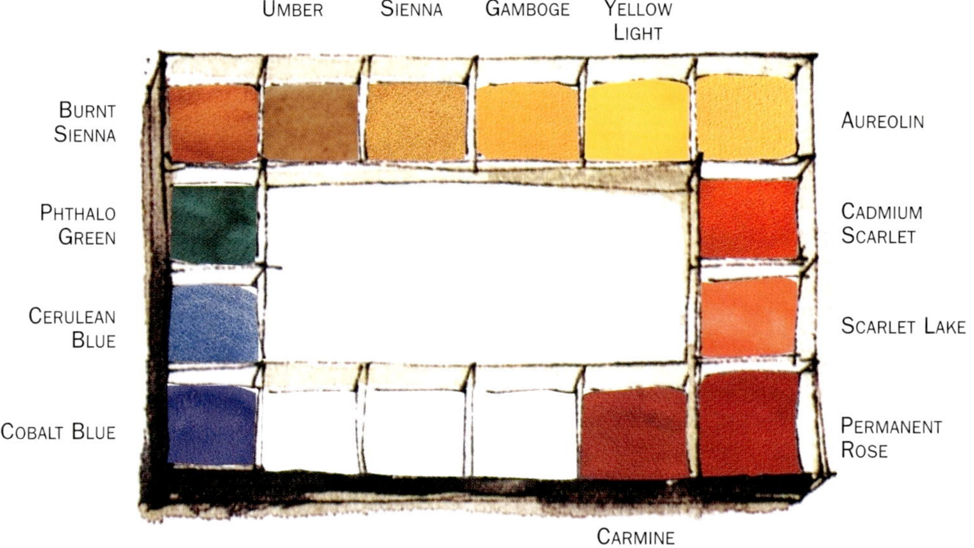

Brush Tips

To distinguish my masking brushes from my painting brushes I wrap a piece of colored tape around the handle.

Protect your brush before masking by dipping it in a mild shampoo. And if you have a lot to mask, then at intervals wash out the brush with soapy water. Allow the mask to dry naturally, because using a hairdryer could cause the mask to permanently stick to the paper.

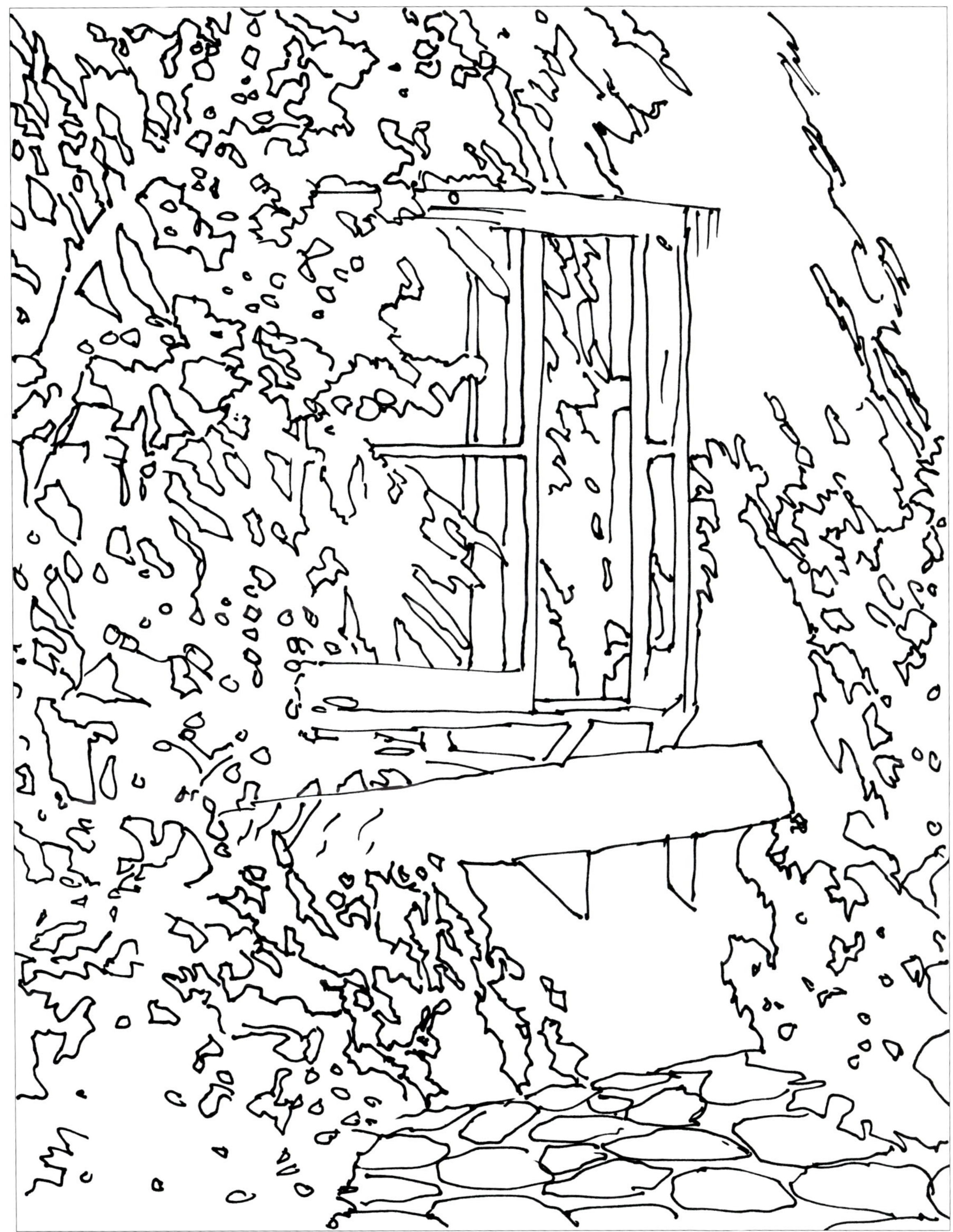

Step 1

Sketch or trace this design onto your paper

In the Introduction, I gave you the option of using a block of paper, taping your paper to a board, or stretching. Whichever method you prefer, we will start on dry paper.

- Carefully draw the scene, taking care to have some of the climbing roses overlap the window. Overlapping helps to unify the separate parts.

I used pen to make this drawing so you can see it properly, but you will use pencil. When drawing architectural details like windows, remember to have all the vertical lines parallel to the edges of the paper. The ground stonework looks authentic when elliptical shapes are used, receding in size as they go back in space.

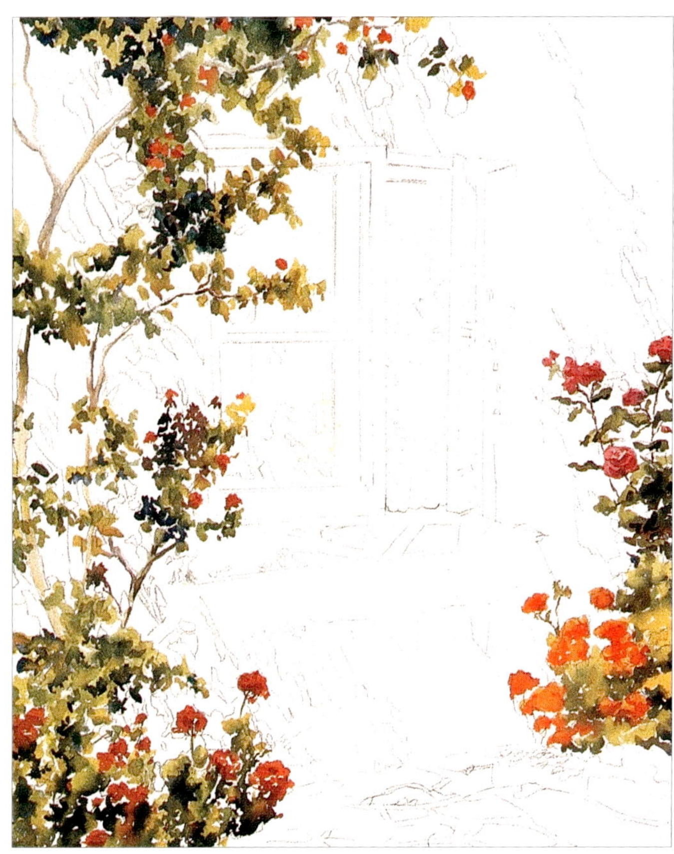

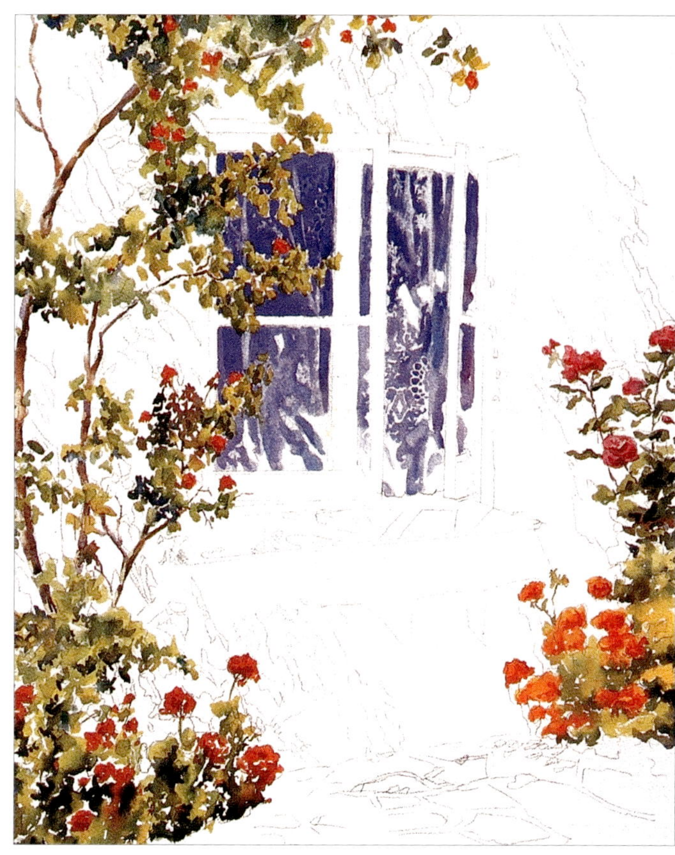

Step 2

Indicate the flower locations

- First spot-in the flower locations with dabs of warm pinks, reds and yellows. When they start to dry, drop in a darker, cooler pink, red or yellow to give the flowers tonal value, shape and substance. Care should be taken with the flowers' placement so as not to have a too-uniform look. Place some flowers in groups of three and some as singles, making sure that the spaces between the flowers are not of equal width.
- Lay down the leaves as dabs of Cadmium Yellow Light with a tiny bit of Phthalo Green and a touch of Raw Sienna. Before they dry add small touches of Raw Umber and Phthalo Green to wet-blend with the first washes.
- When they're DRY, add the darkest greens with Phthalo Green and Burnt Sienna. Because there is so much green, let's add touches of Cobalt Blue and even some cool reds — very sparingly — just for variety and to prevent a stagnant look.

Step 3

Paint the curtains

- Loosely draw only a few of the intricate curtain patterns. Go over the whole curtain area with a mixture of Cobalt Blue and Cerulean Blue, leaving the spots of sun and some of the patterns on the curtains white.
- When that's DRY, deepen some of the darker areas with the same blues and a touch of Permanent Rose, exaggerating the Cerulean in spots. Let this DRY, then wet a few of the fabric folds and gently scrub with your stiff scrubber, then blot with a paper towel for an effective soft lift of color. Soften the sunspot edges with the stiff scrubber.

Cobalt Blue

Cerulean Blue

Permanent Rose

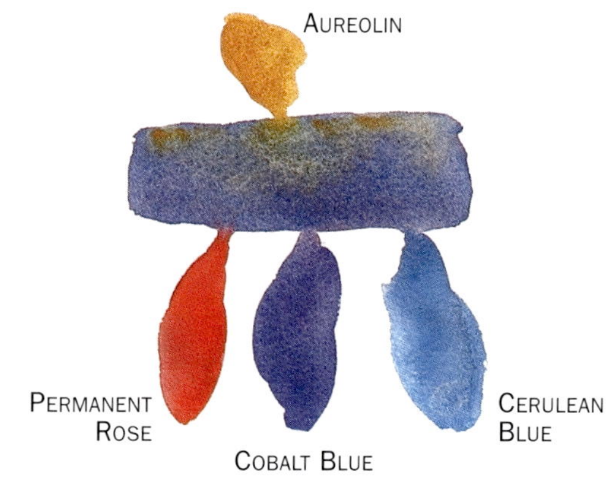

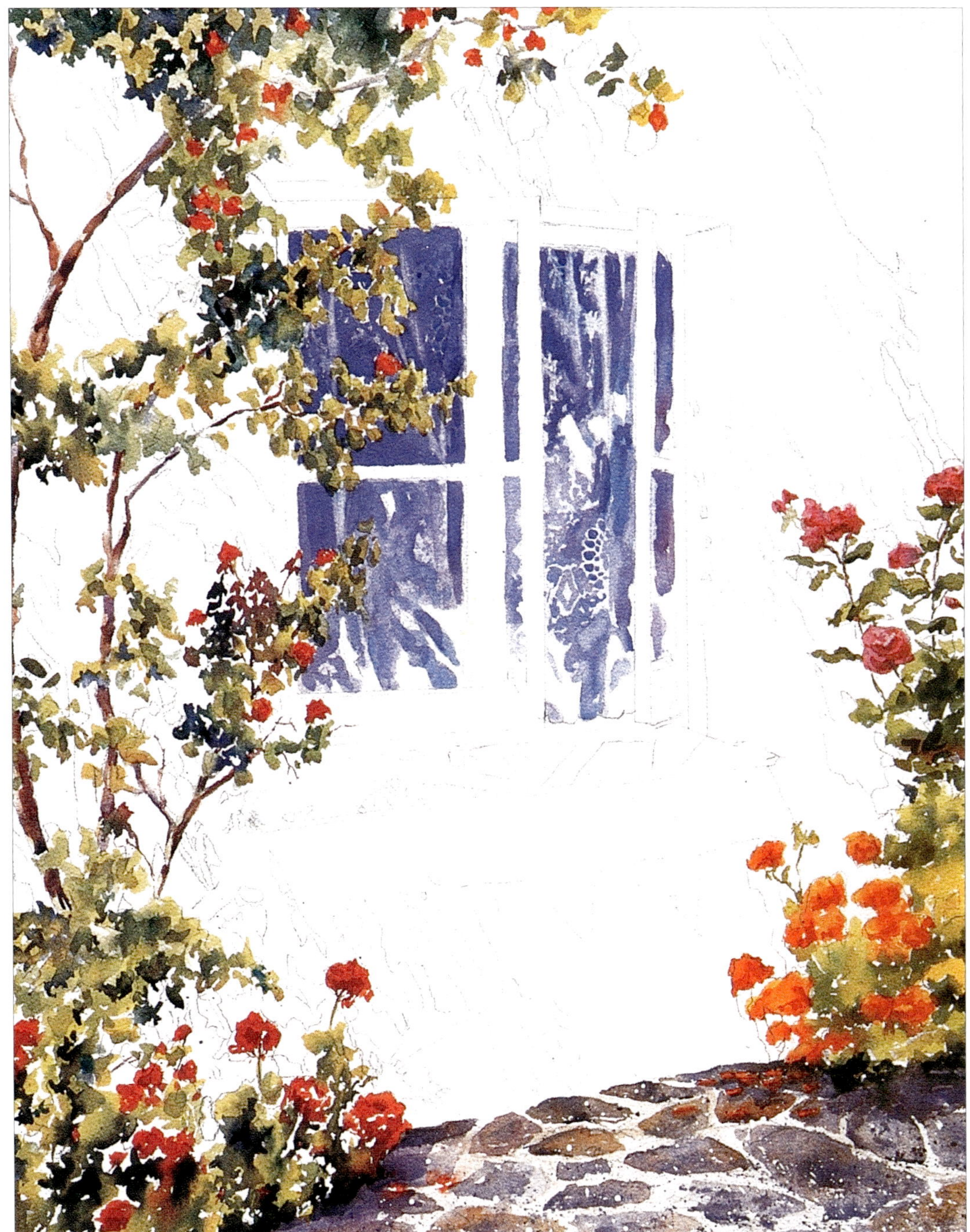

HINT

Another texturing technique is to spray water from an atomizer just as the paper starts to dry. Be careful though, because when it comes to using an atomizer, timing is critical.

Step 4

Paint and texture the patio area

- The next step is to apply the masking fluid in a flicking motion. First dip your stiff round brush in a mild shampoo, and when it is fully coated give it a little shake to remove the excess. Dip it into the masking fluid, and again tap off the excess. Then gently tap the brush against your forefinger, spraying little dots of mask across the patio.
- When those are DRY, use a quick, very watery and very light wash of umbers and grays to color the grout.
- Let it DRY, then paint the stones using various shades of warm umbers and cool grays, at times using a dry brush to scruff in the paint, achieving your first bit of texture.
- After protecting the rest of the painting with waxed paper, again do some splattering onto the stones, but this time with paint. Spatter some paint when the stones are wet and again when they are dry.

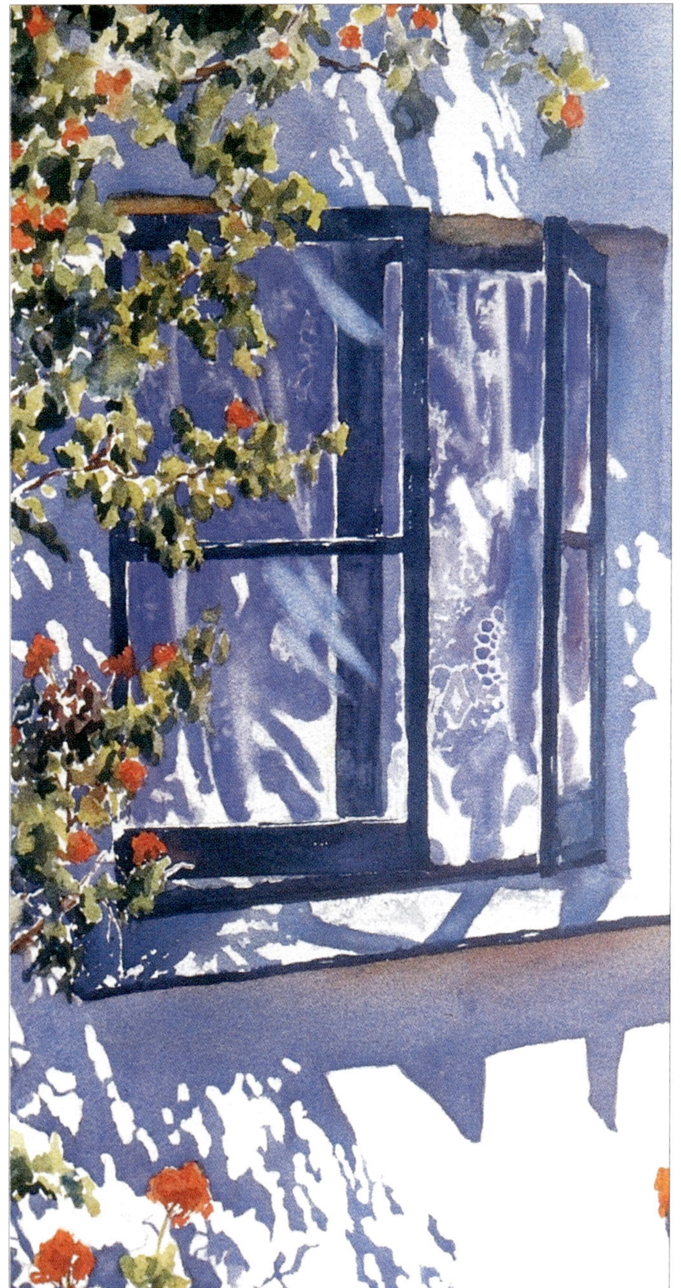

detail

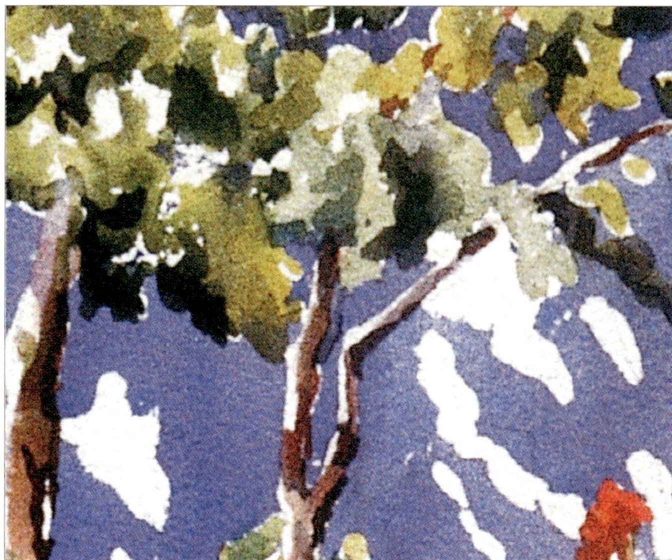

detail

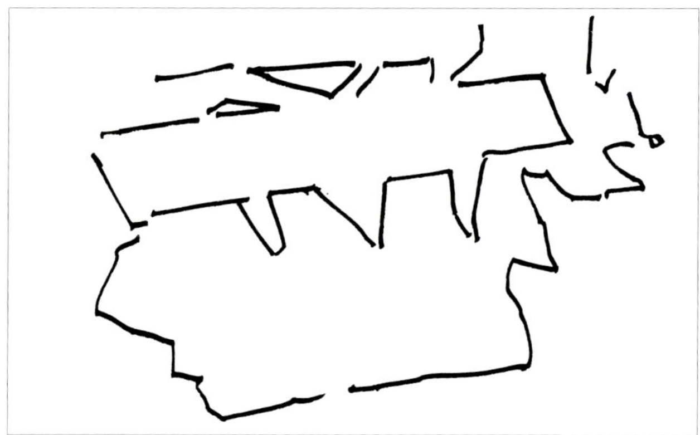

Negative shapes

Positive shapes are objects, negative shapes are the empty spaces between objects. In this instance, the shadows are "objects" and the negative spaces are the unshadowed areas between them. Although our conscious attention focuses on the positive shapes, the negative shapes have strong unconscious emotional appeal. So don't underestimate the importance of negative shapes. They should be interesting and varying in size.

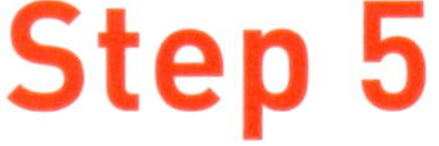

Step 5

Mask the white areas

To prepare for the large mass of shadow that will integrate all of the disjointed sections of the painting, we will continue to spend a bit of time on masking. Mask most of the white parts of the building and many of the already painted leaves, flowers and tree branches. Don't worry about the already painted areas because the mask won't harm the underlying paint.

How to add reflective warmth

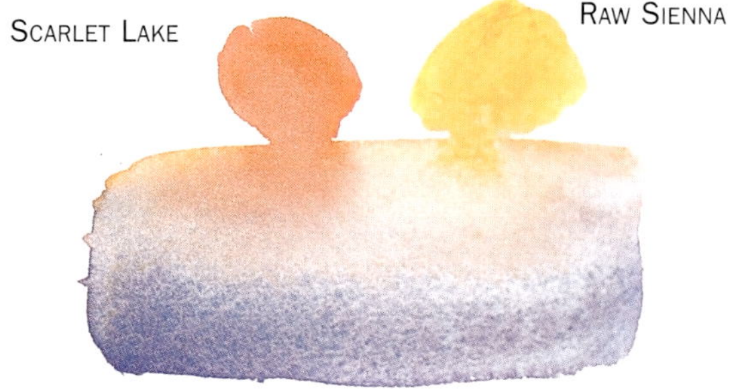

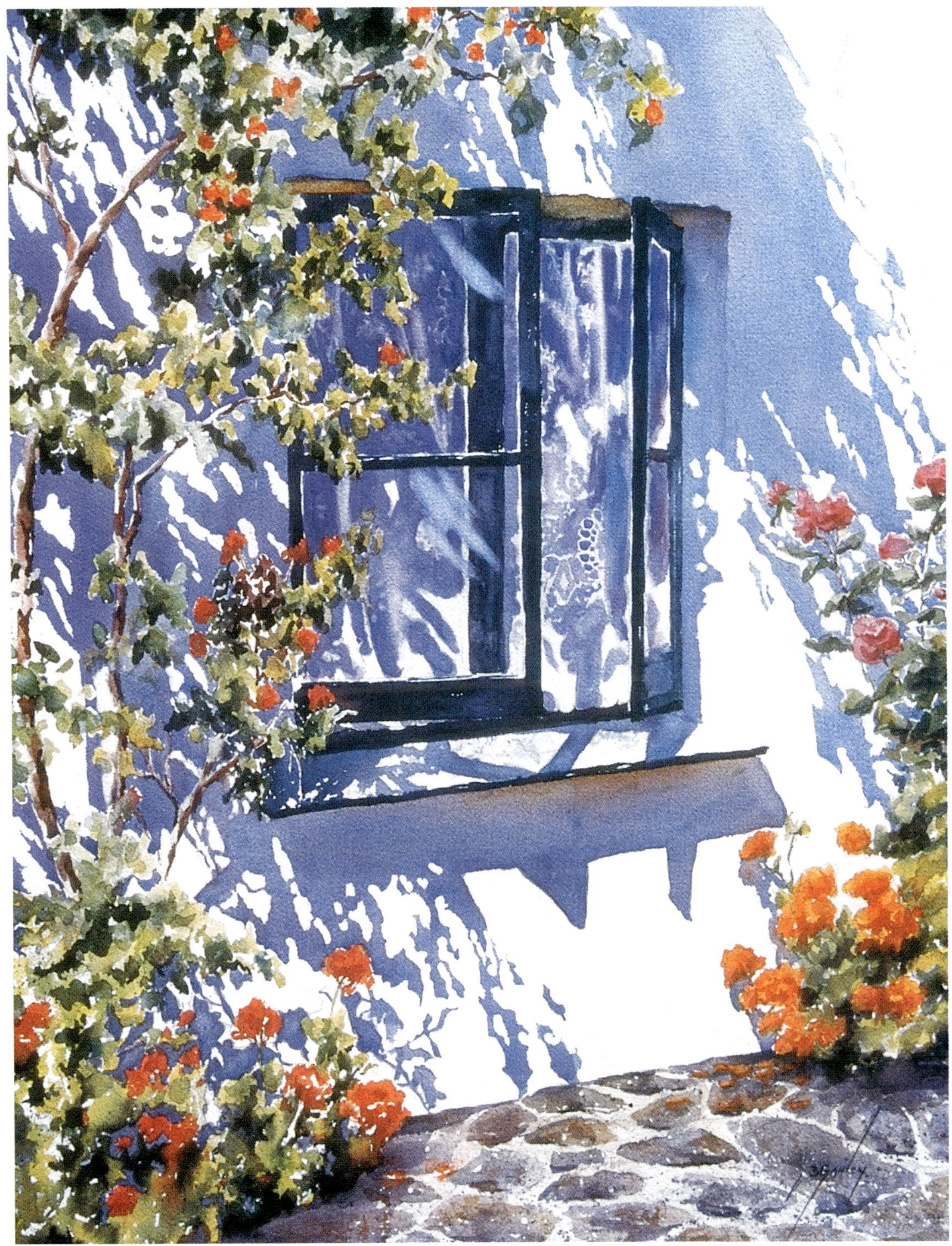

Step 6

Paint the shadows

- When the mask is dry, mix a large puddle of Cobalt Blue and Cerulean Blue with a touch of Permanent Rose. The large mass of shadow will integrate all of the disjointed, unconnected sections of the painting.
- Working on DRY paper and with a juicy loaded brush, apply a slightly darker, warmer mix on the upper left side and gradually cool it with more Cerulean Blue as you work across the paper to the right.
- The ground is usually warm in color, and if there are any horizontal planes that project over the ground then those planes will receive the warm light from the ground and bounce that warm light onto the objects nearby. You usually see this effect in roof overhangs. You should always exaggerate those warm colors. There are a few horizontal planes, on top of the window and under the window ledge. For the areas that bounce warm light, add a mixture of Raw Sienna and Scarlet Lake and let that wet-blend into the blue/violet mixture.
- You will also notice that the right side of the window ledge disappears into the white of the wall, as does the indentation of the window right above it. The viewer's eye will fill those spaces in. Using several of those "missing" details in your paintings adds a bit of mystery and makes the painting more interesting to the viewer.

How to paint opaque backgrounds to intensify your subject

Here's where you learn how using an opaque background intensifies the glowing translucency of the main subject matter.

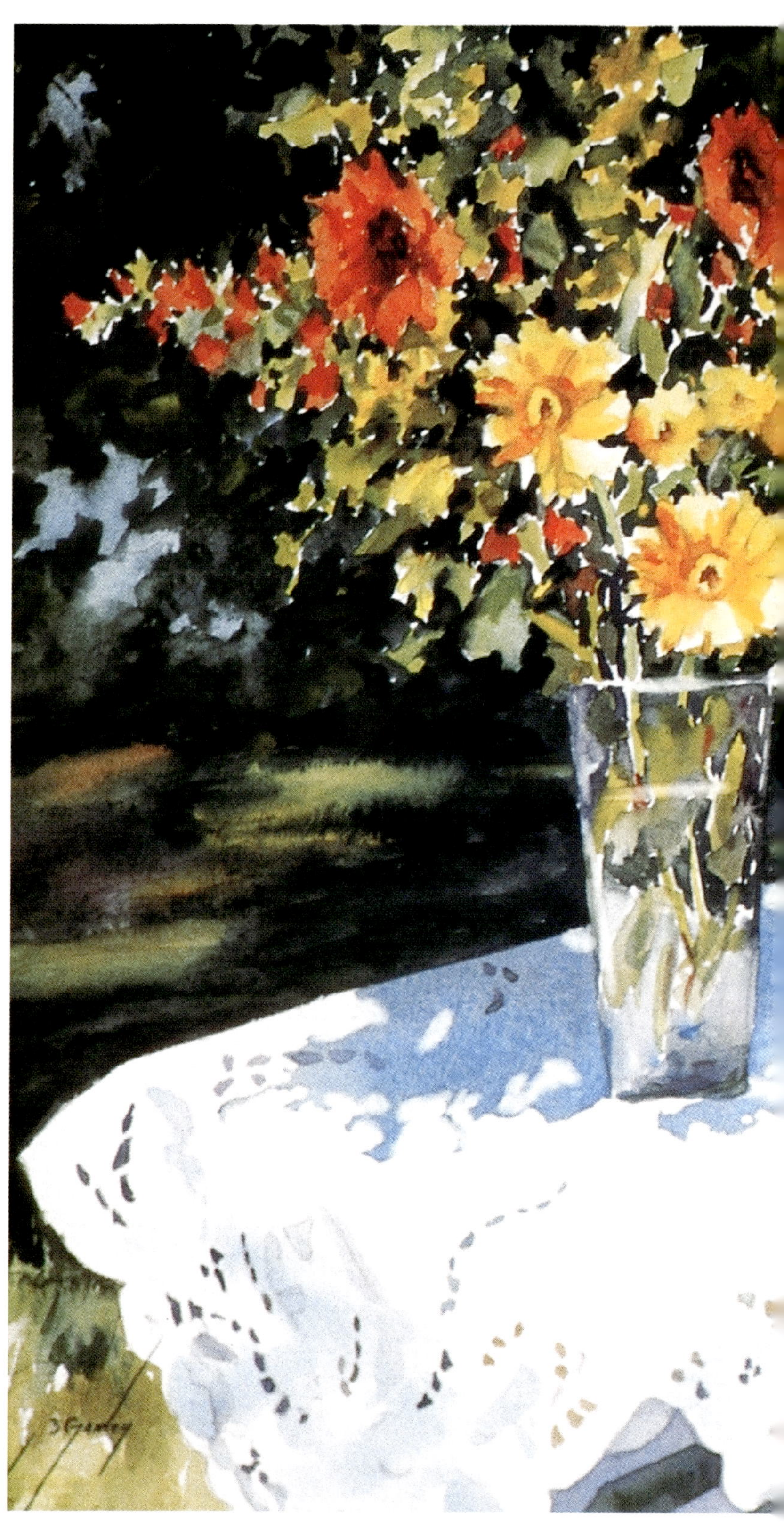

The challenges

- To keep the background interesting, but subdued.
- To keep the background opaque but not "flat" in appearance.

What you'll learn

- How to plan your design.
- How larger washes can be made easy by using lots of masking fluid.
- How to soften the sharp edges left once you remove masking fluid.
- How to make some sunlit areas in shadow to create a sense of depth and add interest.
- How important it is to leave lighter areas in the background foliage to create a greater sense of depth.

The techniques you'll use

- Masking fluid application.
- Opaque washes.
- Lost and found edges.
- Glazes (wet-on-dry washes).
- Translucent washes.
- Wet-in-wet blending.

Before you begin, read the entire project through so you know what's going to happen in each stage.

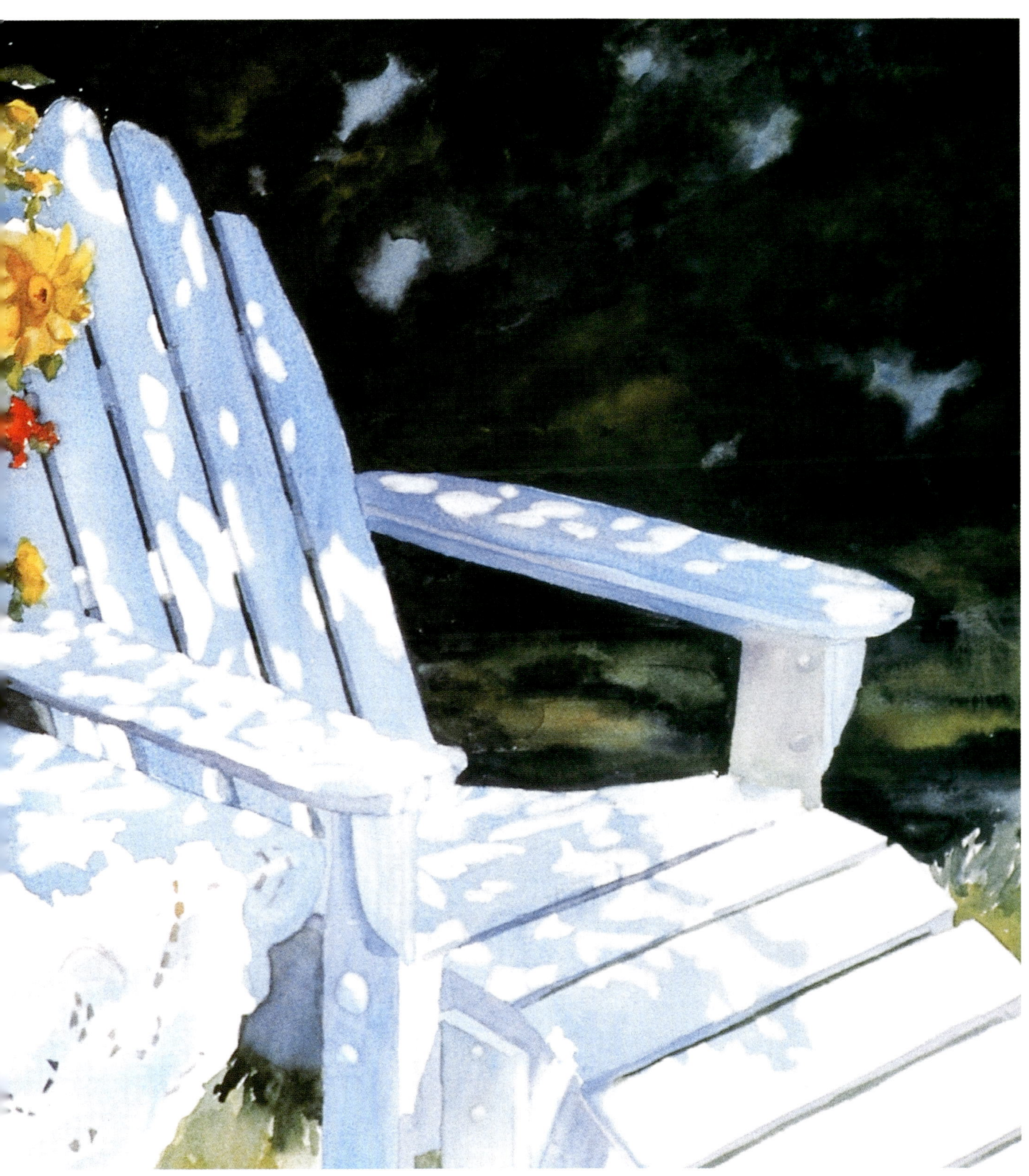

Backyard Invitation, watercolor, 14½ x 21½" (37 x 55cm)

The materials you'll need for this project

Paper and board

- Good quality cold pressed 140lb watercolor paper.
- Gator board as a support for the paper.

Brushes

- Daniel Smith 22-50 Series, Size #8 and #10
- Pro Arte Series 100, Size #12
- Fritch Scrubber (a stiff white nylon bristle brush with very short bristles, sold through Cheap Joe's catalog)
- Stiff round brush for mask application
- ¼", ½" and 1" flat brushes
- 2" hake

Odds and ends

- No. 2 pencil
- Stapler and staples
- Mild shampoo
- Tinted masking fluid

Artist quality watercolors

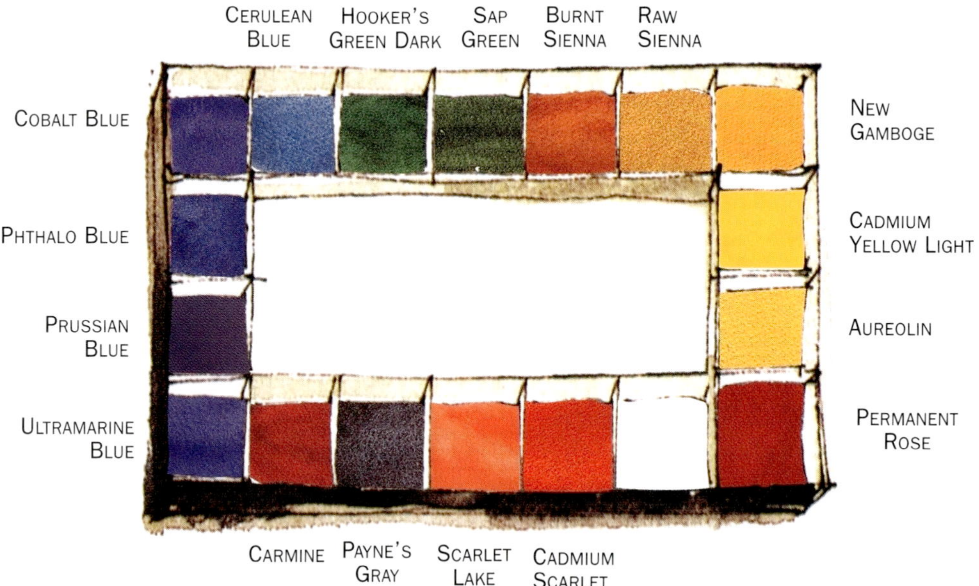

Note: Prussian Blue, Hooker's Green and Payne's Gray are particularly useful when painting opaque backgrounds.

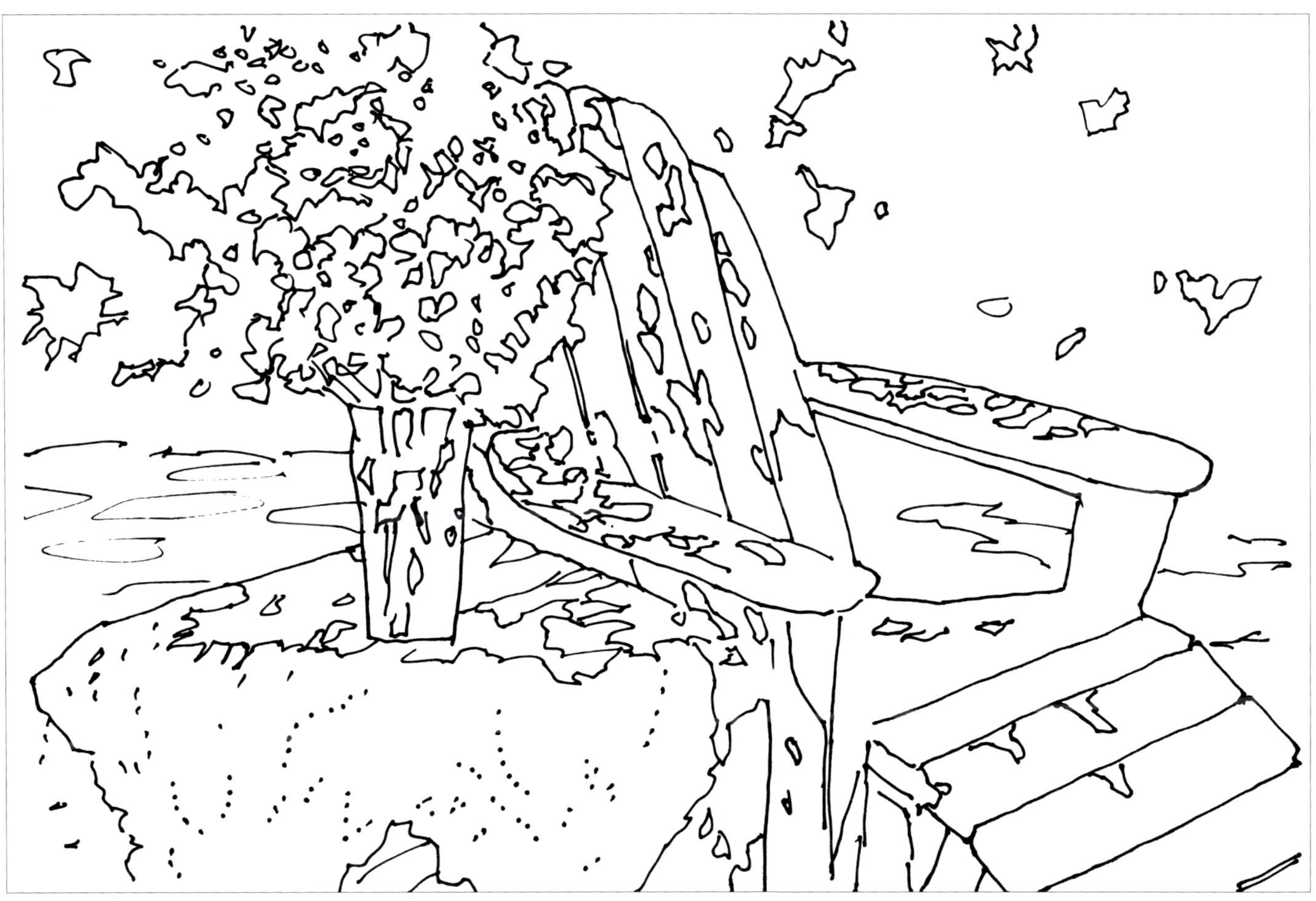

Step 1

Sketch or trace this design onto your paper

- Carefully draw the scene in pencil, making sure the flowers overlap each other and face in different directions. Have some flowers or leaves spill over the top of the vase to unify the flowers with the vase. Notice how the flowers overlap the chair.
- When drawing the flowers in the vase, notice that the flowers near the edge of the painting, and some of the leaves or branches escape the borders of the picture at the top. This creates a more interesting and exciting effect than trying to contain all the wispy edges inside the borders.

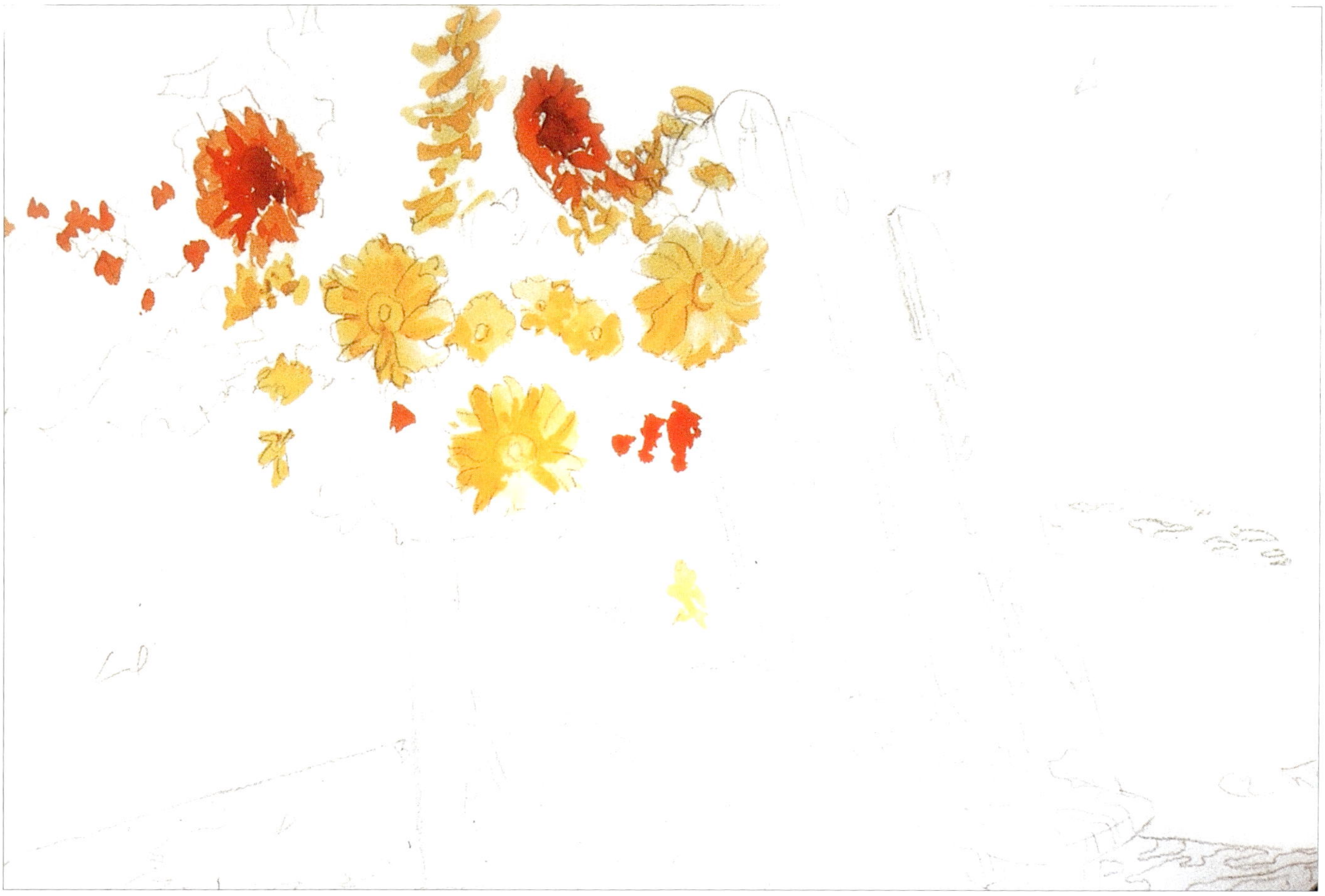

Step 2

Start painting the flowers

• Work from light to dark on DAMP paper. Apply a wash of clean water over the paper, towel off excess water and allow the paper to dry until it is just damp. Give the wispy yellow flowers a pale wash of Aureolin, reserving some of the white paper where the flower petals receive direct sun.

• Before the sheen leaves the flowers, highlight some shady areas with a New Gamboge glaze. Handle the red flowers the same way, starting with Cadmium Scarlet, with a touch of New Gamboge in places for variety.

• Then highlight the shadows with Scarlet Lake and in darker areas with Carmine.

• Use a little Burnt Sienna for the center of the gerbera daisies. Let some edges meld into the petals and drop a trough of Scarlet Lake into one little section of the center.

• Now you can balance the bouquet with yellow red sprays using just little dabs of the brush. Let this DRY before starting on the greens.

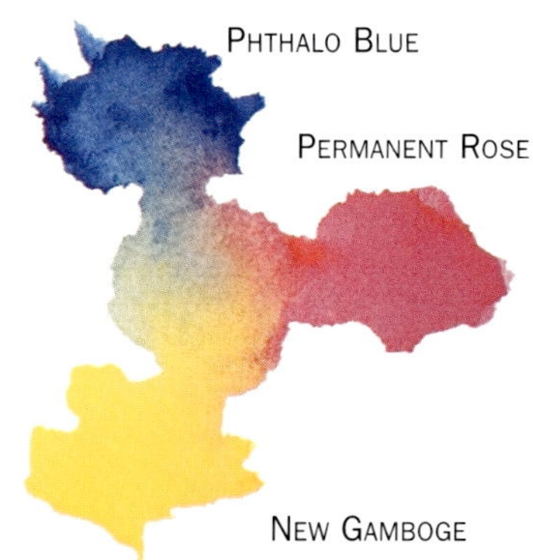

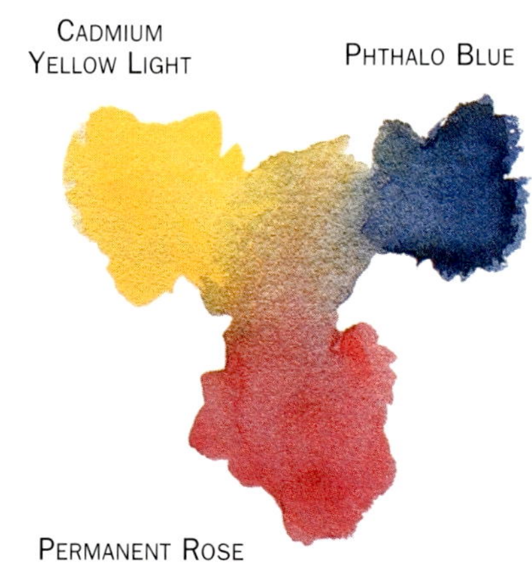

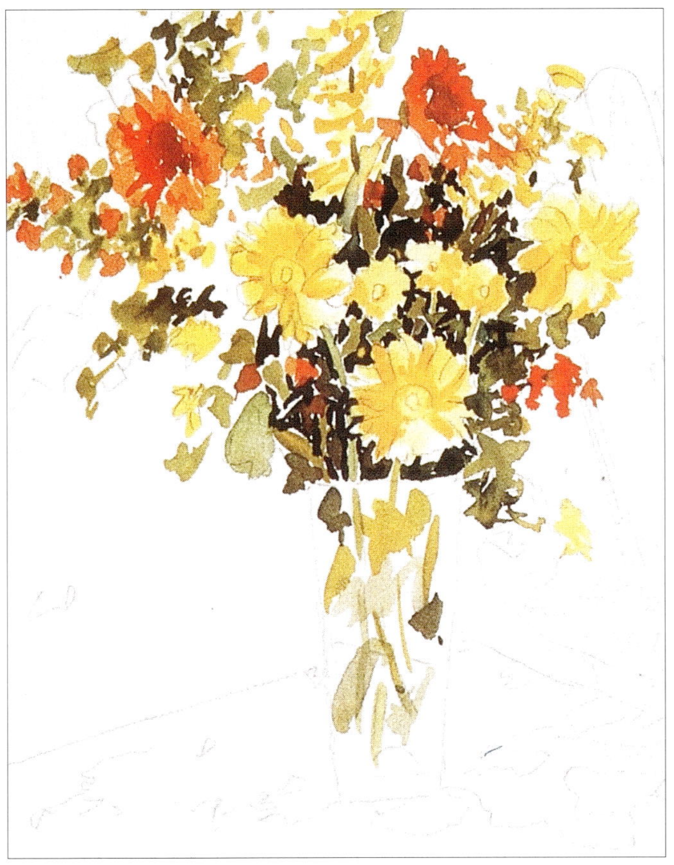

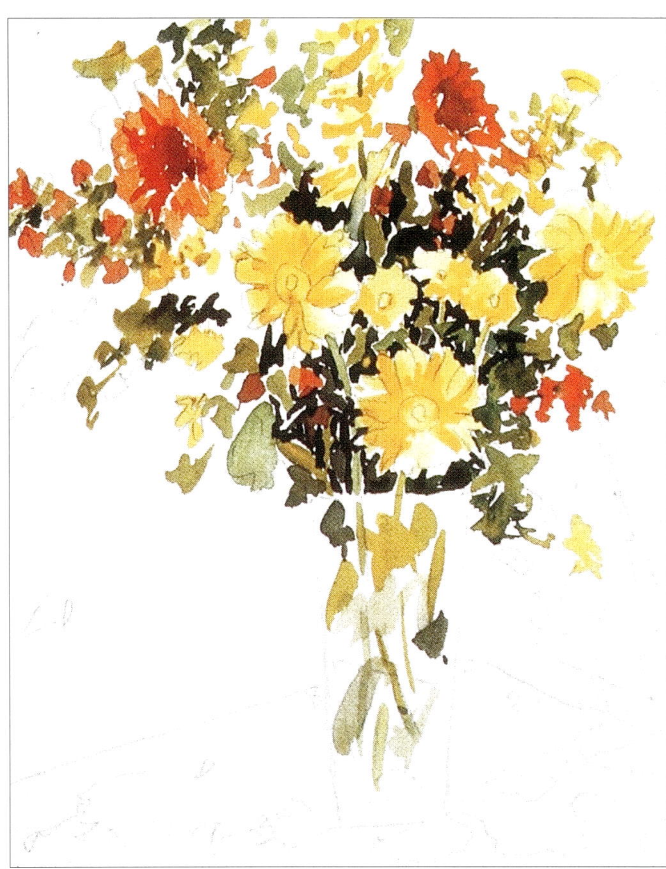

Step 3

Introduce the greens

- When the paper is DRY lay in soft greens for the leaf patterns, changing greens frequently. Try mixtures of Cadmium Yellow Light and Phthalo Blue (with a touch of red or pink to calm it down). You could vary the yellows in the mixture by using New Gamboge or Raw Sienna.
- Start to paint stems and a few leaves in the vase.

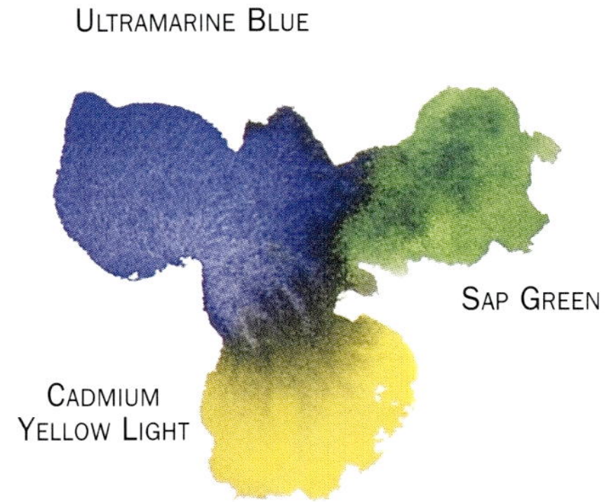

Step 4

Add darker greens

- While the greens are DAMP, add darker ones. Ultramarine Blue and Sap Green make a lovely dark, but occasionally drop in a yellow for leaf variety.
- When DRY, glaze over some of the lighter leaves with a little Cobalt Blue to make those areas recede. This will suggest shadows and soften some of the hard edges.

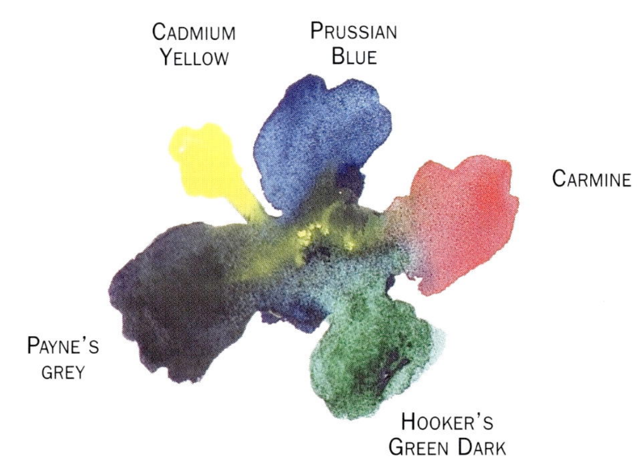

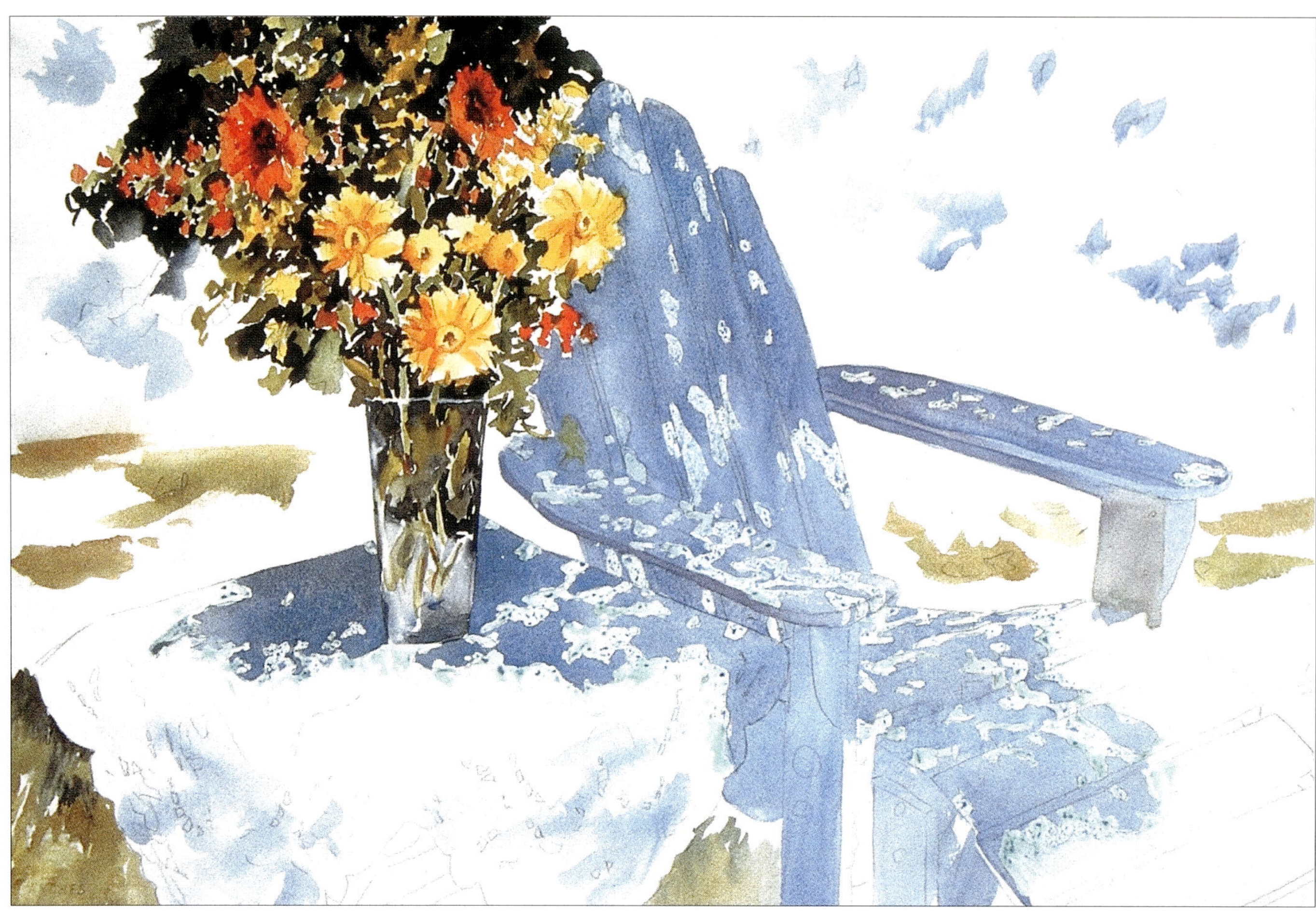

Step 5

Add the light colors

- Add some dark greens around the stems in the vase, noting the distortion of the tablecloth as seen through the clear water in the vase.

Step 6

Mask out the sunlit areas

- When everything is DRY it is time to mask out all those sunlit areas on the tablecloth and chair. Do this all at once, then you can apply one quick, even wash over the chair and tablecloth to introduce the shadows.
- Once the mask has dried naturally, mix a good size puddle of Cerulean Blue and Cobalt Blue. Paint all the shadows on the chair and tablecloth.
- When DRY remove the mask. The edges will look hard, but don't worry, you'll be fixing this later.
- Add some Cerulean/Cobalt Blue mixture to "sky hole" areas in the background foliage. These areas are simple to do and, make the viewer feel they are looking through to something far beyond. "Sky holes" also insinuate an air of mystery and break up the monotony of a large area of dark.
- For the same reasons, add some light green and/or Raw Sienna grasses in the shadowed areas of the background lawn.

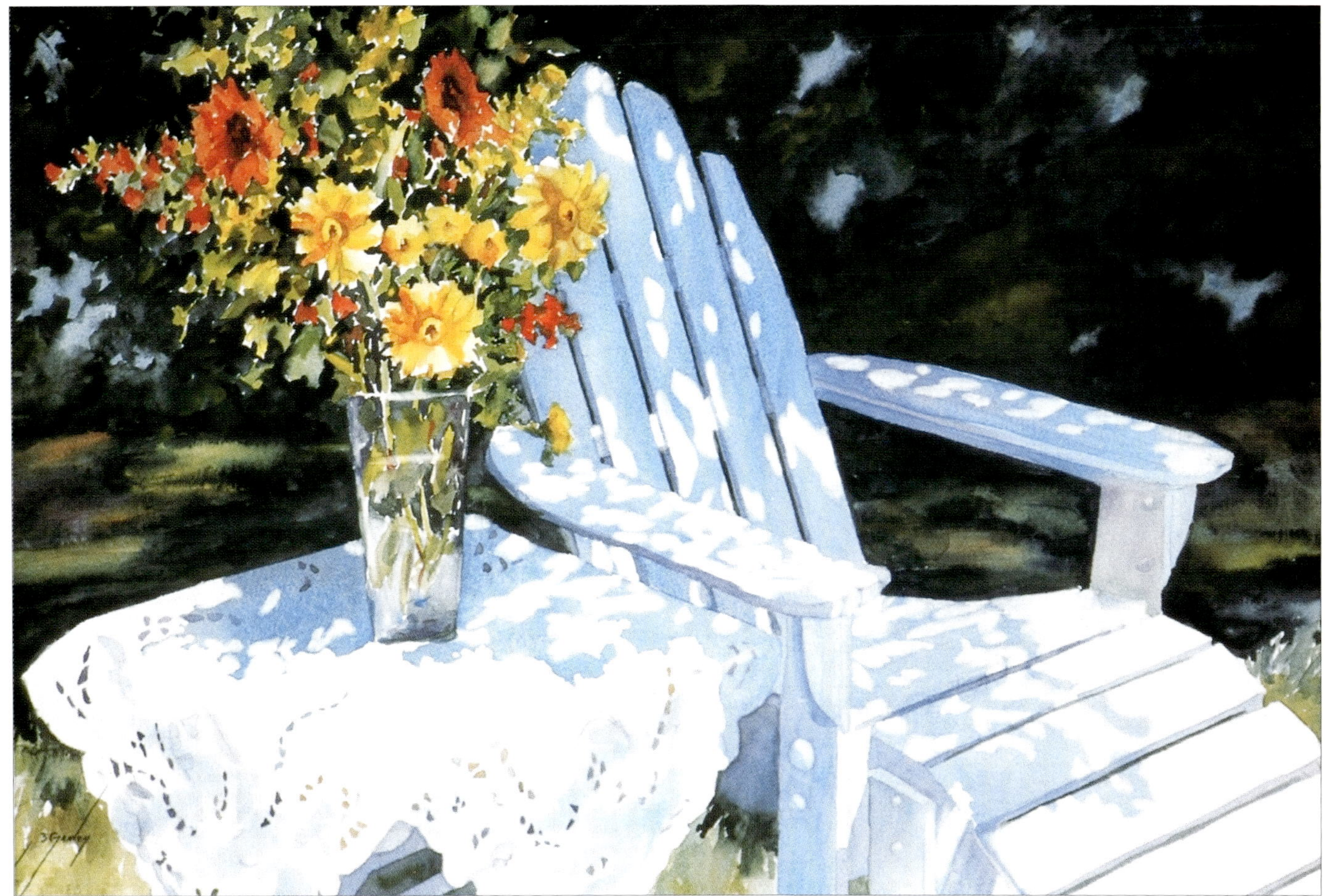

Step 7

Unify with an opaque background

In this painting we are going to subdue the background so it does not compete with the center of interest. You probably know that there should be calm spaces in a busy painting so the eyes can rest. Using an opaque background is one way to do it. It also intensifies the translucent qualities of flowers and emphasizes the center of interest.

- Use thicker consistency paint for this step. Squeeze about an inch of Payne's Gray into a paper cup. Add a quarter-inch ribbon of Prussian Blue and quarter-inch of Hooker's Green Dark. As you paint add touches of Carmine to warm up those spots. Add a tiny bit of water to achieve the consistency of heavy cream. Apply this to the background and BEFORE IT DRIES drop in some Cadmium Yellow Light in a swirling motion. This will turn green and give the impression of lighter areas in trees or leaves.

Step 8

Finish by removing the mask and softening the resultant hard edges

- Remove the mask from the chair and tablecloth. There will be a lot of undesirable hard edges. To soften these,dip your hard-bristled brush into clean water and gently scrub all those hard edges, blotting with a paper towel frequently.

NOTE: Make sure your brush and water are clean before you scrub at the edges.

How to incorporate the rugged textures of old wood and stone in your garden scenes

These textures may look difficult, but if you take them step-by-step, gradually building up layers, then you will achieve them. You'll also find that the resulting rugged look balances the delicacy of the flowers. We will be using rough paper for this project.

The challenges

- To create a sense of depth in the recession of the window.
- To paint realistic looking stonework and aged wood.

What you'll learn

- How to make complementary colors work for you.
- How to take advantage of "bounced" light.
- How to use values to create dimension.

Techniques you'll use

- Masking.
- Dry brush.
- Texturizing with water spray.
- Paint splattering.
- Glazing.
- Sponging.
- Negative shape painting.

Before you begin, read the entire project through so you know what's going to happen in each stage.

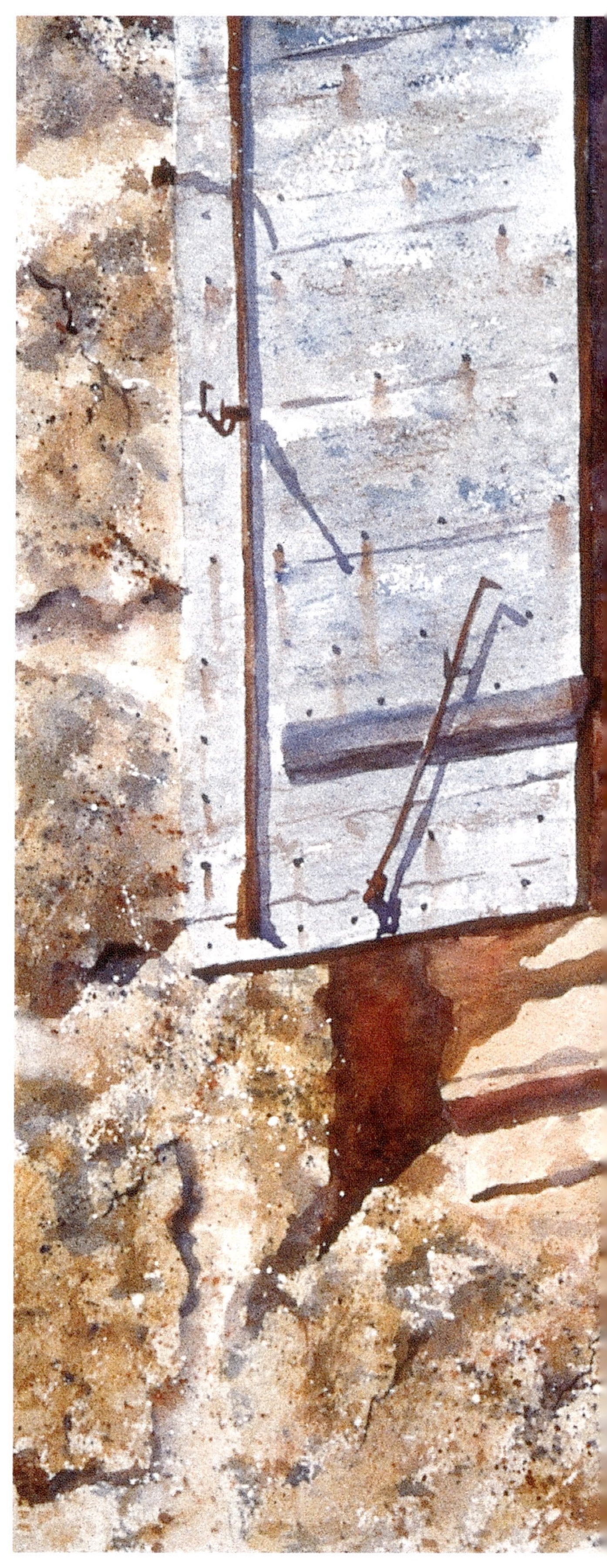

***Window Garden of France*, watercolor, 14½ x 21½" (37 x 55cm)**

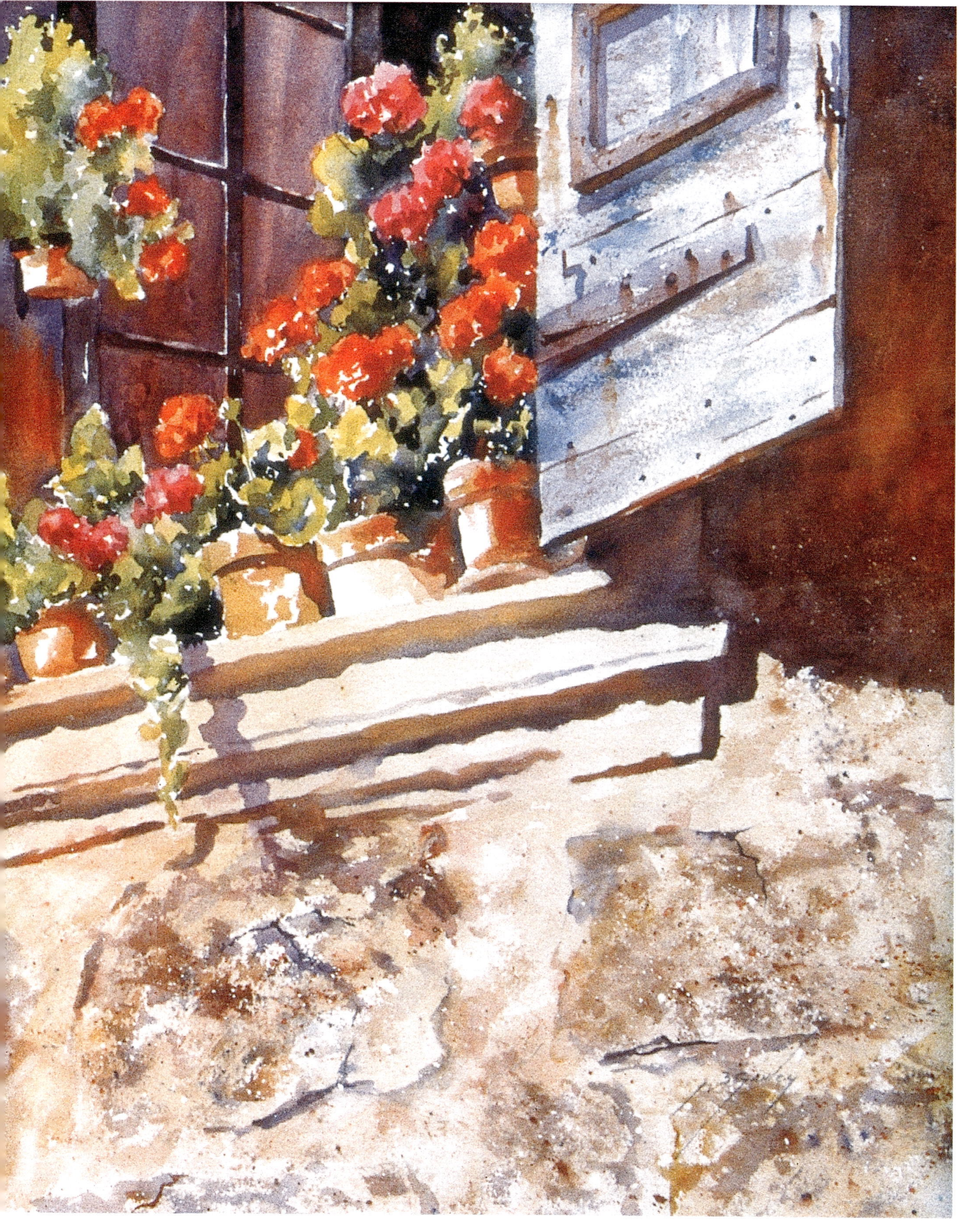

The materials you'll need for this project

Support

- Gator board as a support for the paper
- 140lb (300 gsm) rough watercolor paper

Brushes

- Daniel Smith 22-50 Series, Size #8 and #10
- Pro Arte Series 100, Size #12
- Fritch Scrubber (a stiff white nylon bristle brush with very short bristles, sold through Cheap Joe's catalog)
- Stiff round brush for mask application
- ¼", ½" and 1" flat brushes
- 2" hake

Odds and ends

- No. 2 pencil for the initial drawing
- Stapler and staples
- Tinted masking fluid
- Mild shampoo
- Atomizer for spraying water droplets
- Small sponge
- Waxed paper
- Brown masking tape (or any tape gentle on watercolor paper)

Artist quality watercolors

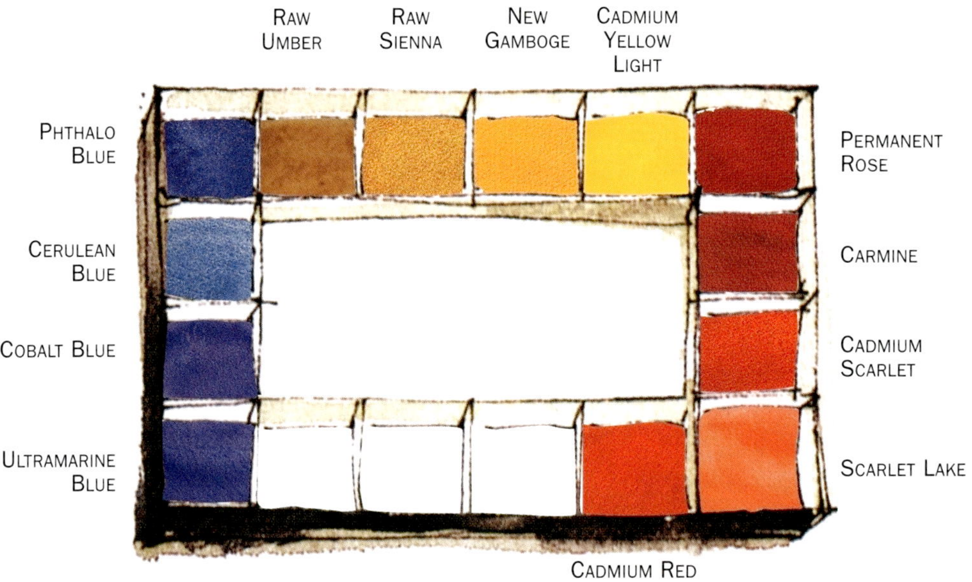

HINT

When you want to achieve a textured look, rough paper gives you a head start.

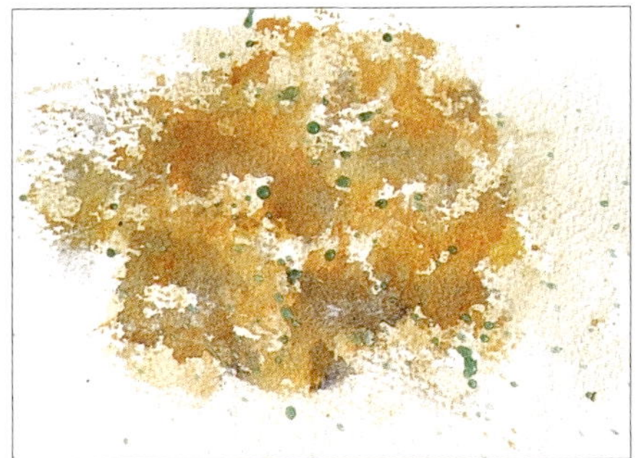

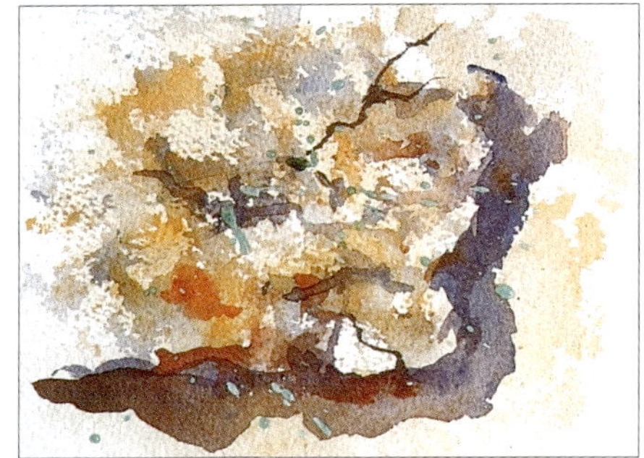

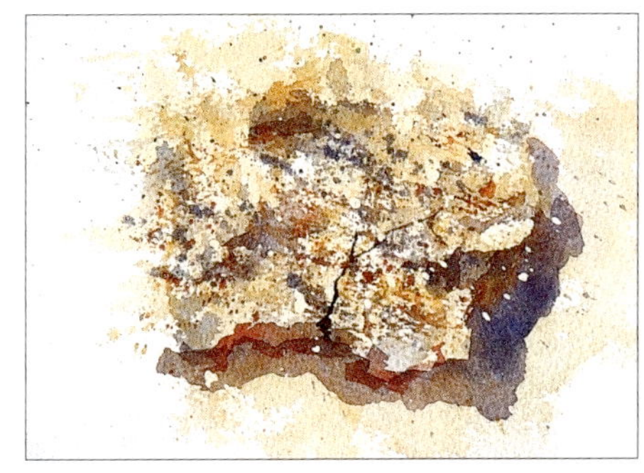

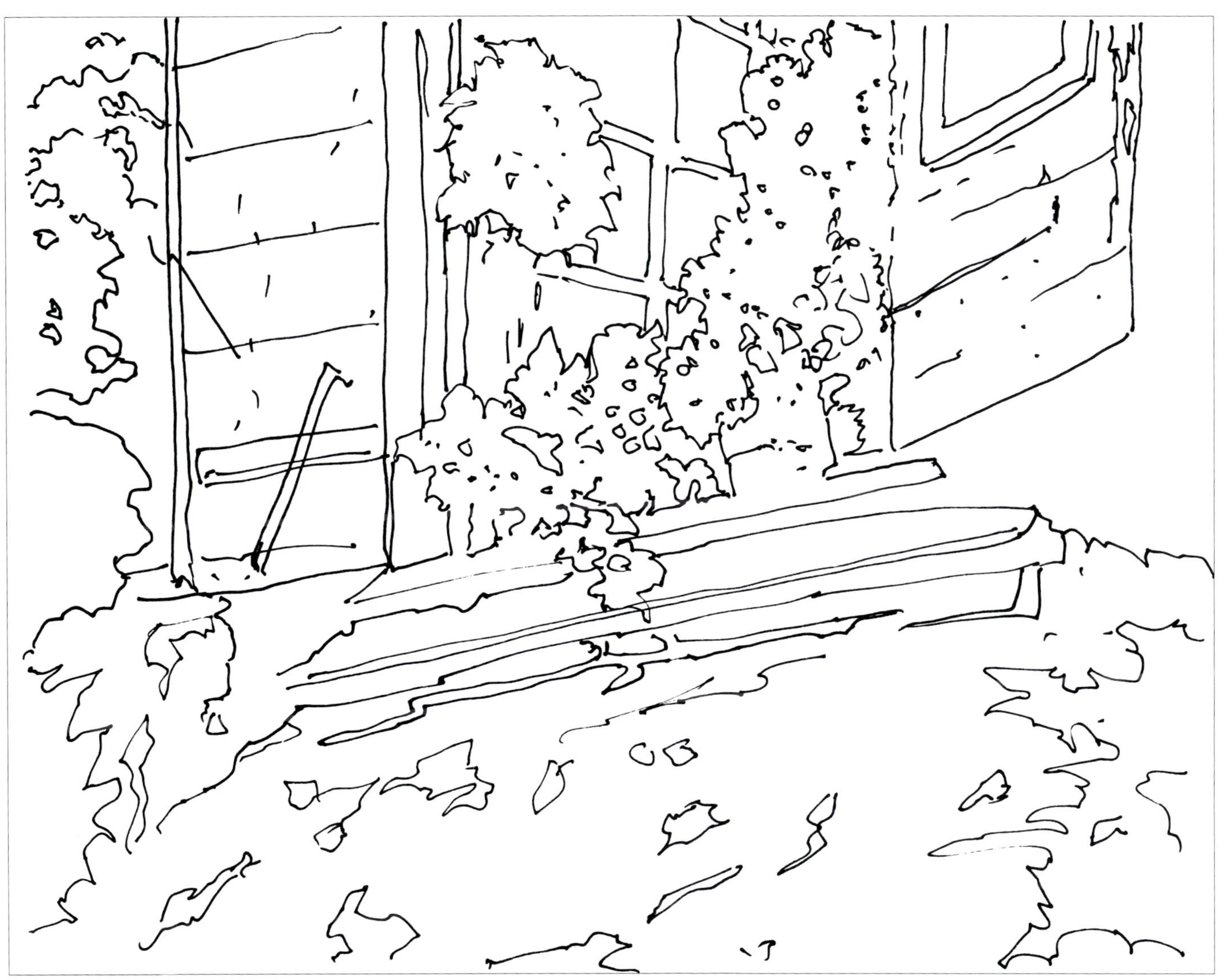

Step 1

Sketch or trace this design onto your paper

- We will be starting on DRY paper. Using a pencil carefully draw the scene on your rough watercolor paper, remaining mindful of the rules of perspective — especially with the placement of the window and shutter angle. (Remember, I used ink, but you'll use a pencil for your drawing.)

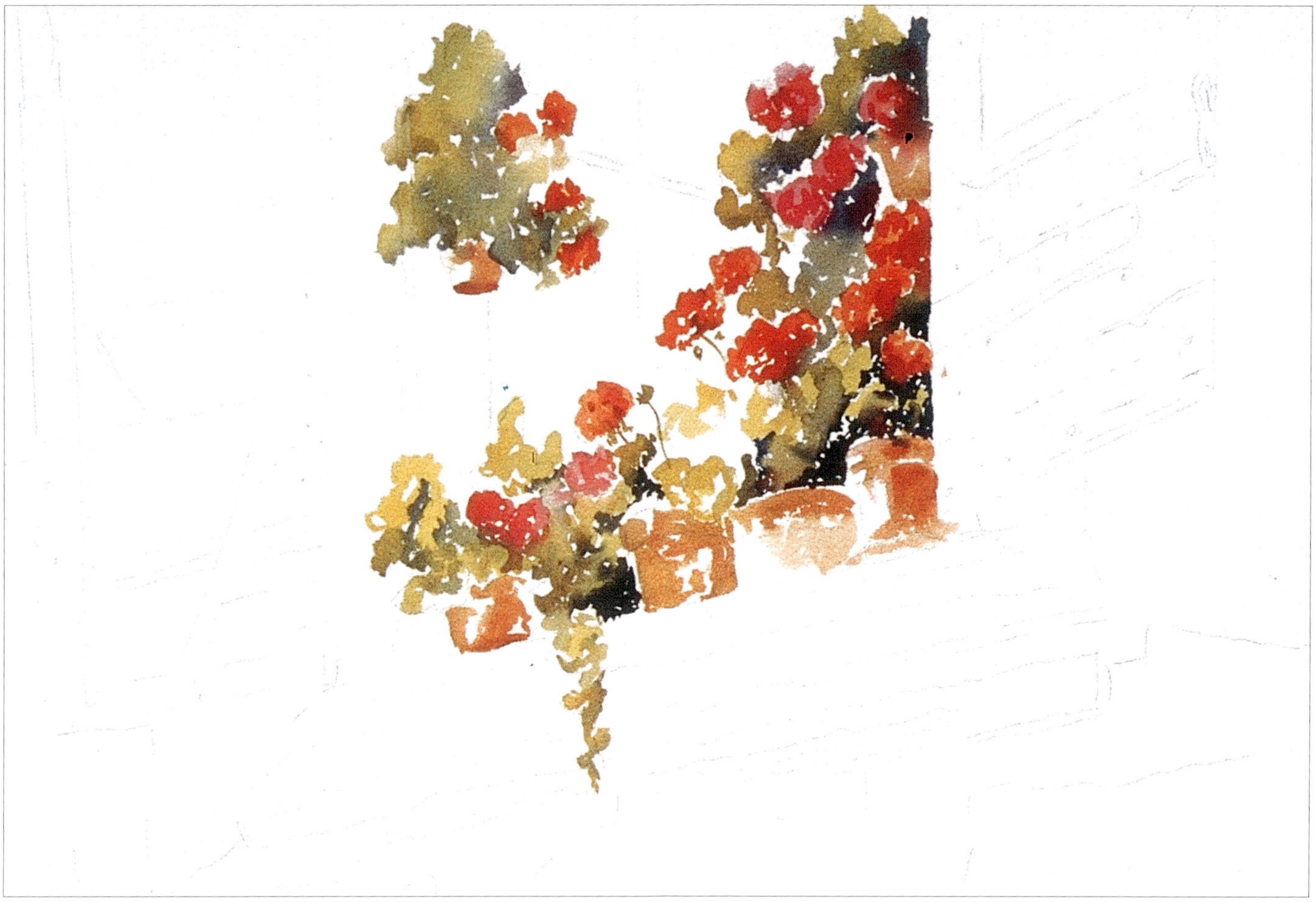

Step 2

Paint the center of interest and the pots

• Start with the center of interest — the bright flowers in the window. Dab in the very warm Cadmium Scarlet for the red flowers and Permanent Rose for the pink ones. Once that starts to dry and lose its shine, start painting the leaves. For the leaves use Cadmium Yellow Light with a tiny bit of Phthalo Blue, and use a touch of New Gamboge instead of the Cadmium Yellow Light, leaving small bits of the paper white. While this settles, start the flowerpots with Raw Sienna and Scarlet Lake in some places and in Raw Sienna and Permanent Rose in others, again leaving interesting negative shapes of white.

Step 3

Start shading

• Start to shade the flowers. Use Cadmium Red as a medium value for the red flowers and Permanent Rose for a deeper value of the pink flowers.

• For the darker greens use Phthalo Blue with Burnt Sienna, adding touches of Carmine for variety.

• Shade the flowerpots with Burnt Sienna and Cadmium Red, adding some Ultramarine Blue in the deeper recesses. The shading in this step will help to give form and substance to the objects. To give the objects a three-dimensional look you must use at least three applications of shading or apply at least three values.

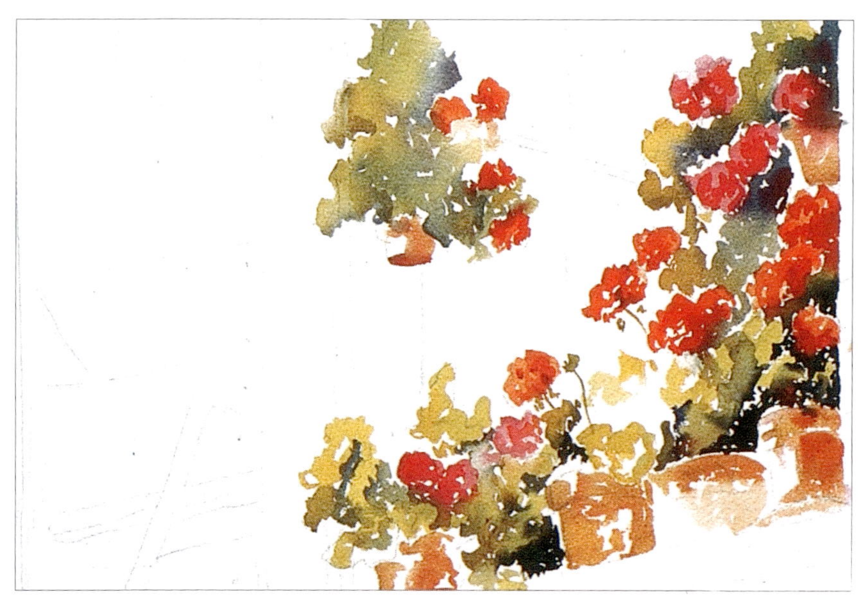

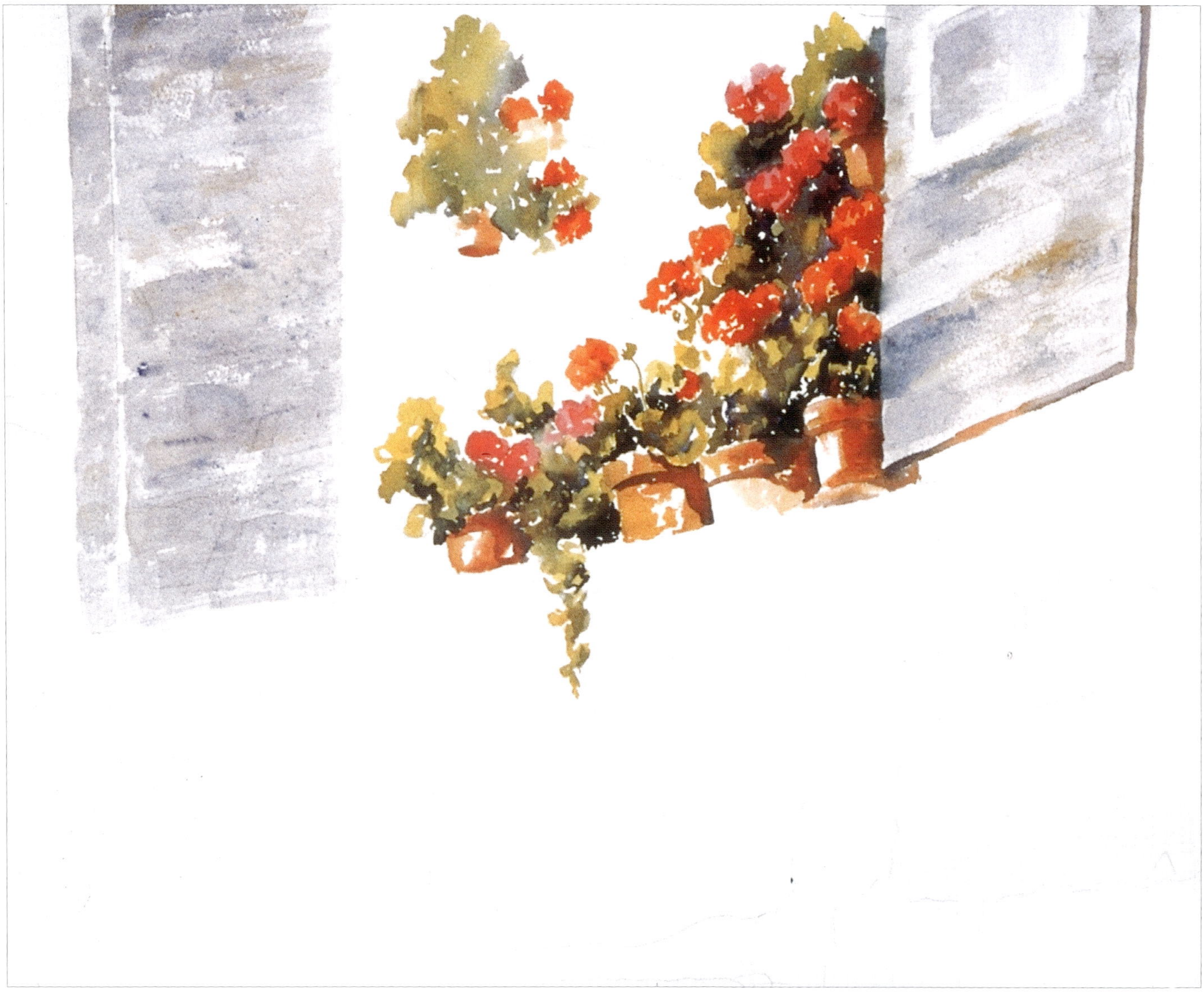

Step 4

Paint the old shutters

- The shutters are cool gray/blue to complement the warmer sienna/orange tones of the stonework. To show the extreme age of the shutters apply the paint in a dry-brush technique. Dip a 1" flat brush in the water and then wipe it gently on a paper towel. Then dip the side of the brush in a blue/gray mixture made of Cobalt Blue/Burnt Sienna and quickly, gently wipe the excess on a paper towel. Barely touching the rough texture of the paper, drag the side of the brush across the shutter, pressing harder in some areas.

Put some Cerulean Blue in some areas and drag some pale Burnt Sienna in dry-brush across other areas. The lower horizontal edges of the shutters will be warm as they receive the "bounced" warm light from the ground.

NOTE: These little texturing tricks can all be overdone, so when you try them make sure to do so in small sections only.

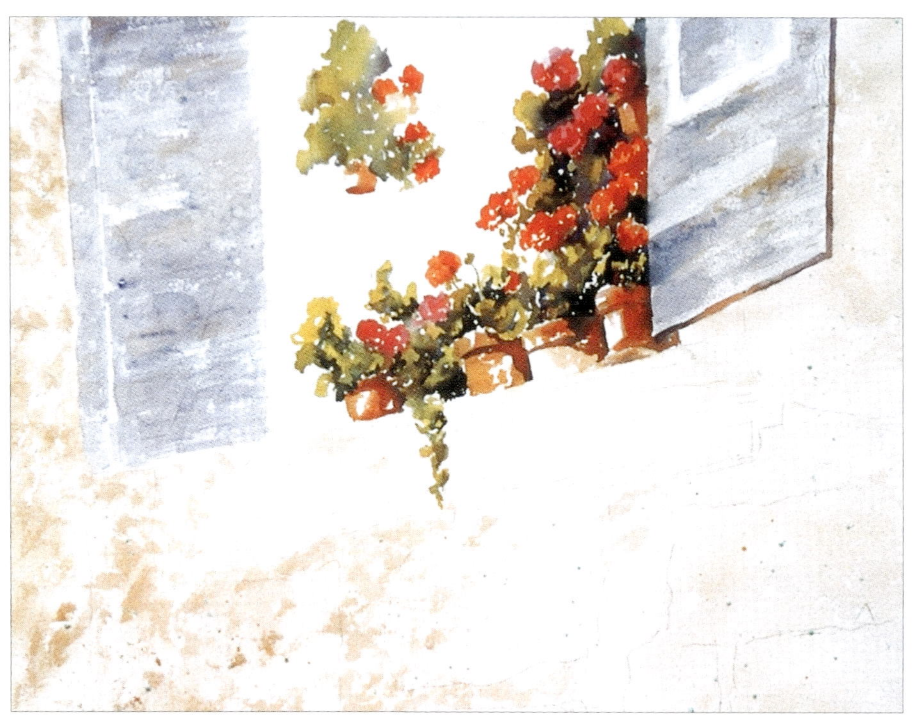

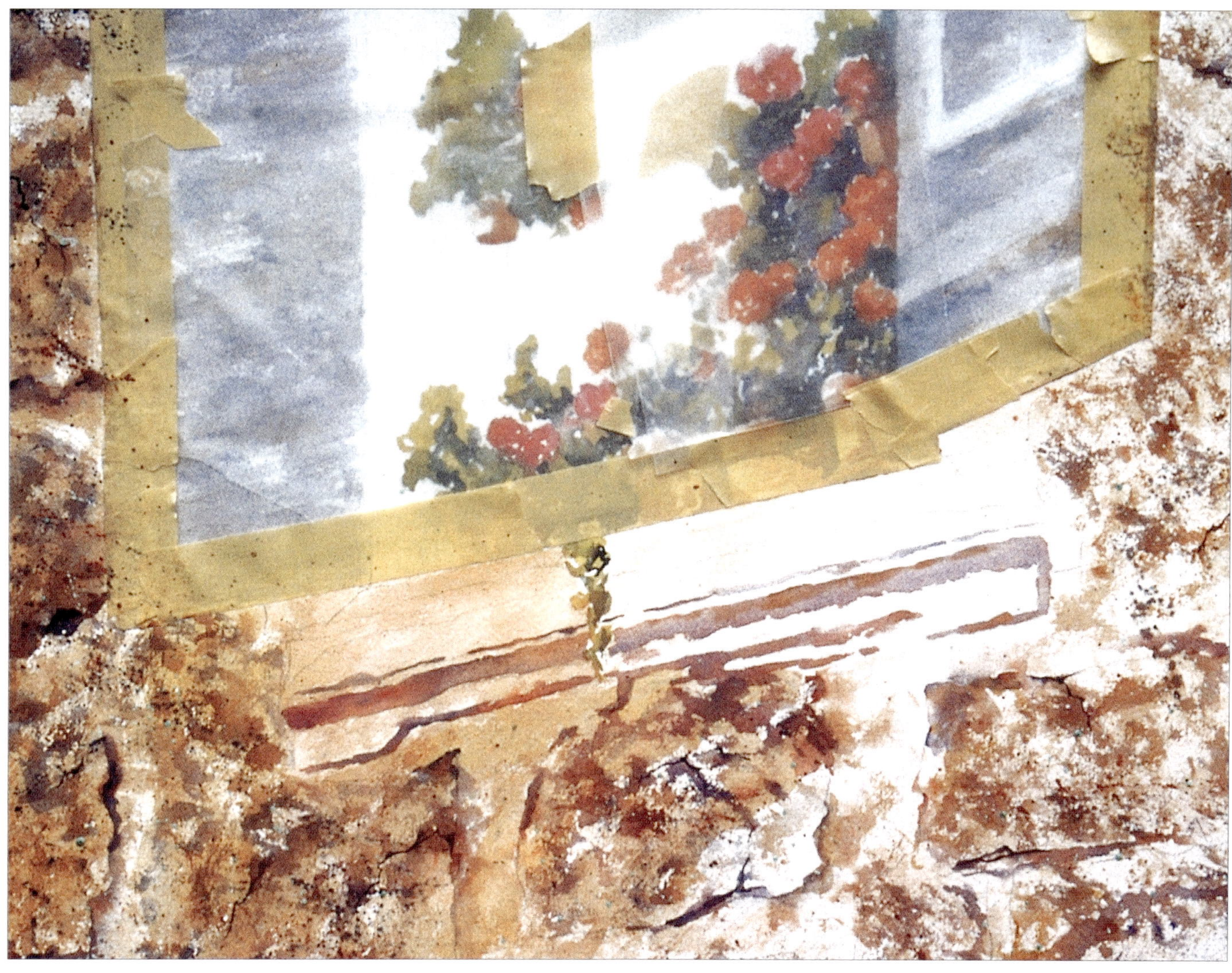

Step 5

Paint the stonework using glazing and splattering

- Since creating the stonework can become a messy task the first step is to use masking tape to fix a large sheet of waxed paper over the open window and shutter areas.
- Dip the brush in mild shampoo then in the masking fluid and splatter it all over the stonework area.
- After that is DRY, lightly glaze all the stonework with a very pale wash of Raw Sienna and Permanent Rose.
- The term "glazing" suggests a very wet wash applied on dry paper with a wet brush, but in this case use a dry-brush technique. As you apply the glaze the brush will skip over some areas. This wash will be the mortar between the stones. Mix various puddles of Raw Sienna/Scarlet Lake and, for a gray, Cobalt Blue/Burnt Sienna. Apply with a sponge and with the side of a round brush in the dry-brush technique, balancing the warm siennas and the cool grays.
- To make an area really sing, the use of warm and cool colors is quite effective. Define the shadows of the stones with warm colors in areas facing the ground and cool colors facing away from the ground. Create interesting rough shapes, but don't overdo it.
- In preparation for the following splattering, again cover the window and shutters with waxed paper. Splatter with reds and with darker Burnt Sienna/Ultramarine Blue grays. Let the splattered areas dry. If you feel at this point that the stonework lacks warmth, when it's completely DRY you can glaze all the stones, here and there with warm Raw Sienna/Permanent Rose.
- Finally, paint in the shutter shadows on the stone and the receding woodwork of the windows. Use Ultramarine Blue/Burnt Sienna with Permanent Rose dropped in for some areas at the top, and Scarlet Lake/Raw Sienna in some areas for warmth.

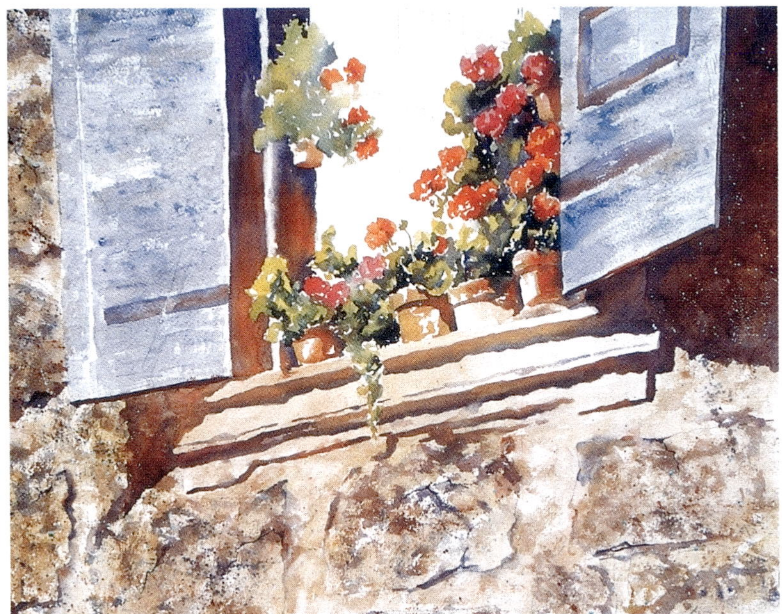

Step 6

Finish the curtains and start the shutters

- The curtains are done with attention to the values, which should be dark enough to make the flowers stand out. Use Cobalt Blue/Permanent Rose, showing lace detail only in a few areas by doing some negative painting around the lace patterns.

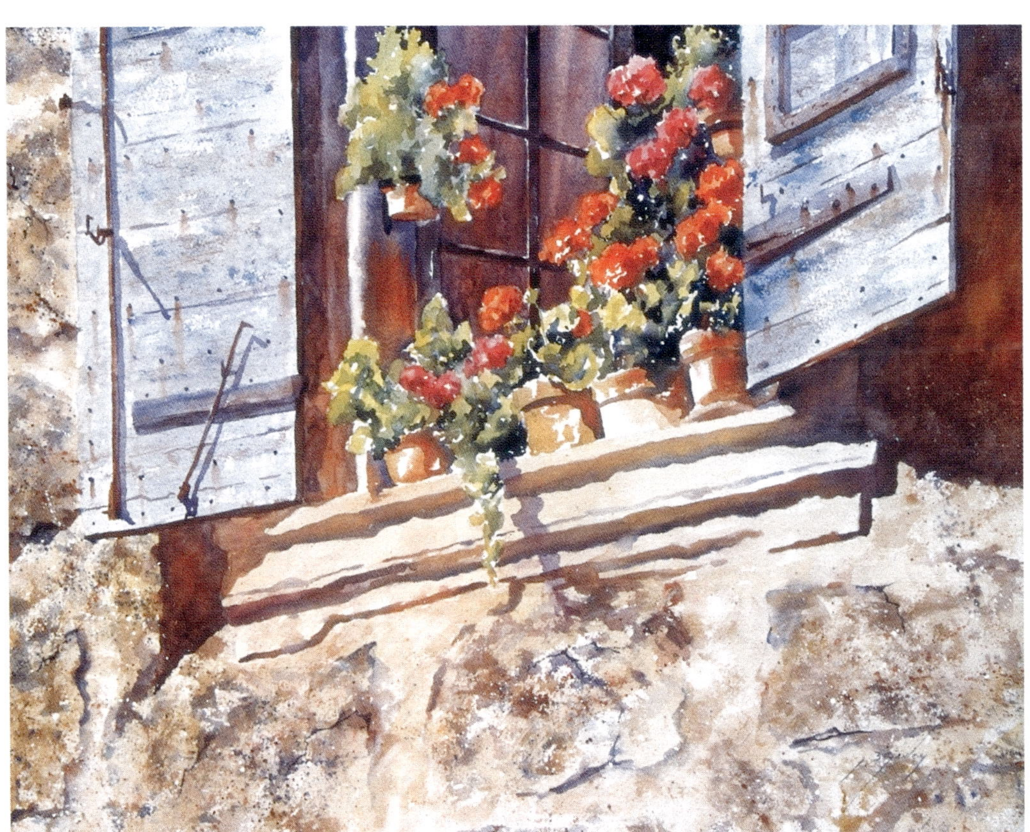

detail

Step 7

Finish the painting

To suggest the rust trails left by the old nails, start with the nail heads by applying dots of Burnt Sienna/ Ultramarine Blue, with a touch of Carmine in spots. Let this DRY. Then with a brush apply a trail of water from the nail head downwards and at the top of this trail drop in a little Burnt Sienna and let it slide down the water trail by itself.

- Remove the mask from the stonework. Some of the dots of mask will have landed in the shadowed area of the stonework and when you remove these there will be too much light for that area. So just apply a clean wet brush over the entire shadow and the little white dots will be glazed — in a way that adds yet another touch of texture.

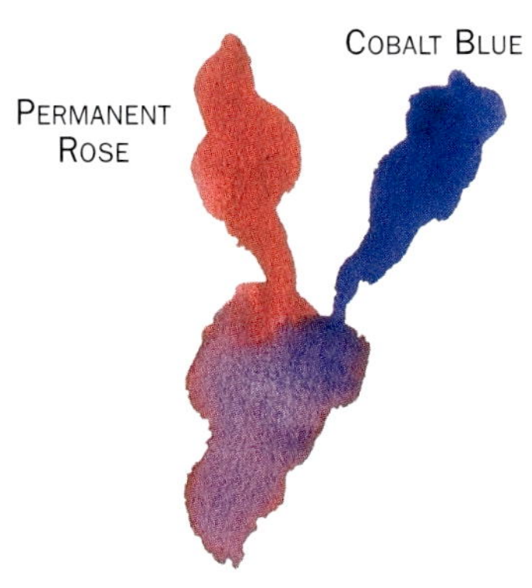

PROJECT 4 THE SECRET GARDEN

How to deal with competing centers of interest

In this scene, the chairs could overpower the flowers. Here's how to paint it so the chairs become the secondary center of interest.

The challenges

- To make one center of interest pop and the others recede and become secondary.
- To make distant areas recede.
- To paint realistic grass without using sawtooth edges.
- To wet-blend edges.

What you'll learn

- How to use values to focus attention on one area.
- How to add sparkle to an area.
- How to use color for emphasis.
- How useful Payne's Gray is.

Techniques you'll use

- Wet-in-wet.
- Opaque edges.
- Texture with thick paint or atomiser spray.

Before you begin, read the entire project through so you know what's going to happen in each stage.

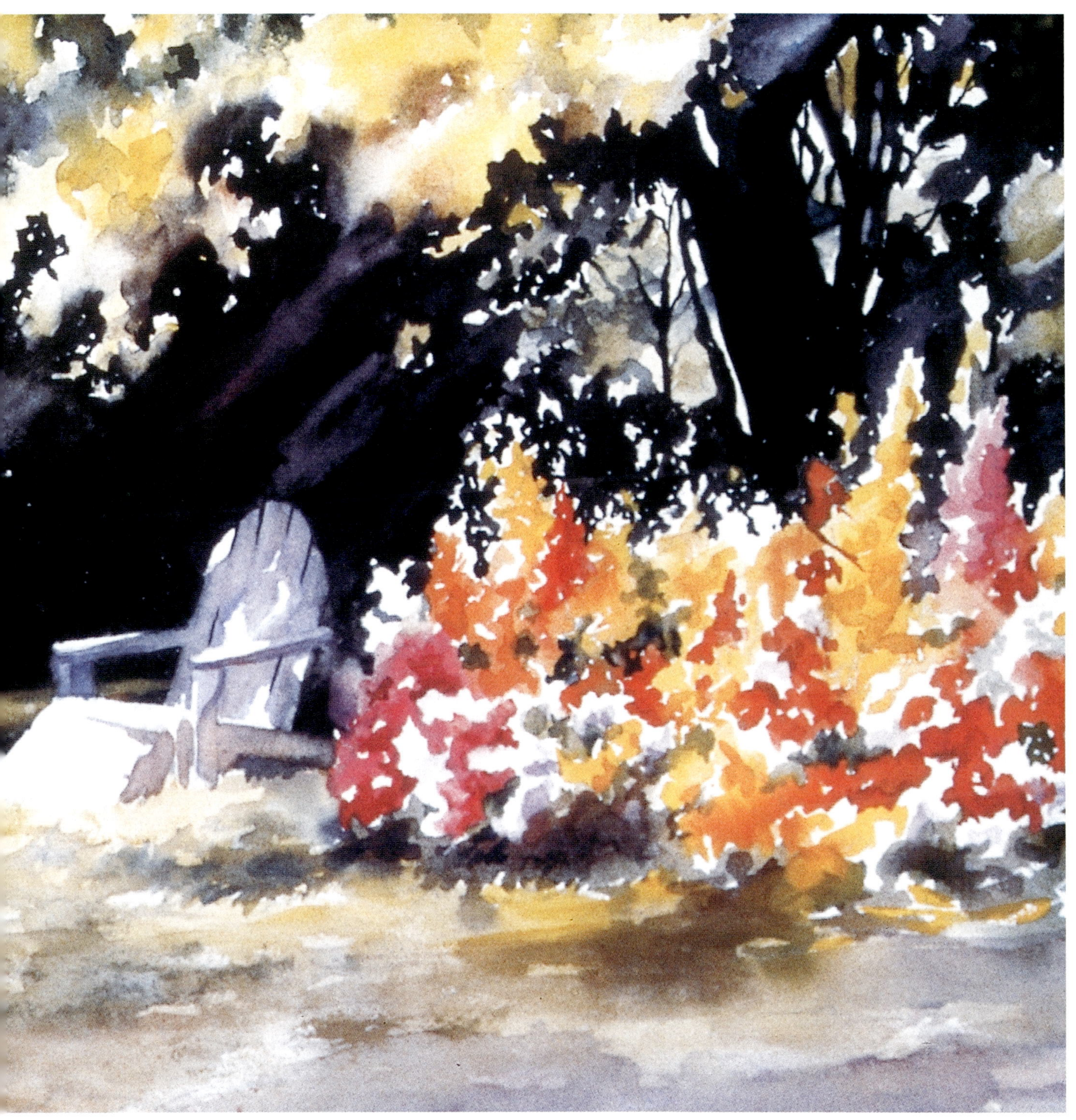

The Secret Garden, watercolor, $14\frac{1}{2} \times 21\frac{1}{2}$" (37 x 55cm)

The materials you'll need for this project

Paper and board

- Gator board as a support for the paper
- 140lb (300gsm) cold press watercolor paper

Masking fluid

- Tinted masking fluid

Brushes

- Daniel Smith 22-50 Series, Size #8 and #10
- Pro Arte Series 100, Size #12
- Fritch Scrubber (a stiff white nylon bristle brush with very short
- bristles, sold through Cheap Joe's catalog)
- Stiff round brush for mask application
- ¼", ½" and 1" flat brushes
- 2" hake

Odds and ends

- No. 2 pencil for the initial drawing
- Stapler and staples
- Large natural sponge
- Mild shampoo

Artist quality watercolors

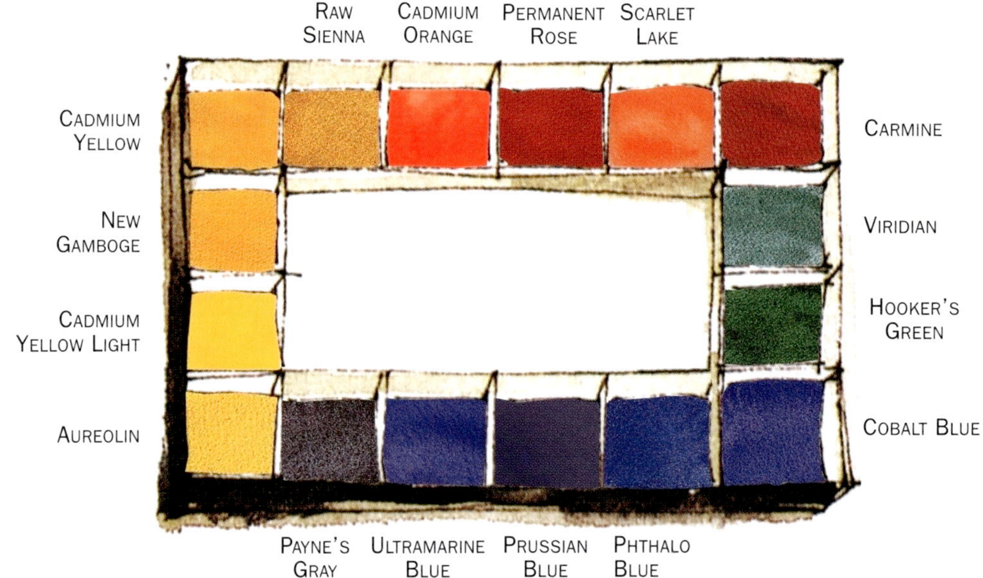

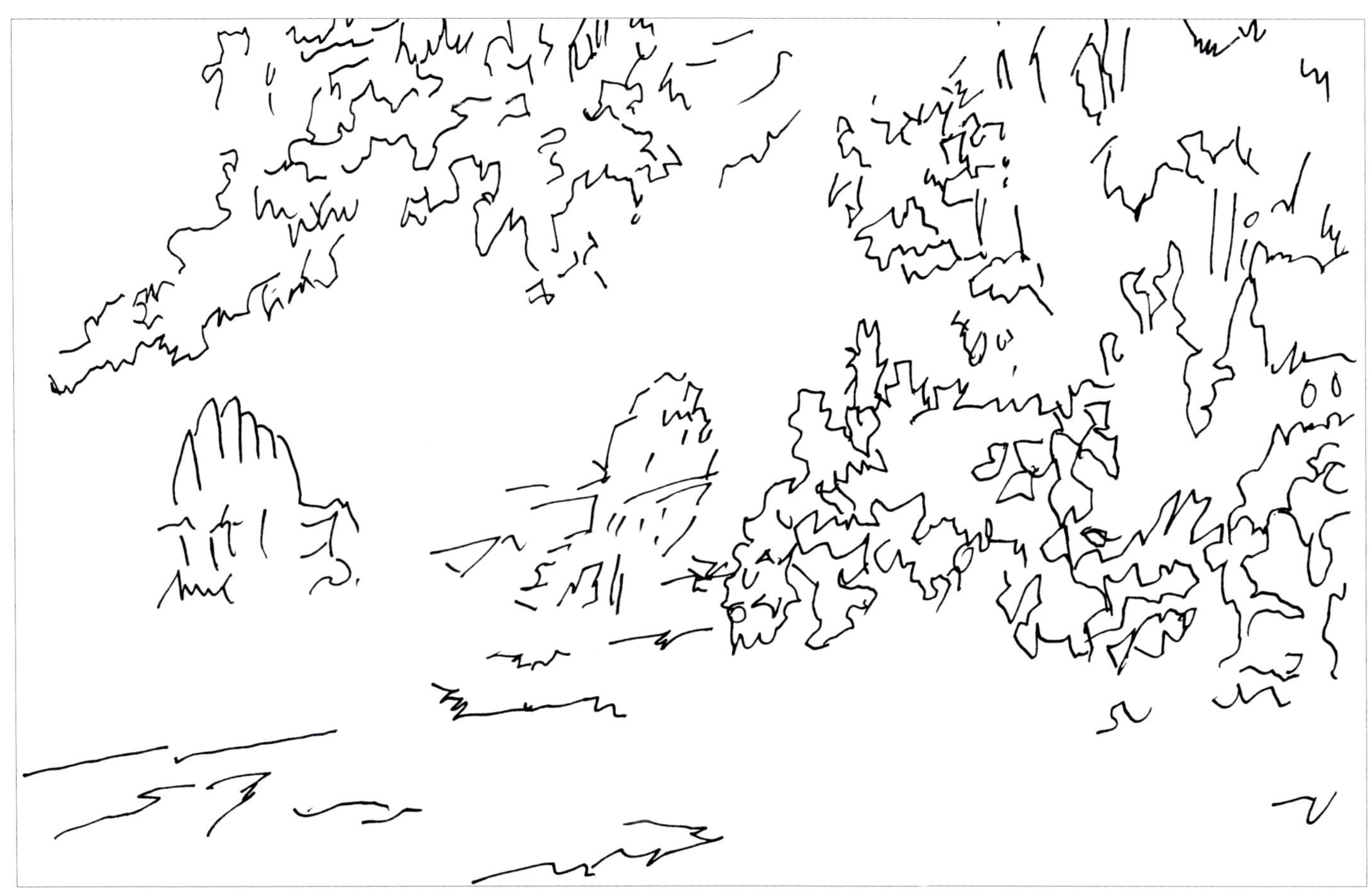

Step 1

Sketch or trace this design onto your paper using pencil

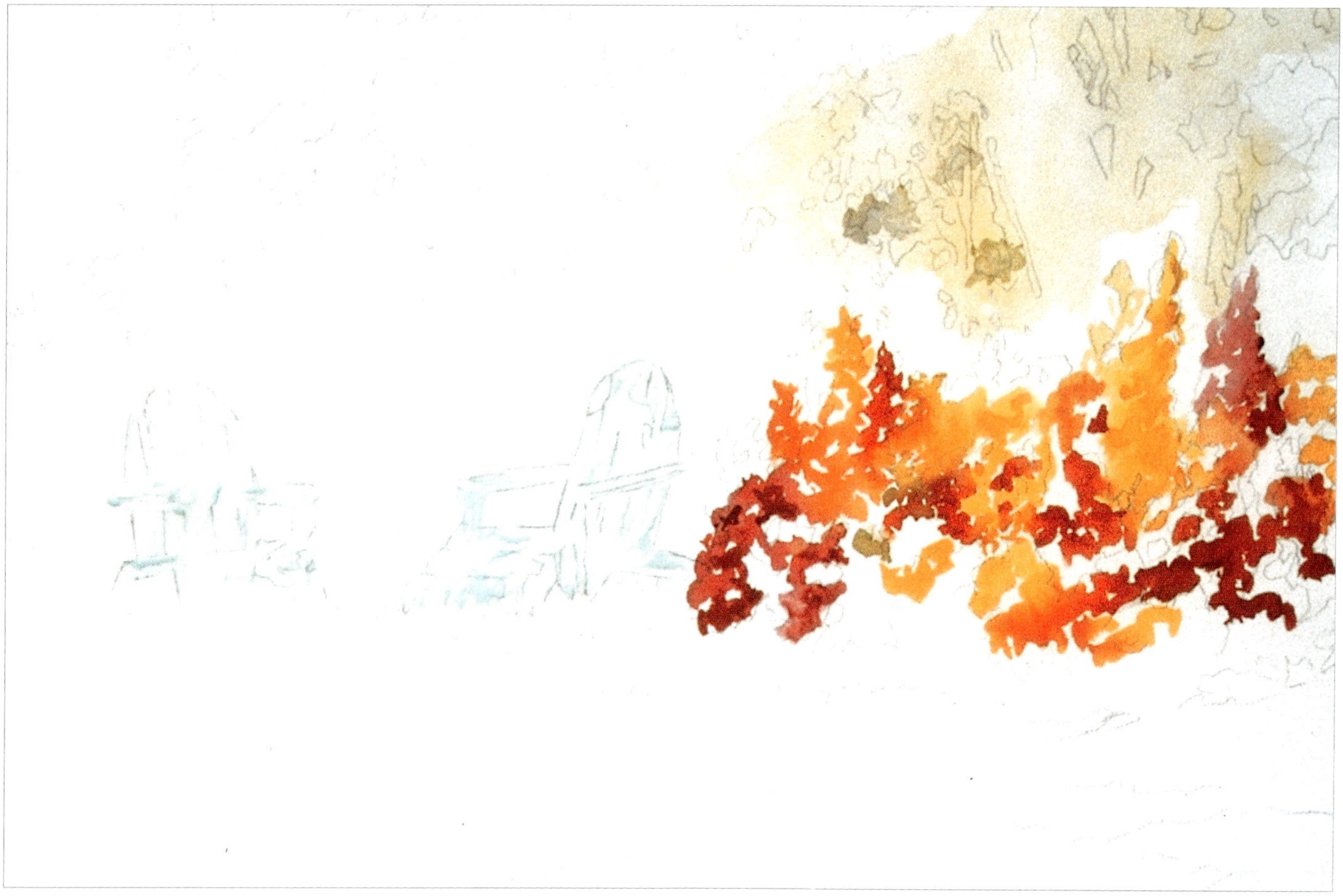

Step 2

Start with light washes

- Wet the area on the right above the flowers. Use your ½" flat brush to drop in some pale grayed yellows.
- Next paint the lightest flowers in Aureolin. Then drop in some New Gamboge.
- Add some orange flowers, and a few Scarlet Lake mounds. Let some edges touch and run together, while trying to make interesting edges and flowerlike shapes, but always save clusters of white. These white "flowers" will be the sparkle in the painting.
- Leave spaces for a few greens which will be added later.

Step 3

Protect the whiteness of the chairs

As a precaution, apply masking fluid to the chairs. Let it dry. Add a few soft blue-greens (Cobalt Blue and Viridian) as leaf clusters in the distance beyond the tree trunks.

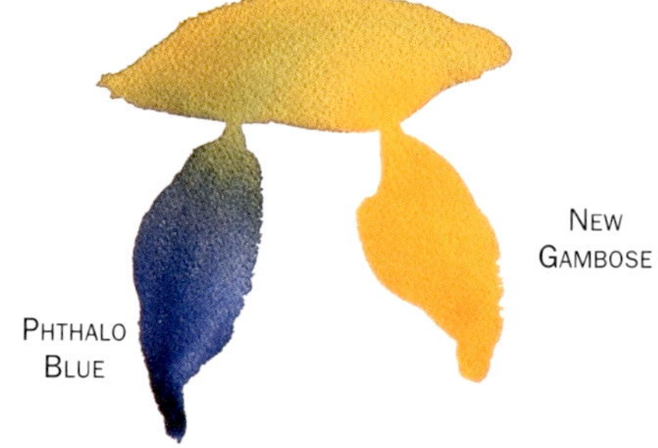

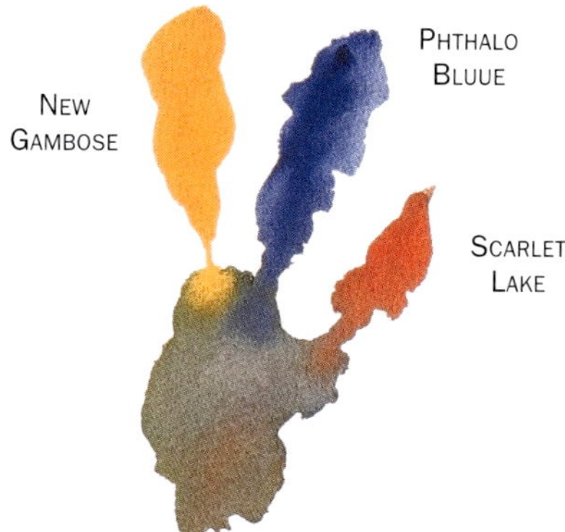

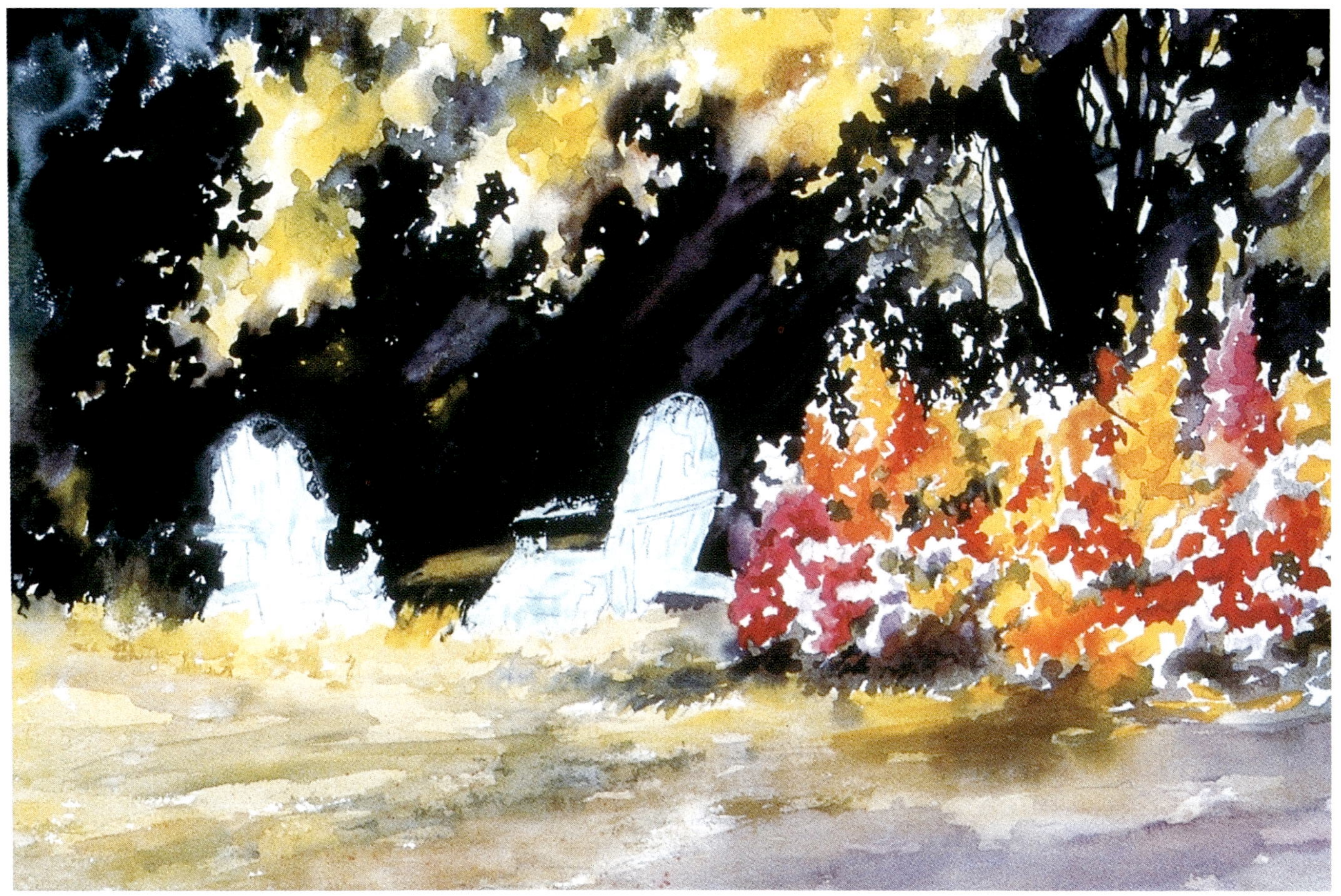

Step 4

Paint the branches and grasses

- Wet the area of the overhanging branches using clear water.
- Use your #12 round brush and drop in palest Aureolin, then add a little New Gamboge, Cadmium Yellow and Raw Sienna. Use the Aureolin as the palest yellow at the top of each branch, and Raw Sienna as the deepest yellow at the bottom.
- Mix a small bit of Phthalo Blue with your yellows and gradually add a touch of green to some of the still-damp yellow edges and let them wet-blend.
- For some darker areas, paint darker greens by adding a touch of Ultramarine Blue into the greens. This will help those areas recede while the yellow areas will come forward.
- Add some Raw Sienna with just a touch of Scarlet Lake, mix and touch this to some edges.
- For the grasses, use a 1" flat and paint some warm yellow on the upper left part of the lawn. Gradually change yellows and eventually add some soft greens as you work your way down the paper. Add just a touch of pink to this mixture to gray it as you work to the right. Go right into the garden foundation greens with a darker green (Phthalo Blue, New Gamboge, and just a hint of Scarlet Lake), letting these wet-blend only in some places with the grasses.
- Here's a tip: when doing the grass, don't overdo the typical sawtooth pattern edges. Instead, wet-blend some of those edges.
- Now add a variety of greens in the flowerbed — remembering to save those whites!

Step 5

Develop the darks

- Once your paper is DRY you can start on the darks. Mix into a small plastic cup a one-inch squeeze of Payne's Gray, a quarter-to half-inch of Prussian Blue, and a quarter-to half-inch of Hooker's Green, plus a smaller amount of Carmine. Add 8-10 drops of water and stir. The paint will be a little thicker than usual. Change the proportions of the Hooker's Green and the Carmine as you work in different areas.
- In the areas where there is more Hooker's Green than Carmine you can drop in some Cadmium Yellow Light while the darker color is still WET. The yellow will hit that dark mixture and turn green as it twirls around and settles down, resembling interesting leaf patterns.
- When this is DRY you can wet certain areas and gently brush out sunrays, leaving a lighter area of the predominant color (in this case Carmine). You can also wet areas that meet the green leaves and wet-blend some of these edges. For more texture in the Payne's Gray area, spray tiny droplets of water and, after ten seconds, blot.

HINT

On any painting you always want the color to change, usually from warm to cool or dark to light, as you go from one side of the paper to the other.

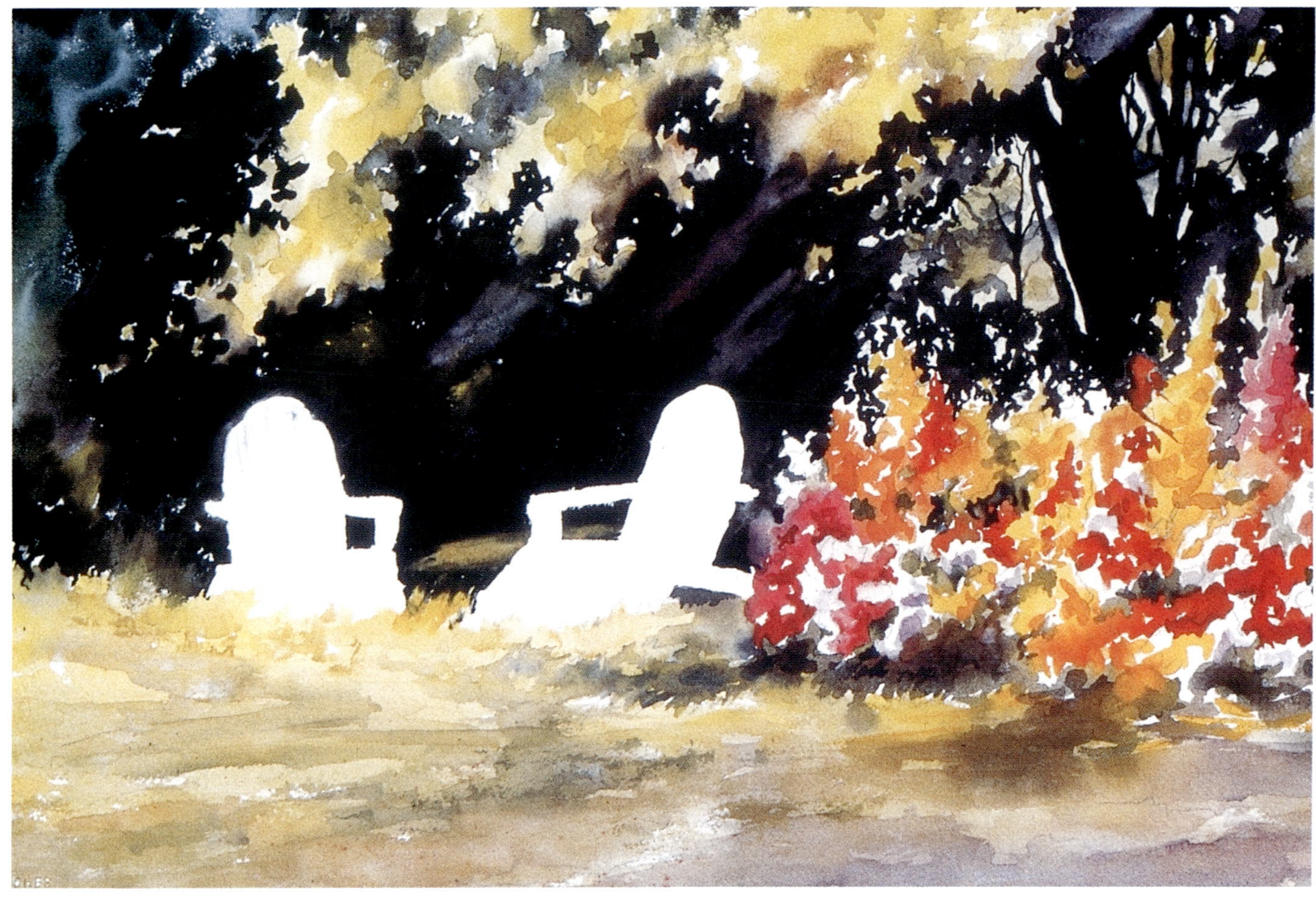

Step 6

Glaze the lawn

It's a good time to glaze over areas of the lawn with a variety of light greens and some violets (Cobalt Blue and Permanent Rose).

Emphasizing the larger center of interest

- Let's review how we emphasize a center of interest. We decide what the focal point will be, then we create it by using the brightest complementary colors in that area (blue/orange, red/green, yellow/violet), and using the strongest light/dark contrasts and more detail. Not all those techniques need to be used in every painting — one will work.
- Here, the brightness and lightness of the flowers against the darkness of their immediate surroundings, as well as their busyness, makes them the center of interest. The shadows on the chairs help them to recede and remain secondary.

Step 7

Paint the chairs

- The next step is to remove the masking fluid from the chairs. It was a smart move after all! Using masking fluid allows you more freedom in applying the staining background in a loose manner.
- To ensure the chairs do not compete with the flowers as the center of interest, you have to make them recede and subdue them. The way to do it is to use very little detail on the chairs — mostly shadows with a touch of dappled sunlight, keeping some of the edges soft enough to blend into the background.

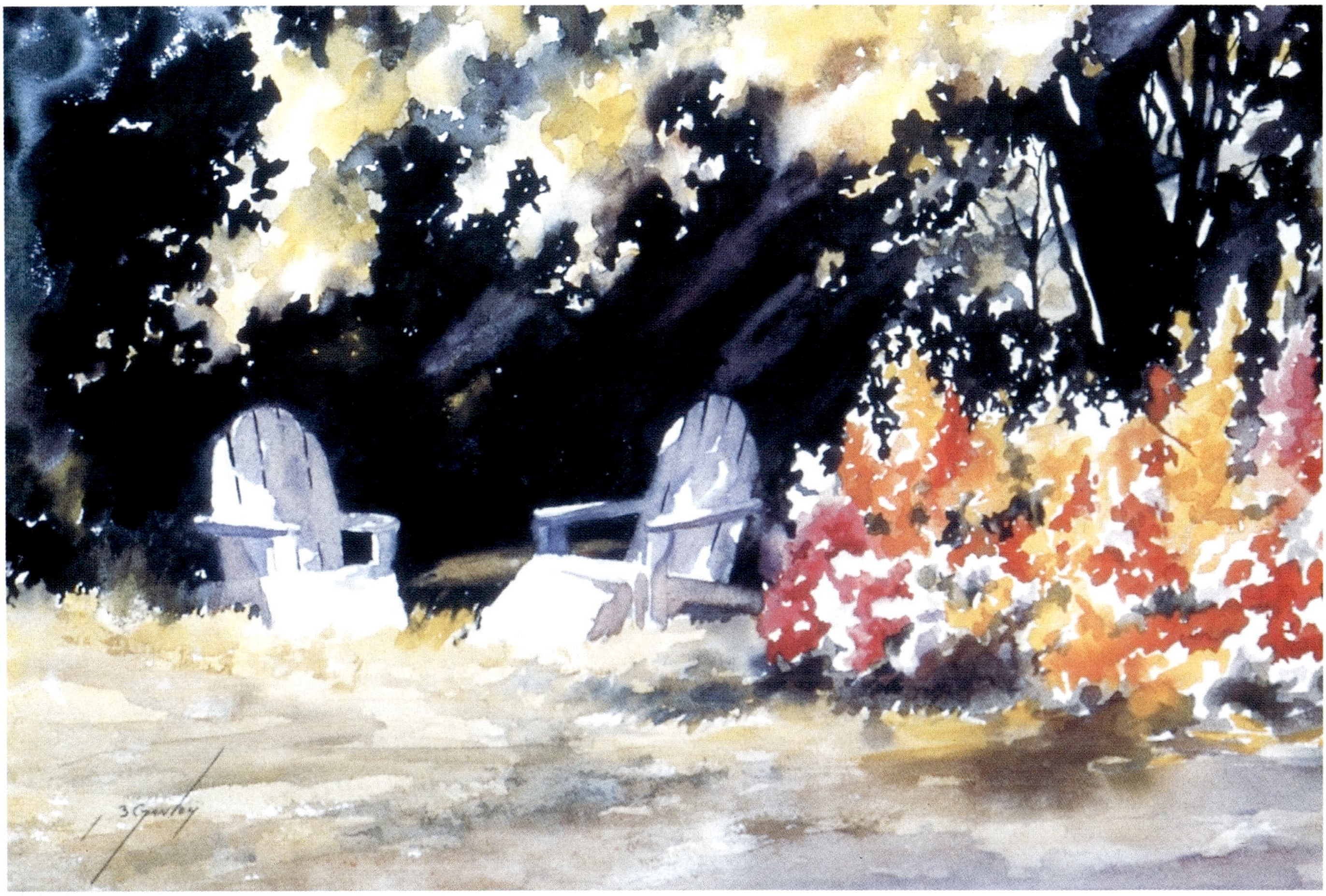

Step 8

Paint the shadows on the chairs

- For the shadows use a mix of Cobalt Blue and Permanent Rose, dropping in a little Raw Sienna on the left chair for warmth and variety.
- On the part of the right chair nearest the flowers, drop in a tiny touch of red for a reflective glow.
- Soften some of the chair edges by dampening some of the nearby dark background and letting the chair edges blend into the background.

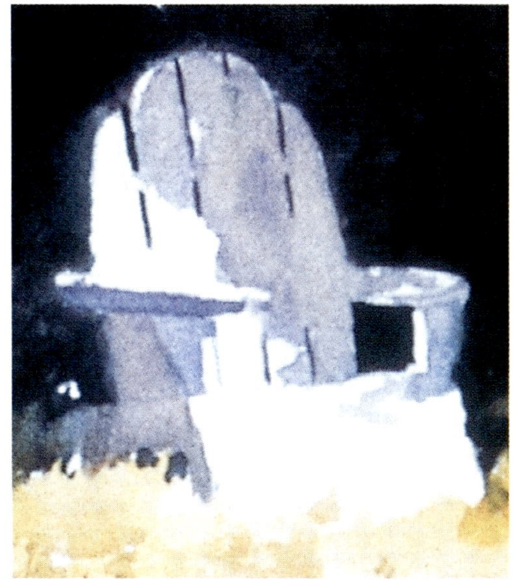

Detail

PROJECT 5 THE ORCHID GAZEBO

How to achieve balance in a painting

Through good design, complementary colors, hard and soft edges, color repetition, and a variety of textures, you can achieve the overall unity and balance that is so desirable in any painting. For this project, we'll be working on rough paper.

The challenges

- To break up a confusing mass of green vegetation into simple shapes.
- To make large masses of green more interesting.
- To achieve balance.
- To paint intricate shadow patterns while keeping the edges soft.
- To make a realistic transition from one very distinct area of a painting to another.

What you'll learn

- Why saving whites is so important.
- How to add vibrancy to large masses of green.
- Why it's important to evaluate your design as your work progresses.
- How to gray too-vibrant colors by mixing three translucent primary colors.
- How to deal with problem areas.

Techniques you'll use

- Wet blending.
- Lifting.
- Splattering.
- Painting wet on dry paper.
- Spraying water dots on dry paper and then adding color for the creation of both hard and soft edges.

Before you begin, read the entire project through so you know what's going to happen in each stage.

***The Orchid Gazebo*, watercolor, 29⅛ x 21¼" (74 x 54cm)**

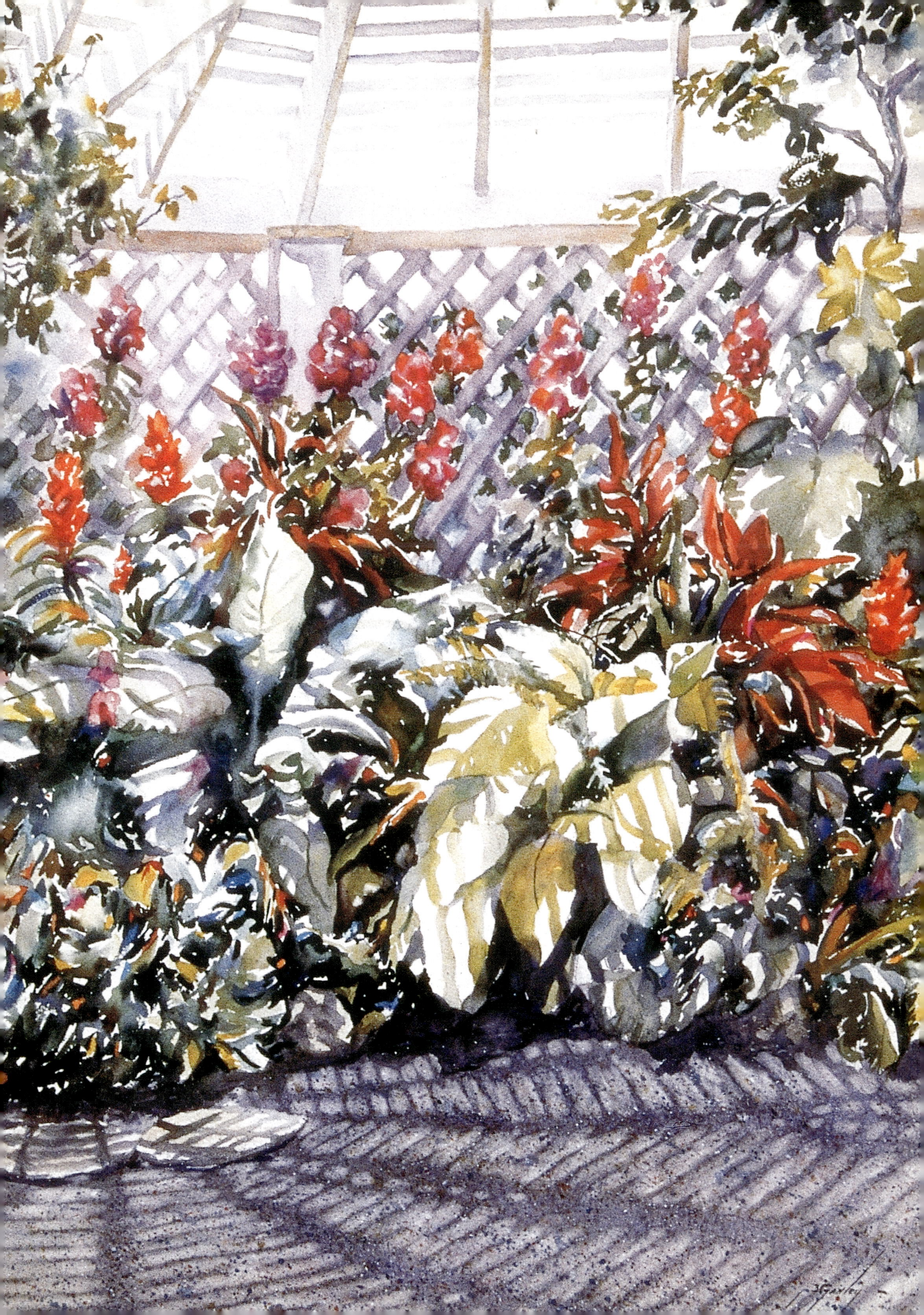

The materials you'll need for this project

Support

- Gator board as a support for the paper
- 140lb (300gsm) rough watercolor paper

Brushes

- Daniel Smith 22-50 Series, Size #8 and #10
- Pro Arte Series 100, Size #12
- Fritch Scrubber (a stiff white nylon bristle brush with very short bristles, sold through Cheap Joe's catalog)
- Stiff round brush for mask application
- ¼", ½" and 1" flat brushes
- 2" hake

Odds and ends

- No. 2 pencil for the initial drawing
- Stapler and staples
- Waxed paper
- Permanent White gouache

Artist quality watercolors

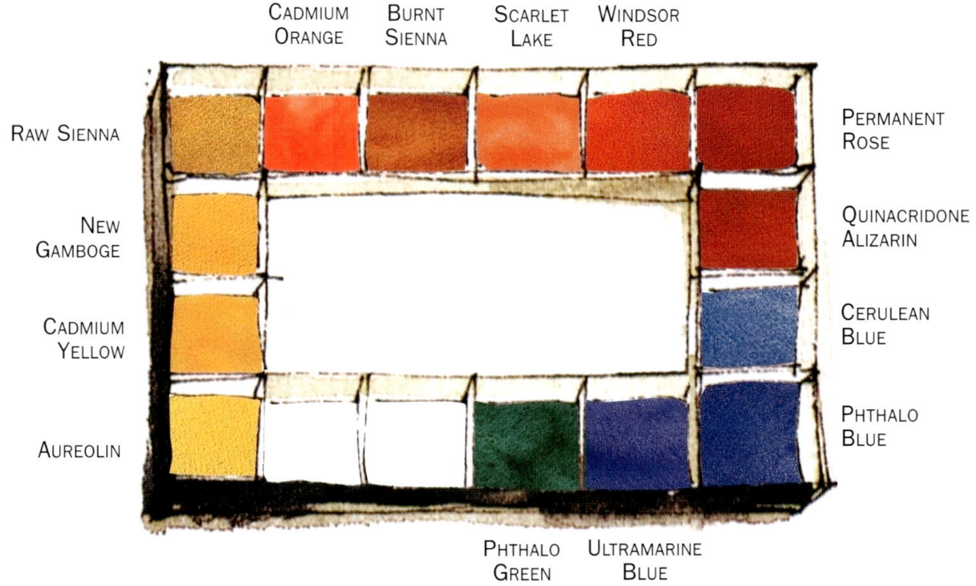

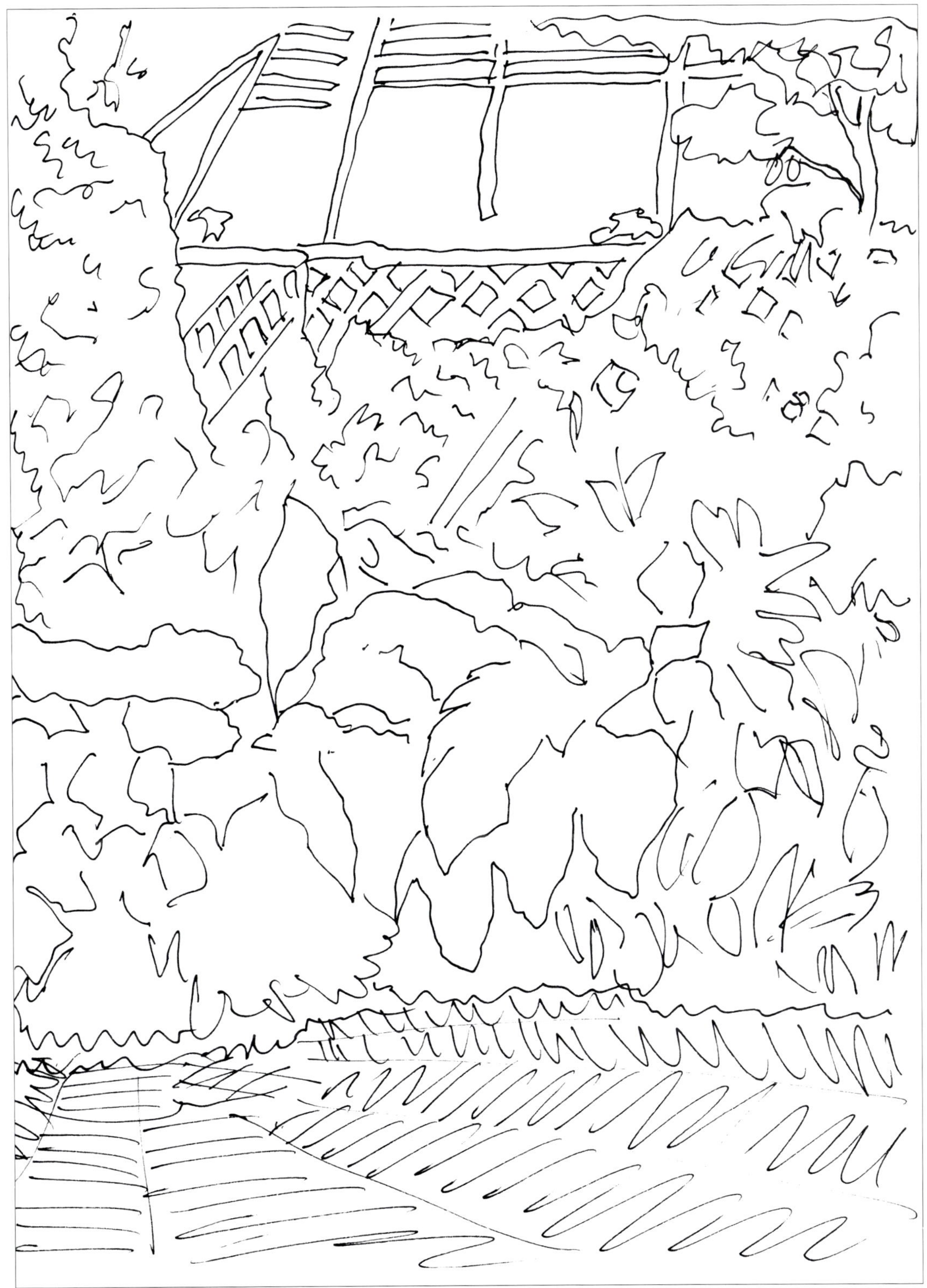

Step 1

Sketch or trace this design onto your paper using pencil

- This scene consisting of massed vegetation and patterns was confusing and it took me a while to decide how best to approach it. I decided to break it down into its obvious sections: the vegetation, the overhead lattice, and the shadows on the ground. Note the various interconnecting shapes.

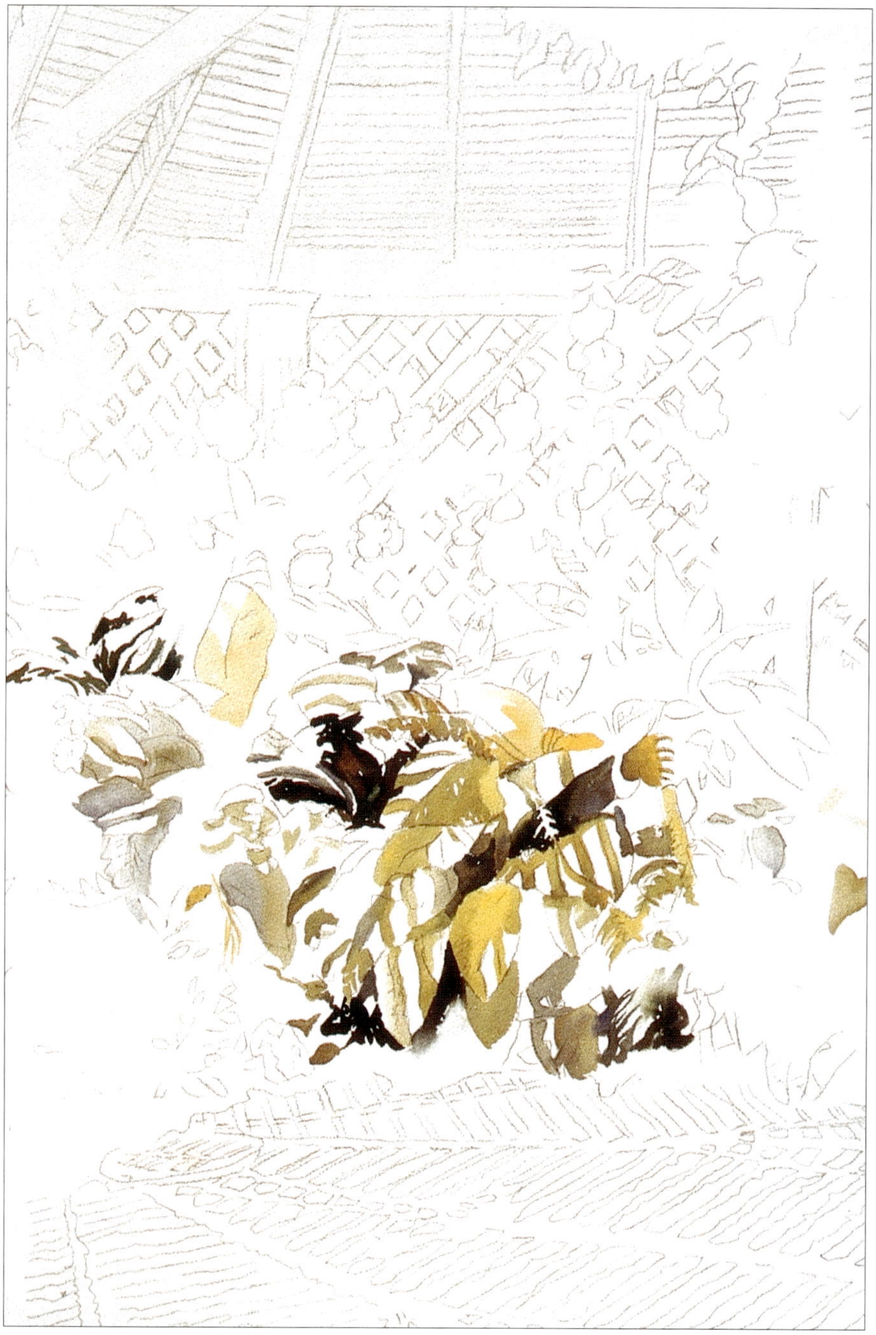

For your lights

For your lights you may use either Cadmium Yellow Light or Raw Sienna with Phthalo Green or Phthalo Blue, at times taming these colors with touches of Permanent Rose. In some washes you may add Cobalt Blue to the palette mix. The idea is to vary the pale greens.

For your darks

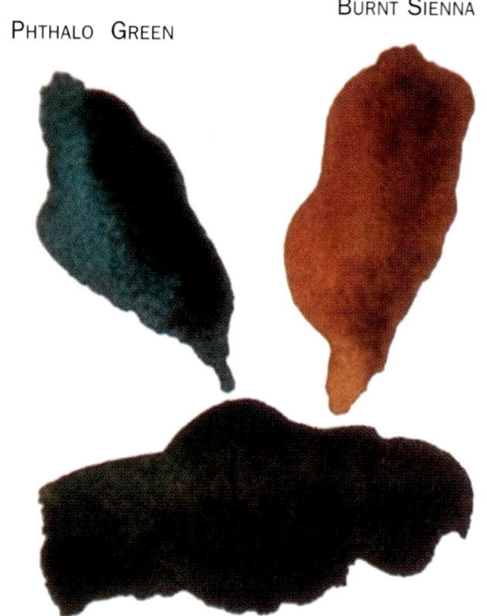

Step 2

Starting by mixing some darks

- The first painting step is mixing the colors you'll need for the very dark areas. Use Phthalo Green with Burnt Sienna, and substitute Phthalo Blue or Ultramarine Blue for Phthalo Green. Occasionally add Quinacridone Alizarin for a little spice in the darks. These early dark additions help define leaf clusters and make recognizable landmarks.
- Keep using a variety of these greens for the shrubbery on the left, starting with lights, and gradually going darker. Leave various shapes pure white, especially in the smaller shrubs. This will read as pure light bouncing off the leaves. Leaving small white triangles in the midst of a dark area of foliage will suggest the tips of hidden leaves, and will also serve to break up and add interest to larger masses of dark.
- Some of the white areas that are left will be filled in with small bits of vibrant color (orange, red, turquoise, purple and yellow) in a variety of tiny shapes. These small dashes of color will relieve the tediousness of all the green, help to liven up the painting, and give it that daring dash of originality. This method works especially well with tropical vegetation in which you may often catch glimpses of a Bird-of-Paradise or another bright lush flower. When you do drop in darks, keep some of them on the warm side by adding a little Alizarin and allow for wet-blending of darks with the still-damp lights. The idea is to strive for balance: warm vs. cool colors, soft vs. hard edges, and intricate vs. simple areas.
- You will also notice a few red fronds in the background. A little splash of red, as red is the complement to green, is needed to counteract and add balance to the vegetation. But remember, only a small amount of red is necessary to accomplish this balance. Always avoid using equal amounts of complementary colors, unless you want mud.

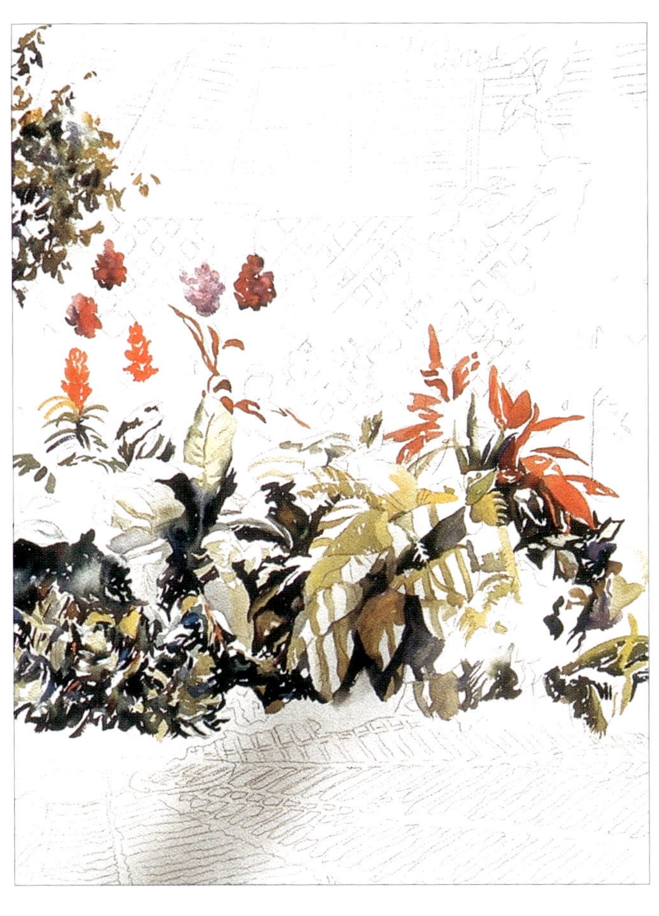

Step 3

Create a unifying bridge of green

- For the bit of green tree foliage on the left, give one quick spray of water to the dry paper in this area, then add the leaves. These dots allow some soft blending of edges and, where the paper isn't touched by water dots, hard edges form. Again, the key is balance. However, these overhead trees accomplish another purpose: they act as a bridge connecting the greenery of the shrubs in the middle section. Thus the top and bottom are connected, and at the same time the shape of the top section is broken up and made more interesting.

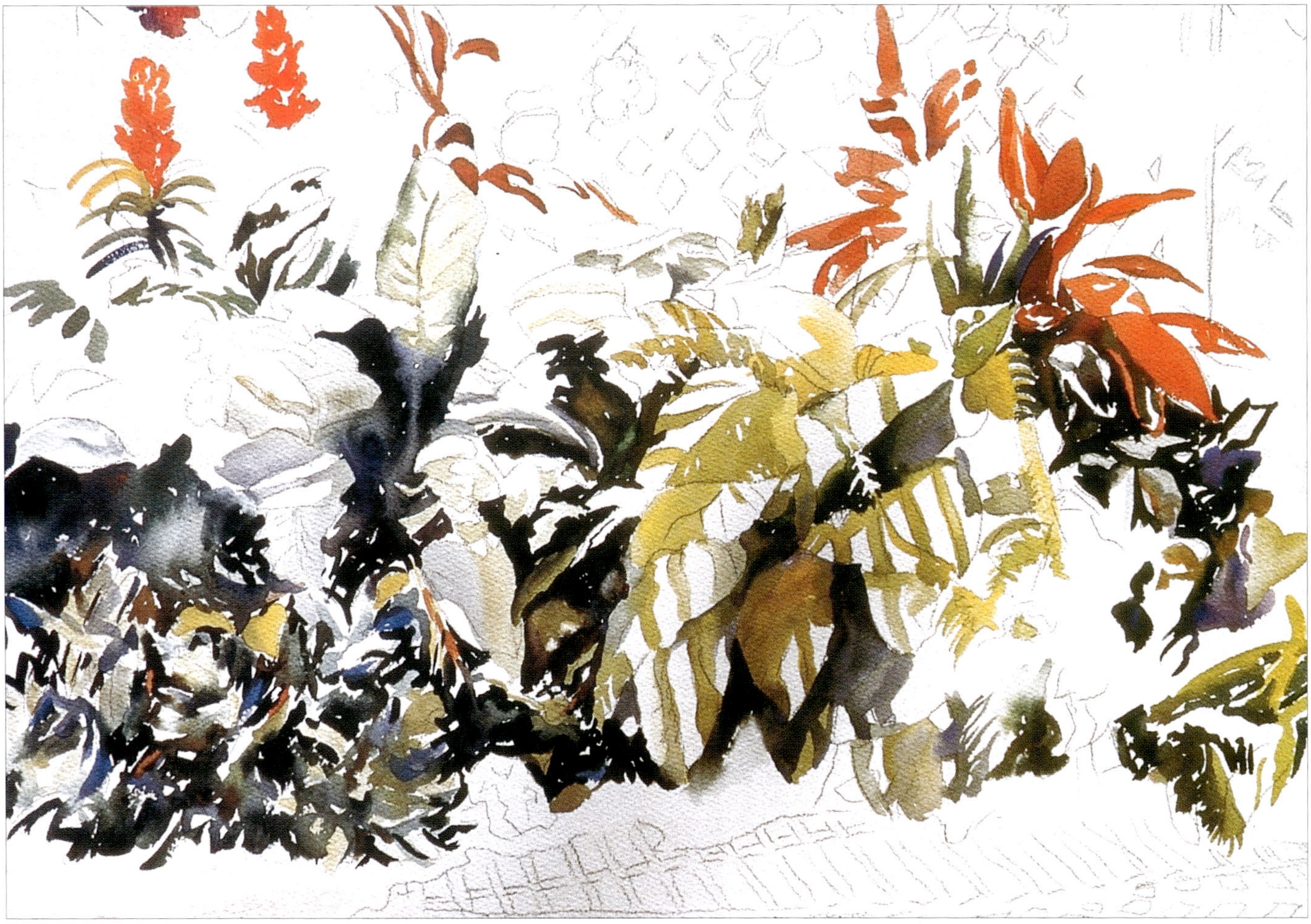

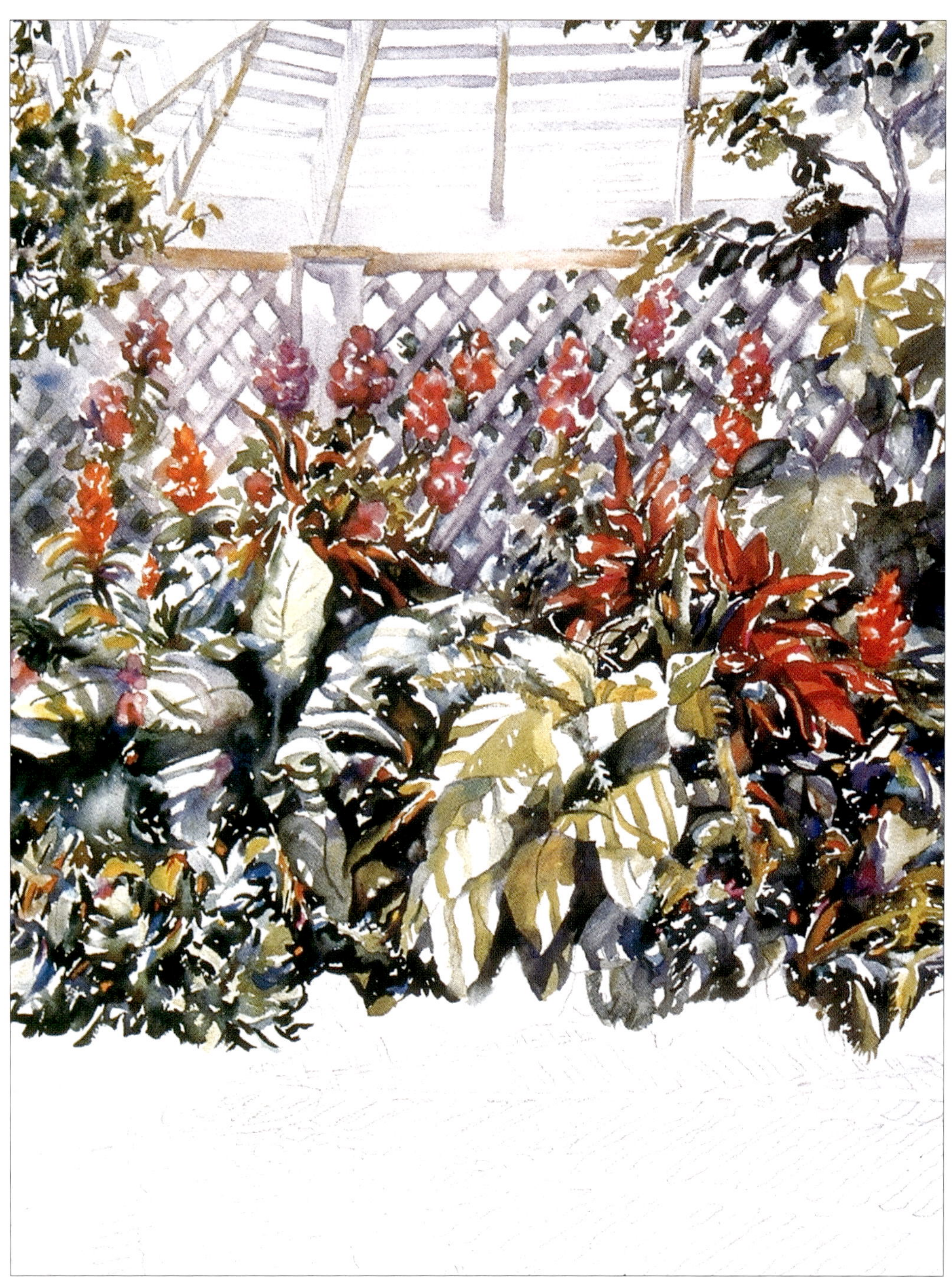

Step 4

Add the orchids

When adding the orchids, be careful to scatter them about in a pleasing pattern — not uniform or symmetrical. If you make them too dark, simply add a little water and blot! Choose a variety of pinks, violets and reds. Add the tree foliage on the right.

Step 5

Paint the latticework

For the overhead latticework use a mix of Cobalt Blue and Permanent Rose with a touch of Aureolin to gray the mixture. So that the lattice will not appear stagnant or boring, change the value as it progresses upward, from very pale to a medium value. This gives the impression of the glare of light radiating from beyond. Use the lattice color to paint the trunk of the tree on the right .

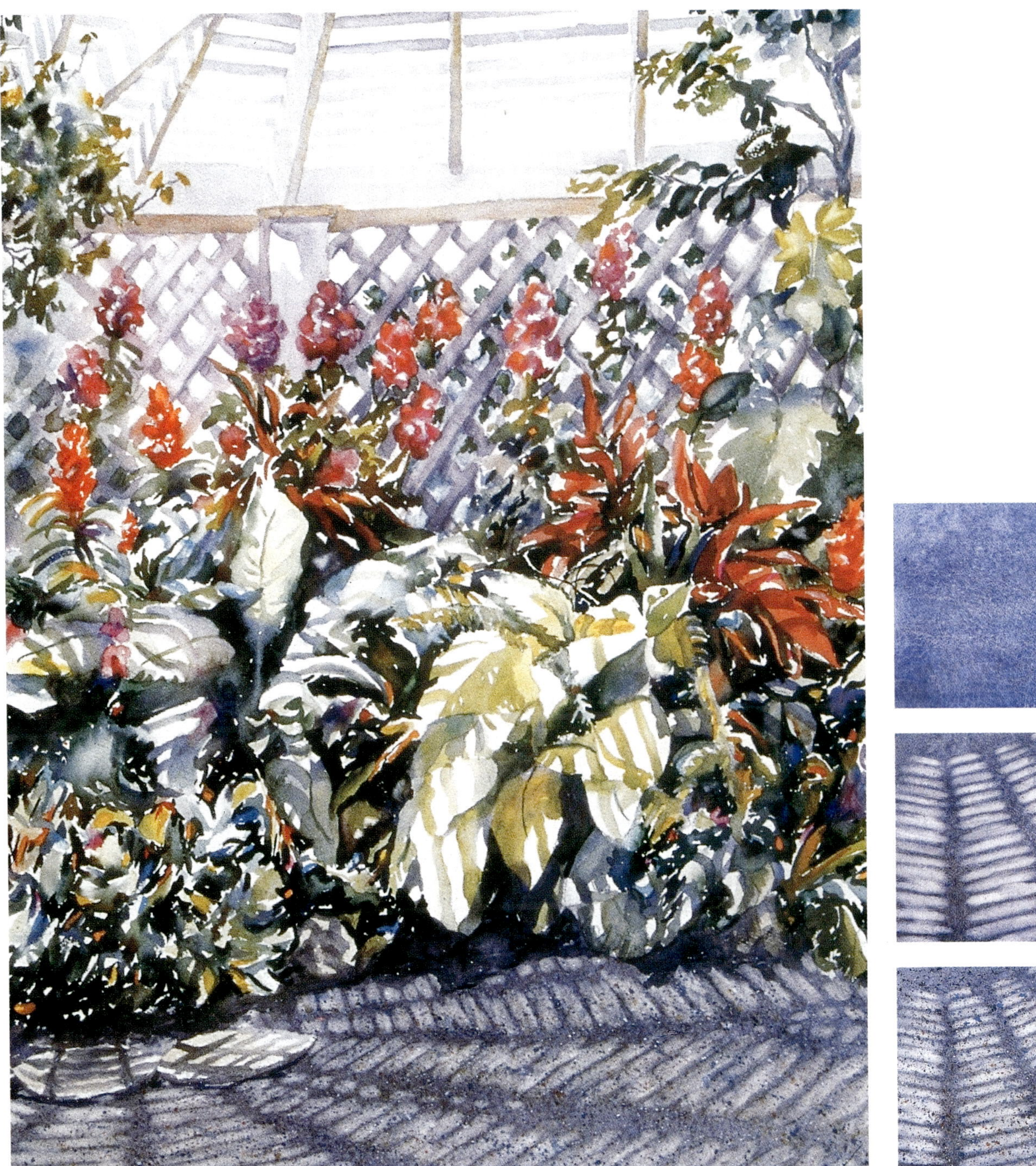

Step 6

Darken the shadows and lift the lights

- For the shadows on the ground you could paint the ground and then mask out the lighter areas. But then you end up with all the hard edges the mask leaves. Instead, mix up and apply a fairly dark gray using Ultramarine Blue for its sedimentary qualities and Burnt Sienna.
- When this is totally DRY, wet the lighter areas one at a time, and gently scrub with a stiff scrubber, then blot, thus lifting the lighter areas out. Lifting color will give a much softer edge than masking, and that combined with the splattering to follow (which will soften the edges even more) will give a very realistic and visually compelling look to the heavily shadowed gravel ground.
- When that rather large job of lifting is complete, add darker grays to the shadowed areas of the shrubs, thus making a nicer transition from the shrubs to the graveled floor. This simultaneously offers the opportunity to use the shadows to make a more interesting shape at the bottom portion of the painting. It no longer looks to be an equal third of the painting.
- Cover most of the painting with waxed paper and splatter on a variety of values of blue-grays, then a few pure blues, then a little red and, when everything is entirely DRY, add Permanent White gouache.

PROJECT 6 FESTIVAL OF COLOR

How to build up glazes to give color, form and substance

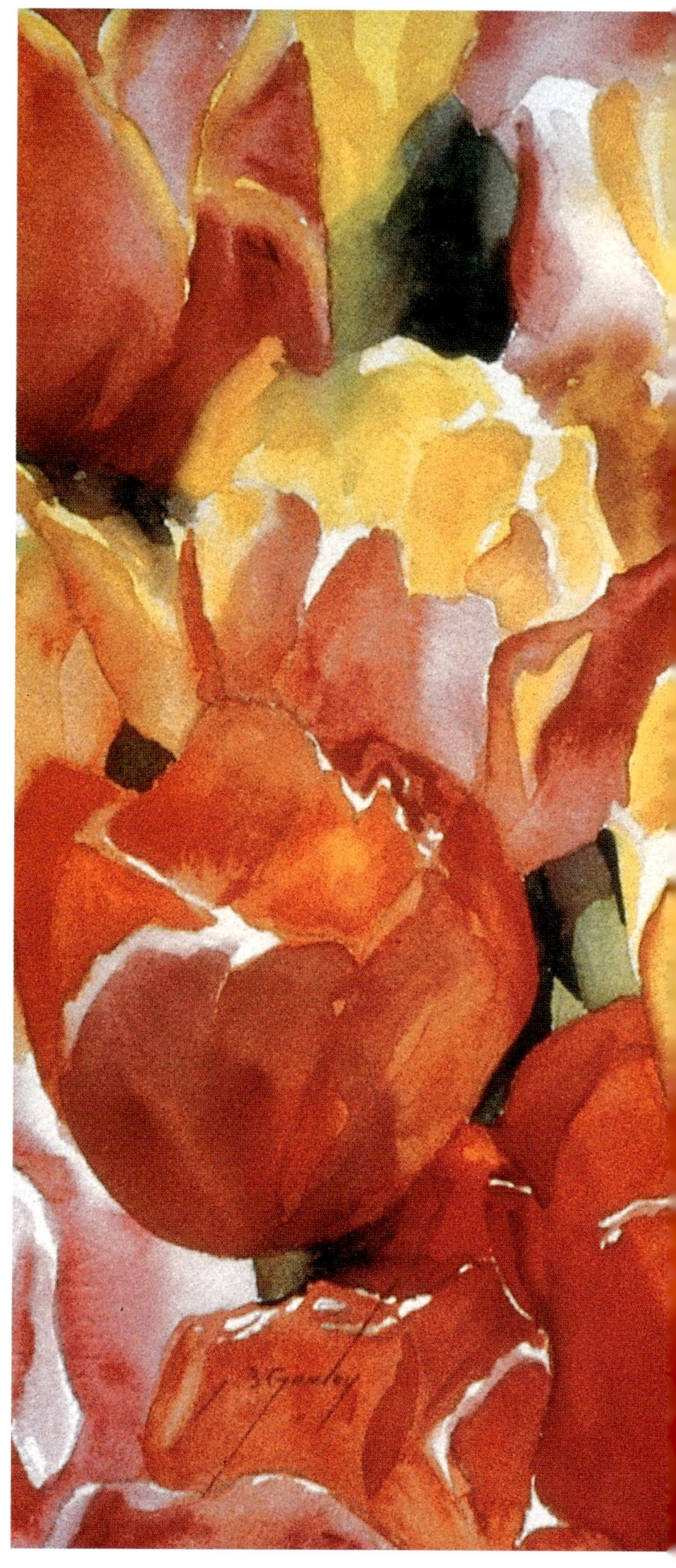

The challenging news is that because each previous layer must thoroughly DRY before you glaze on the next one, patience and time are two essential ingredients for a glazing project. The best news is that the end result will be worth the effort.

We will be using cold-pressed paper for this project.

The challenges

- To preserve the center of interest.
- To make some areas recede and others advance.
- To learn which of your colors are transparent and which are opaque.

What you'll learn

- The importance of using the right paper.
- Why you use transparent colors instead of opaque ones.
- How to isolate the center of interest.
- The importance of continuity of color from one flower to another in order to unify the painting and to form a mass of flowers rather than a bunch of individual ones.

Techniques you'll use

- Glazing — wet over dry.
- Wet-in-wet.
- Gradual build-up of colors from light to dark.

Before you begin, read the entire project through so you know what's going to happen in each stage.

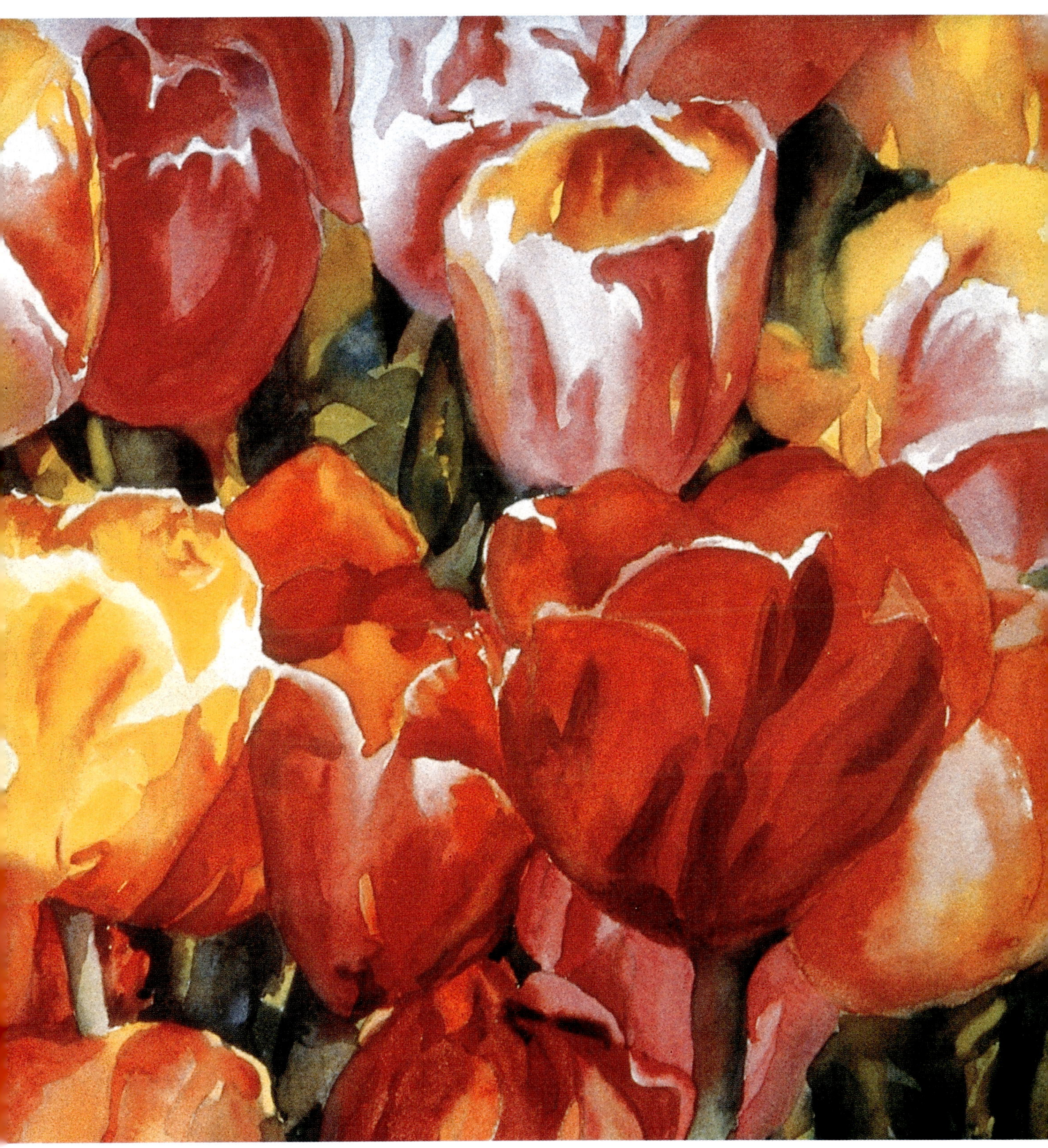

Festival of Color, **watercolor, 14½ x 21½" (37 x 55cm)**

The materials you'll need for this project

Support

- Gator board as a support for the paper
- 140lb (300gsm) cold-press watercolor paper

Brushes

- Daniel Smith 22-50 Series, Size #8 and #10
- Pro Arte Series 100, Size #12
- Fritch Scrubber (a stiff white nylon bristle brush with very short bristles, sold through Cheap Joe's catalog)
- Stiff round brush for mask application
- ¼", ½" and 1" flat brushes
- 2" hake

Odds and ends

- No. 2 pencil for the initial drawing
- Stapler and staples

Use heavier paper when you want to do lots of glazing

Because you'll be using repeated glazes or wet washes, your choice of paper is quite important. 140lb paper versus 300lb paper. The added weight of the heavier paper means that there is more substance for the glazes to sink into, and that means that the glazes on 300lb paper usually don't end up as vivid as ones done on 140lb paper.

Artist quality watercolors

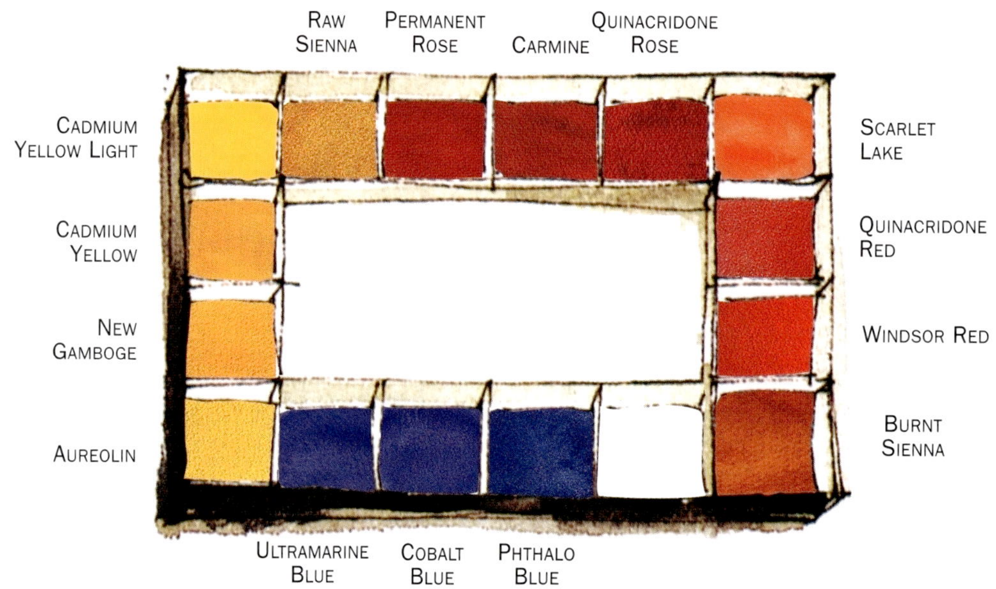

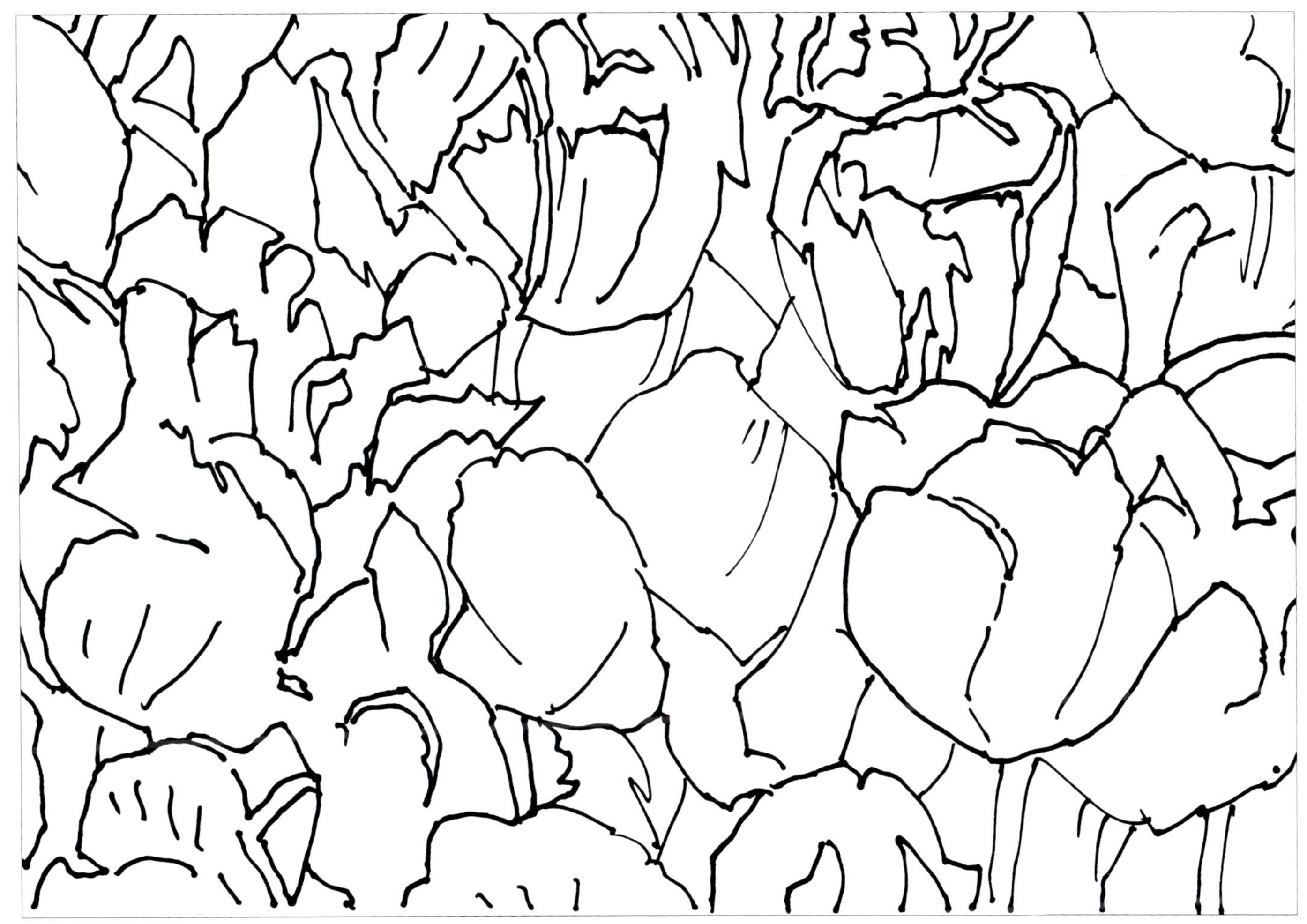

Step 1

Sketch or trace this drawing using pencil

Vary your viewpoint

When searching out wonderful garden ideas don't overlook more close-up compositions. I confess I am usually drawn to these fabulous cameos of flowers in a garden rather than the whole garden. Paintings like these take much longer to complete due to the fact that every petal of every flower receives multiple glazes, but the end result makes it worth the extra time.

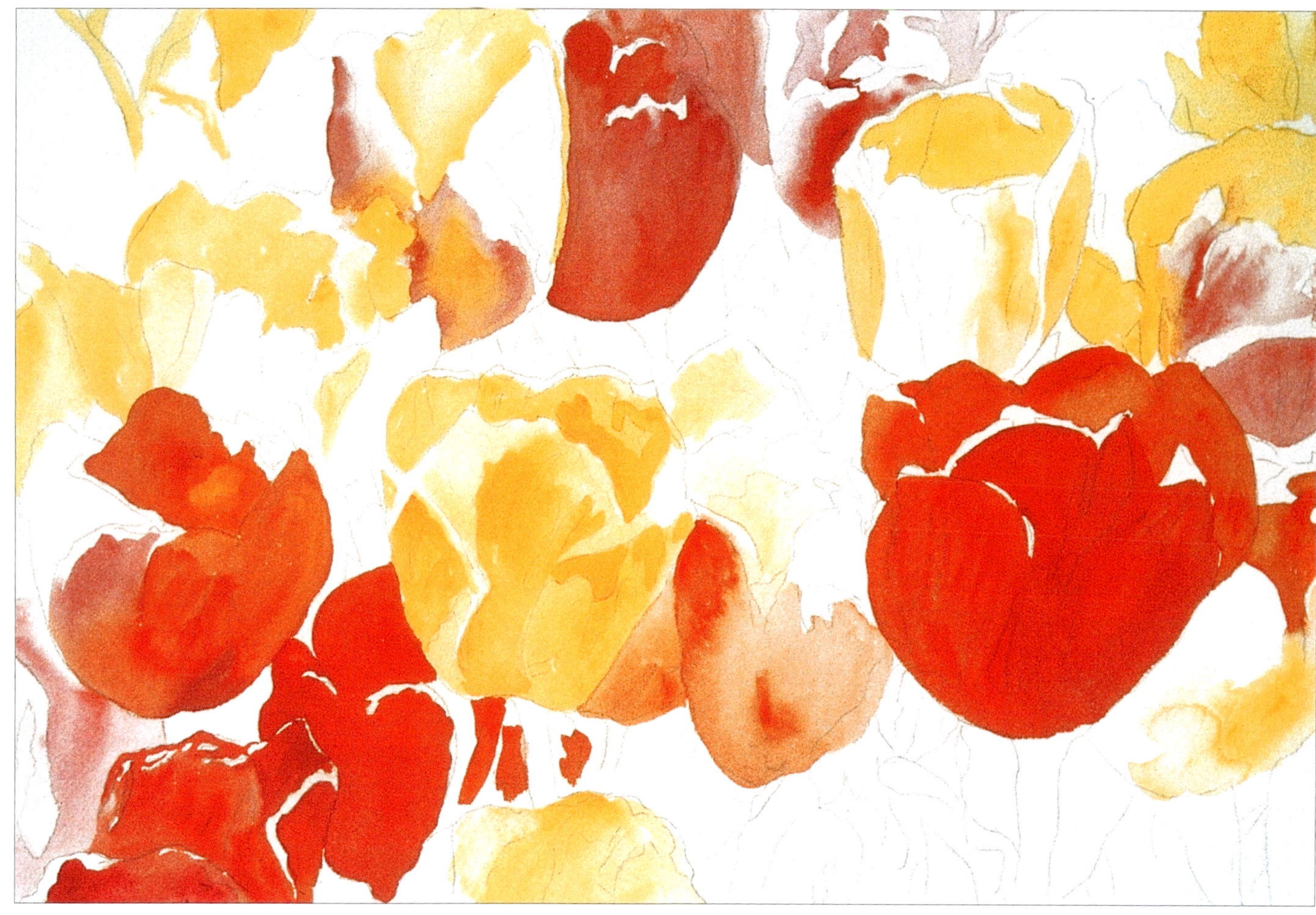

Step 2

Appreciate the pathways, then glaze

Before starting note the little pathways of white throughout the painting. These pathways are thoughtfully arranged so that they wander in a pleasing pattern throughout the whole painting. It's a good idea to reserve more whites than you think you'll need. At the end you'll glaze over some of these areas to just barely cover the white glare.

- Start with light transparent layers of the base color and then add many glazes. Starting with the lightest value of the chosen color, apply it on wet or dry paper with the largest brush possible, a No. 12 round or a 1" flat. Let the first glaze DRY thoroughly and then apply another wash over it.
- Depending on the size of your painting, select either a 1" flat or a round No. 8 or 12. Wet it and dip it into paint varying from quite thin to the consistency of cream and apply it onto the DRY first coat, leaving some areas unpainted so that the first wash peeks through.
- For the yellow flowers, start with Aureolin, which is the palest of yellows and quite transparent. Putting it on the paper, it appears very bright, but it's really quite tame after it's dried. When it is DRY, glaze some areas with New Gamboge, and while that's still WET add Raw Sienna into some of the creases, allowing for wet-into-wet blending. Gradually add a few warm reds to the yellow flowers.
- For your two pinks, use Permanent Rose with Quinacridone Rose blending wet-in-wet in some areas and adding cool reds in other areas.
- The red flowers may be started with yellow undertones, then blending with or glazing with the warm Scarlet Lake, or the cooler Quinacridone Red. And for the very darkest area dip into Carmine or even Carmine with a touch of Ultramarine Blue.

Use transparent colors

It's your choice of colors that determines whether you will wind up with the desirable glow that is so sought-after by watercolor artists. Part of the trick is to use transparent colors. Because opaque colors in any underlying glaze will cause dullness, opaques can be used, judiciously, for the top coat only. In fact this is where I often dip into Cadmium Yellow for a brilliant touch of yellow on the top coat.

NOTE: If you are unsure if your colors are transparent or opaque, look at the label on your paint tube.

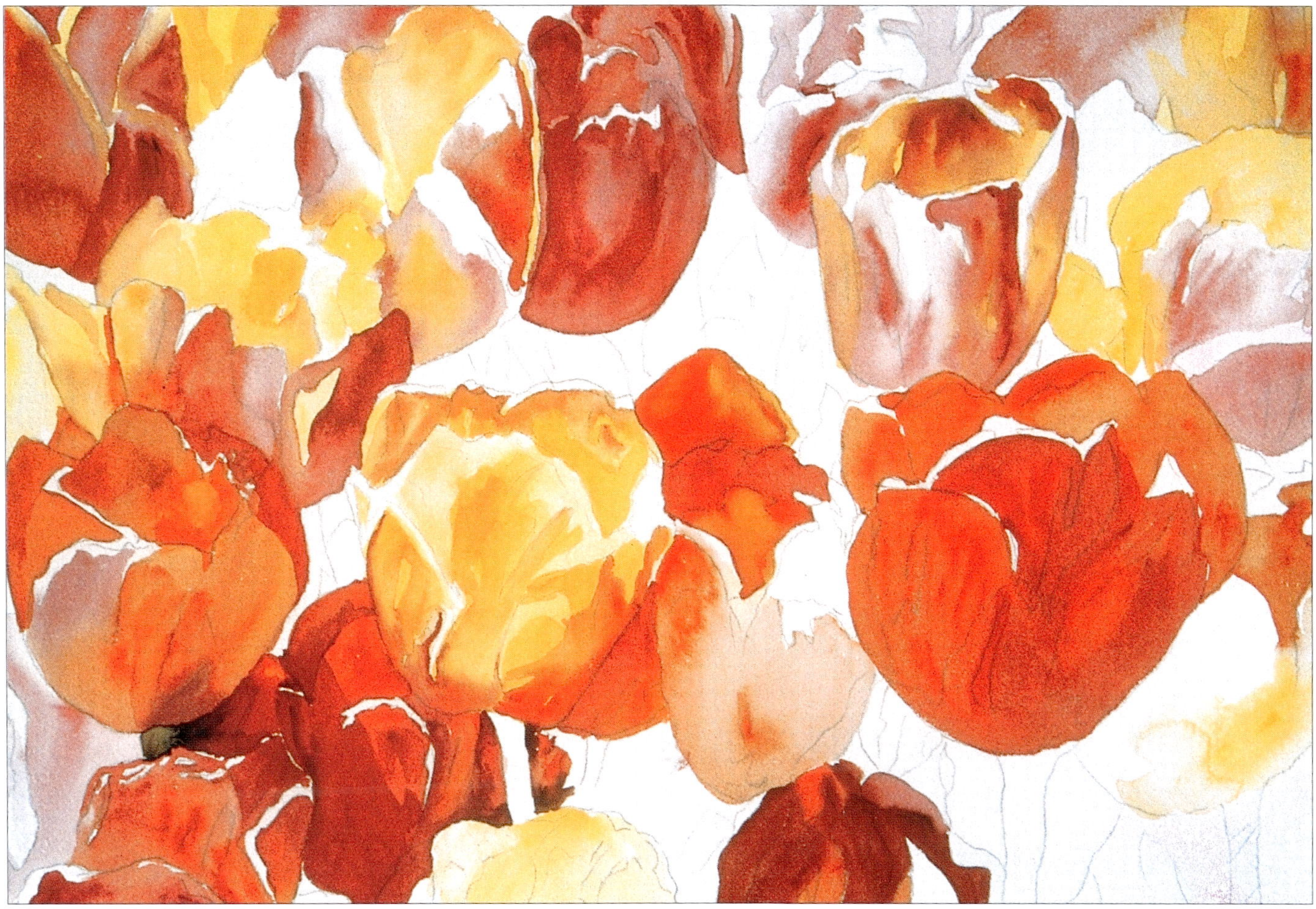

Step 3

Paint flower masses and the center of interest

- After the first coats have dried continue to glaze layers of deeper yellows, pinks and reds, always waiting until the first glaze has dried thoroughly.
- It's also best to work the whole painting for the first glaze and then the whole painting for the second, and so on, rather than trying to complete one flower at a time.
- When you're glazing flowers it is often effective to skip little strips of color, letting the pure color from the bottom layer show through in of interesting shapes.
- As you work toward the darker reds, introduce the darker and cooler Windsor Red. At this late stage of glazing it's a good idea to let the red or pink glaze from the petal of one flower continue on into the petal of the next flower. This helps to unify all the flowers into one interlocking mass, which is more effective than a painting of individual unconnected flowers.

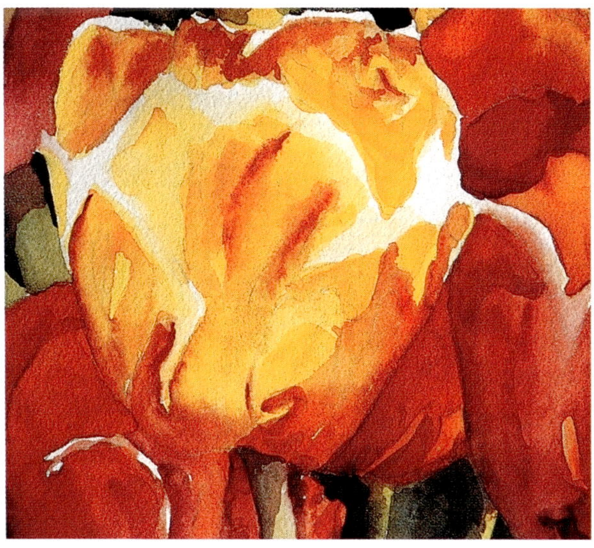

Glazes emphasize your center of interest, which in this painting is the rather large yellow flower to the lower left of center. Use color to emphasize this flower, downplaying the other yellow flowers. Giving them a soft warm red glaze to integrate them into the mass of pink and red flowers while leaving the main flower mostly yellow will make it stand out. For balance and cohesiveness the yellow will still be repeated throughout the painting, although nowhere else will it be in as large an area or have the same intensity.

Step 4

Bring in the green

- Now it's time to introduce the green foliage.
- Once again start with the palest color, this time the greens, using either Phthalo Blue with Cadmium Yellow Light, with a touch of Permanent Rose, or Phthalo Blue and New Gamboge. As you work towards the darker greens, you can start reaching for Phthalo Blue and Burnt Sienna.
- Next it's time for a little push and pull. Through the step of glazing or dulling or darkening an area, you will push it back, simultaneously making any adjacent area appear to advance. This is often accomplished with a glaze of a "receding" blue such as a Cobalt Blue or a very thin wash of Phthalo Blue.
- Here's another little secret: glaze the stem, where it attaches to the flower, with the color of the flower, thereby showing reflected color. Do this especially with red or pink flowers.

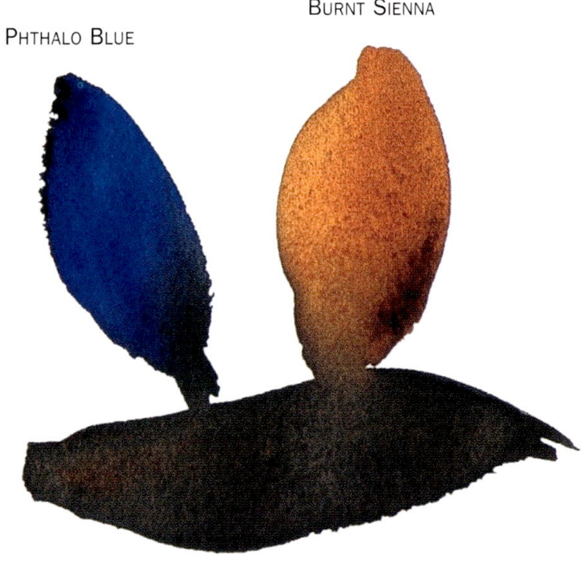

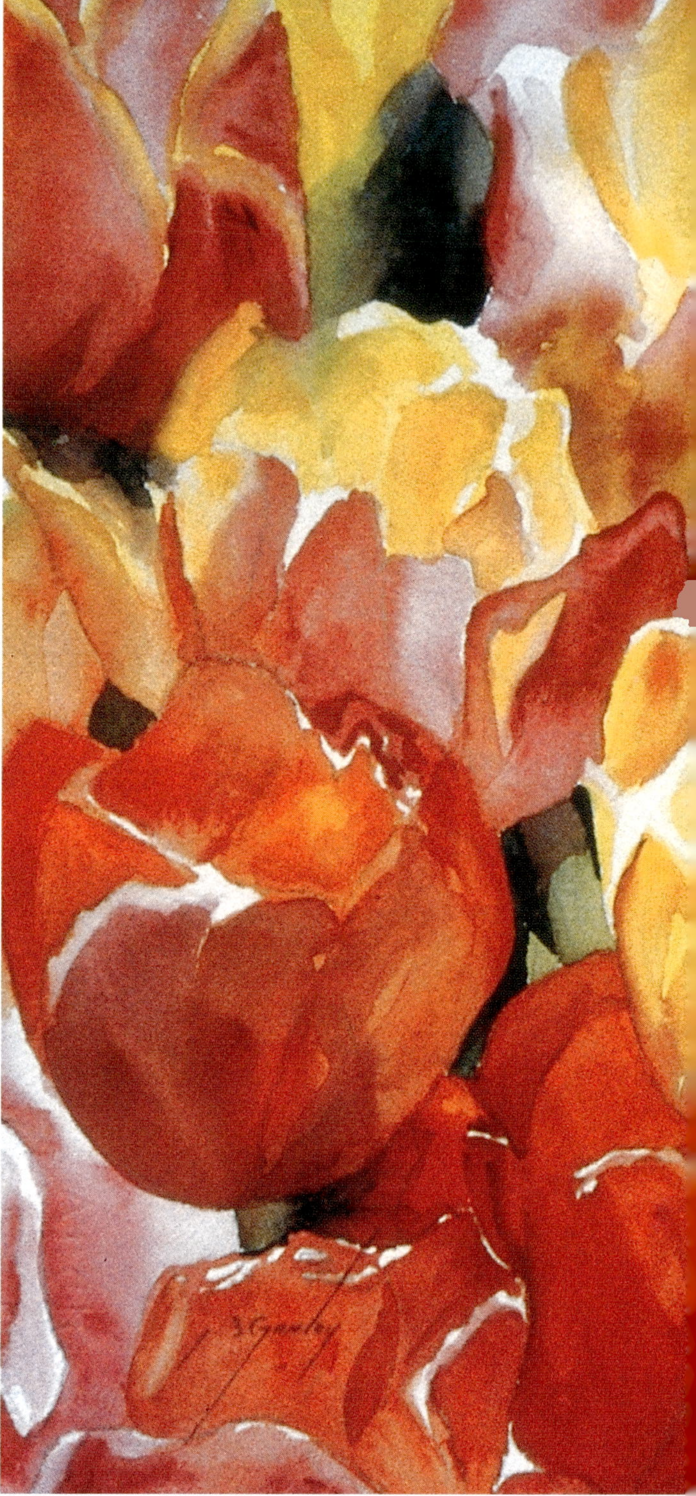

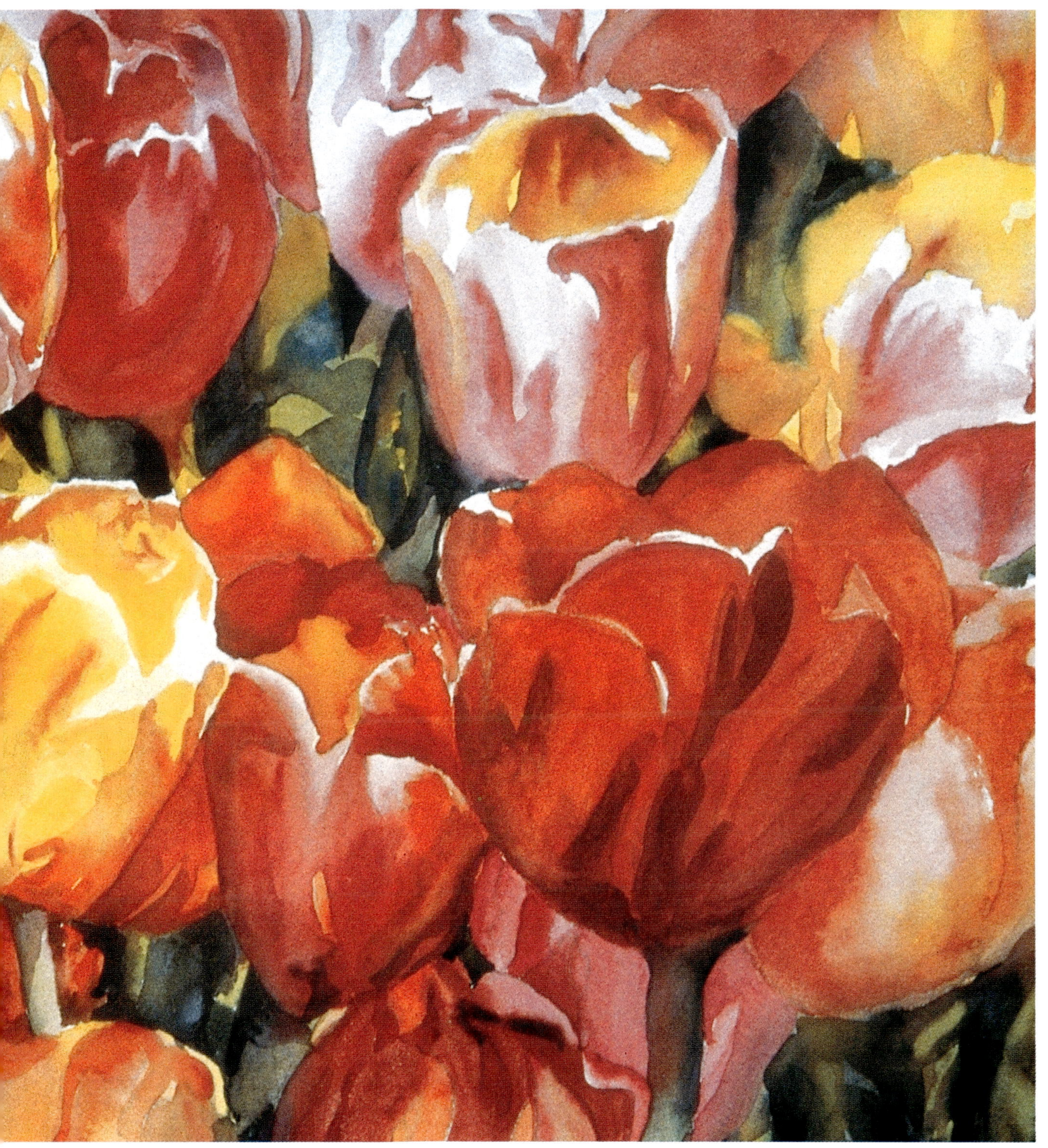

The importance of experimenting

I've always been a strong advocate of experimentation, because to experiment is to grow. So my own personal rule is that every fifth painting is strictly for experimenting. There can be no expectation that these paintings will be for sale or for competition. They are simply to learn — and to have fun! So try a new paper or board, or a new technique, or try a landscape — go wild, splash around, break rules, and learn!

How to create the look of dappled sunlight and distance

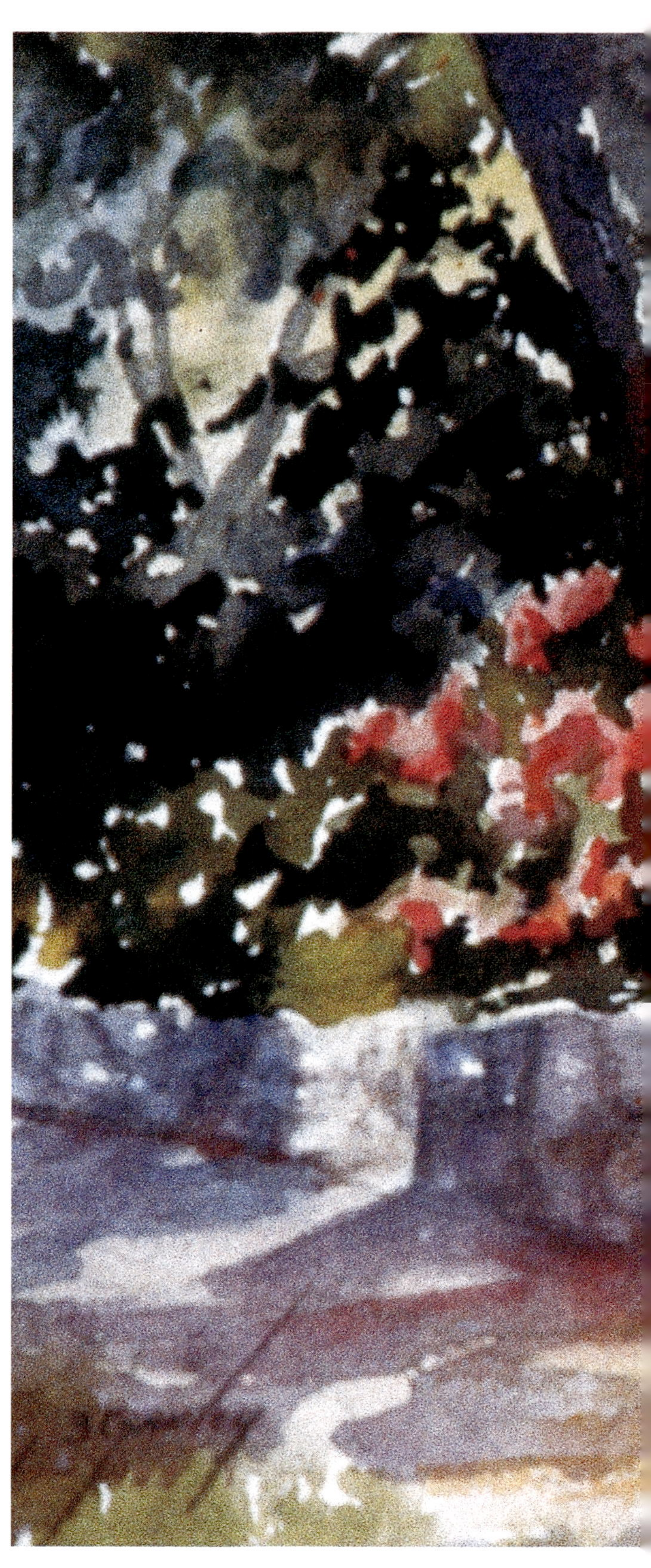

Using shadows and saving white sparkling areas enhances the look of dappled light, and leaving "sky holes" creates the effect of distance.

We will be using rough paper for this project.

The challenges

- To create texture in a mass of green foliage.
- To learn the specific qualities of your paints in order to achieve the maximum effect.
- Preventing a "cool" painting from becoming "cold."

What you'll learn

- How to get the maximum effect from a flat brush.
- Why "sky holes" are important in a heavily foliaged area.
- How to mix grays and keep them luminous.
- How to give form and dimension to your foliage.
- Why it's important to repeat a color in various areas of a painting.
- Why it's important to frequently step back to view the whole painting.
- How to add some "painterly" touches like bright colors in your splattering.
- Tips on adding your signature.

Techniques you'll use

- Lightly spritzing an area before adding paint.
- Scraping for texture.
- Using reflected lights.
- Splattering mask and paint.
- Blotting static lines for variety.
- Softening occasional edges.
- Wet-on-dry paper.

Before you begin, read the entire project through so you know what's going to happen in each stage.

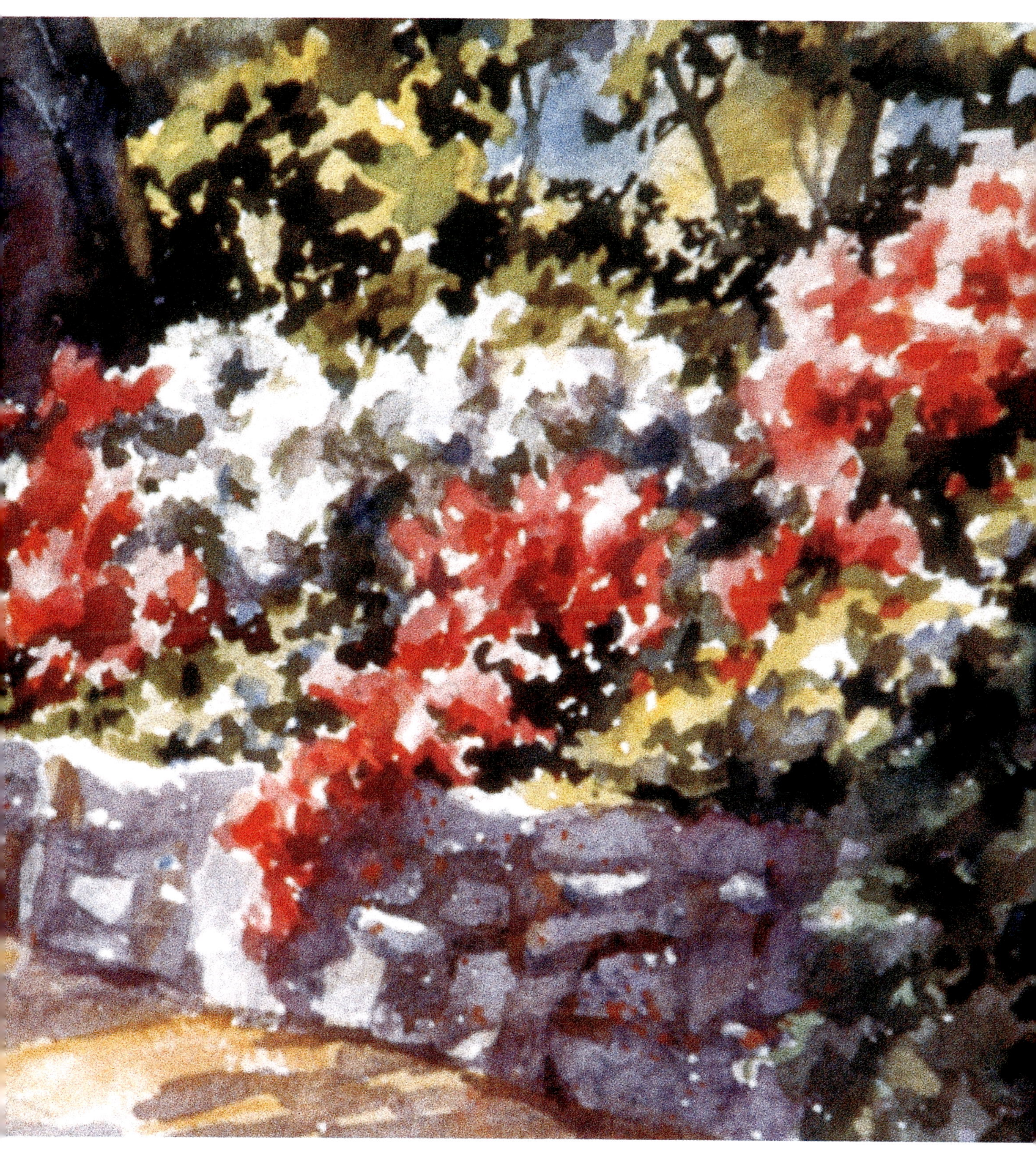

***Dappled Light in Arlington*, watercolor, 7¼ x 10¾" (18 x 27cm)**

The materials you'll need for this project

Paper and board

- Gator board as a support for the paper
- 140lb (300gsm) rough watercolor paper

Masking fluid

- Tinted mask

Brushes

- Daniel Smith 22-50 Series, Size #8 and #10
- Pro Arte Series 100, Size #12
- Fritch Scrubber (a stiff white nylon bristle brush with very short bristles, sold through Cheap Joe's catalog)
- Stiff round brush for mask application
- ¼", ½" and 1" flat brushes
- 2" hake

Odds and ends

- No. 2 pencil for the initial drawing
- Stapler and staples
- Small bottle of mild shampoo
- Palette knife
- Atomizer

Artist quality watercolors

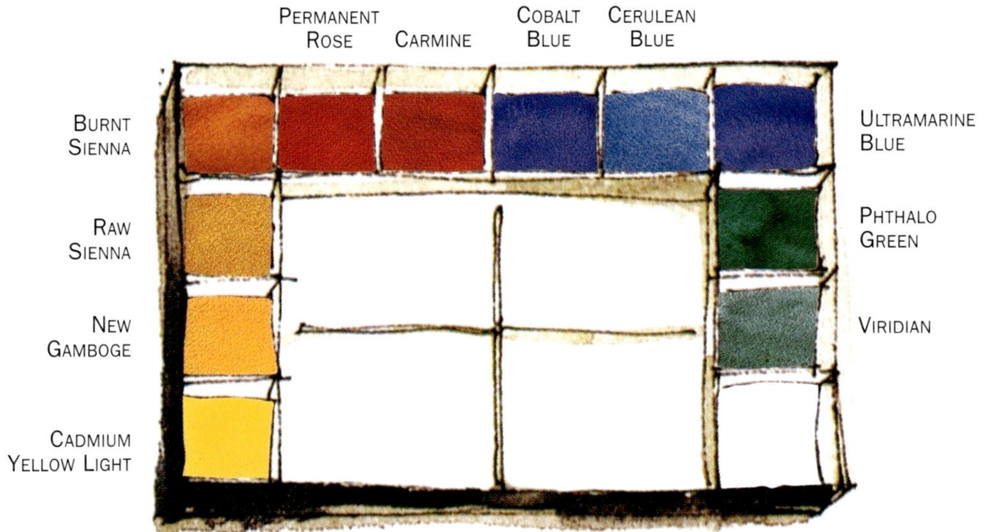

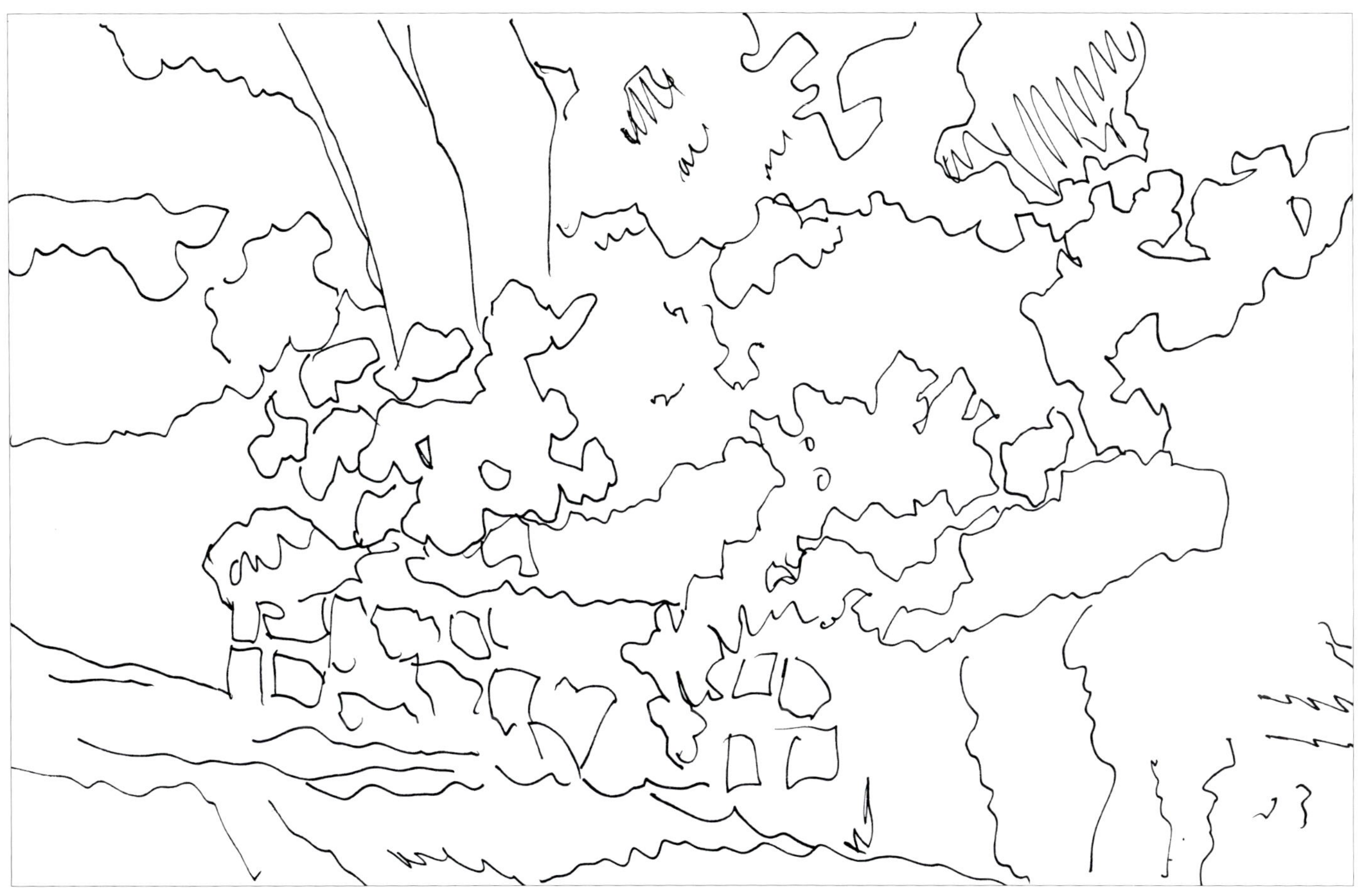

Step 1

Sketch, photocopy or trace this drawing in pencil

In this step, all we can see is a somewhat confusing mass of lines. It will be our task to make this flat drawing look three-dimensional.

Drawing secrets

There is always the temptation to race through the initial pencil drawing, or even skip it altogether, and to plunge right into the actual painting. But there are a number of important reasons for taking the time to do your drawing right, and the first is that it's a dry run for your painting.

Another reason for not rushing through the drawing stage is that using your pencil you can visually compose your scene — then change it. This was expressed by the author of The Cat in the Hat books that my granddaughters love, Dr. Seuss, who once said, "I start drawing, and eventually the characters involve themselves in a situation. Then in the end, I go back and try to cut out most of the preachments." As visual artists, we also are prone to "preachments," meaning unnecessary forms or colors, and the drawing stage allows us to cut these out before we even start painting.

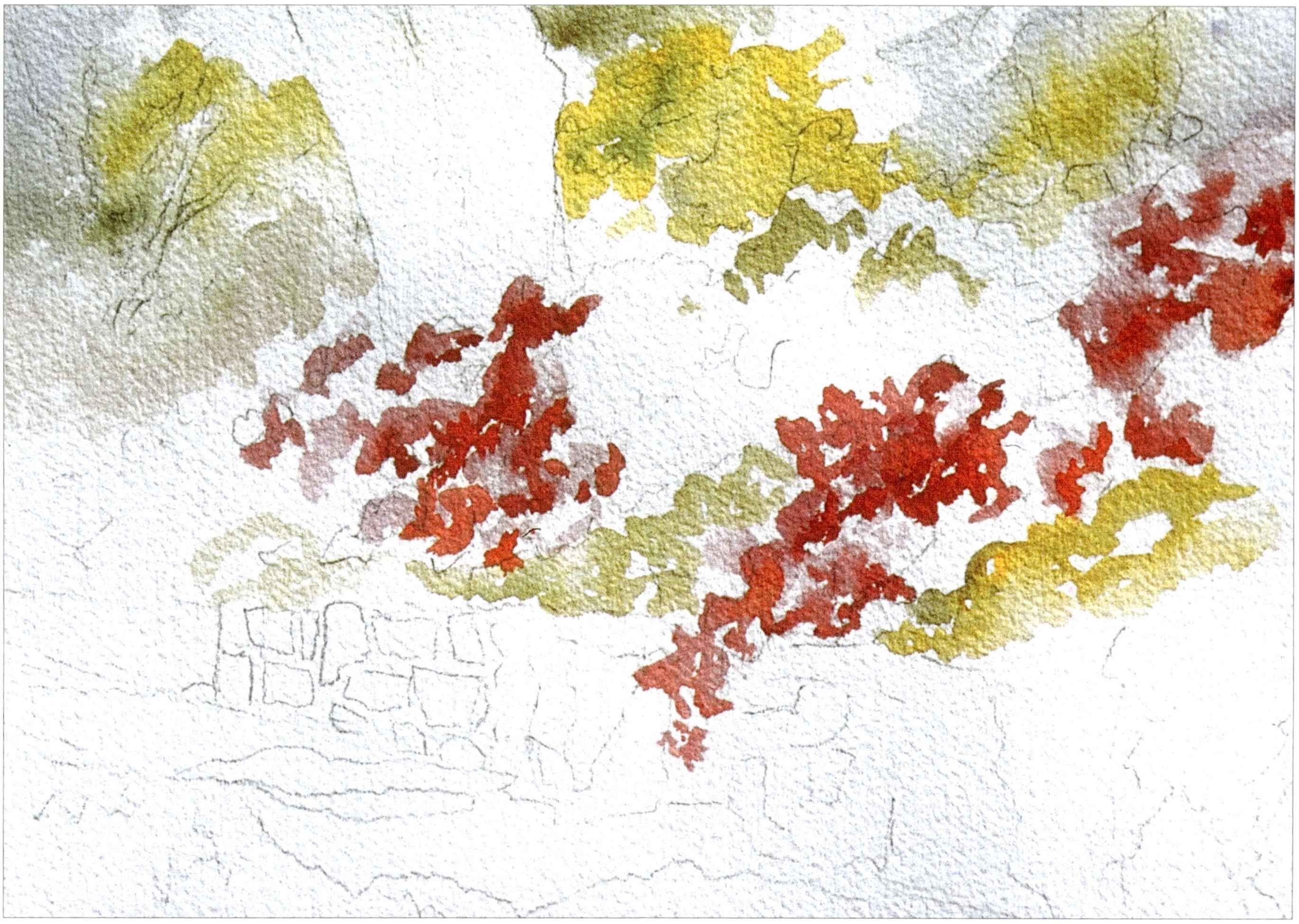

Step 2

Map out the pinks and greens

- To begin, we'll use a pale wash of Permanent Rose to map out the graceful sway of the azaleas. Working on DRY paper, give a quick spritz of water to the area of the pink azaleas.
- Then, because this is a small painting, we'll use a No. 8 round to drop in some pale pink blossoms in irregular patterns, following the contour of the two pink bushes. While that's still DAMP, add deeper Permanent Rose at some of the blossom bases.
- While that dries, mix up some pale spring-like greens with Cobalt Blue and Cadmium Yellow Light.
- Because the painting is quite small, we'll use a flat 1/2" brush most of the time for the greenery. By twisting the flat brush and using all of its different sides you can get a variety of strokes.
- When placing the greens, remember to save the "sky holes." I see these areas as important because their simple addition to or presence in a painting adds another dimension, it's as if you are looking through to something beyond. In this case the something is the distant sky. Sky holes also act to break up the monotony of all that greenery and to make this heavily shrubbed area look less forbidding and more inviting. Just think: these tiny sky holes do all that work for us! To create them use pale mixture of Cobalt Blue and Cerulean Blue. Just WET the sky holes and drop in a little of this mixture. Remember that you want to keep this very light, so use plenty of water in your mixture. Let it DRY thoroughly before adding the green leaves to the edges of these areas.

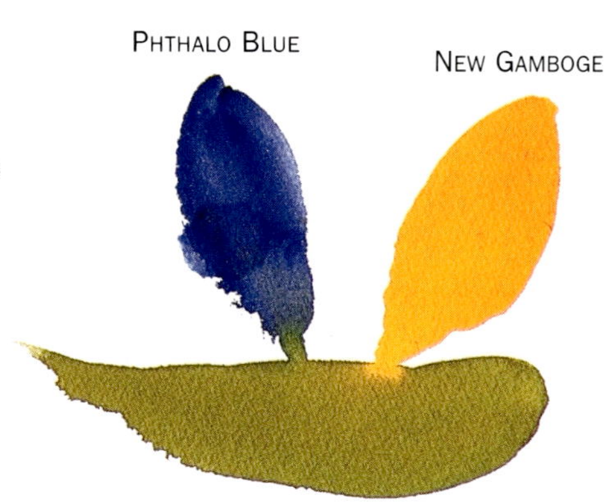

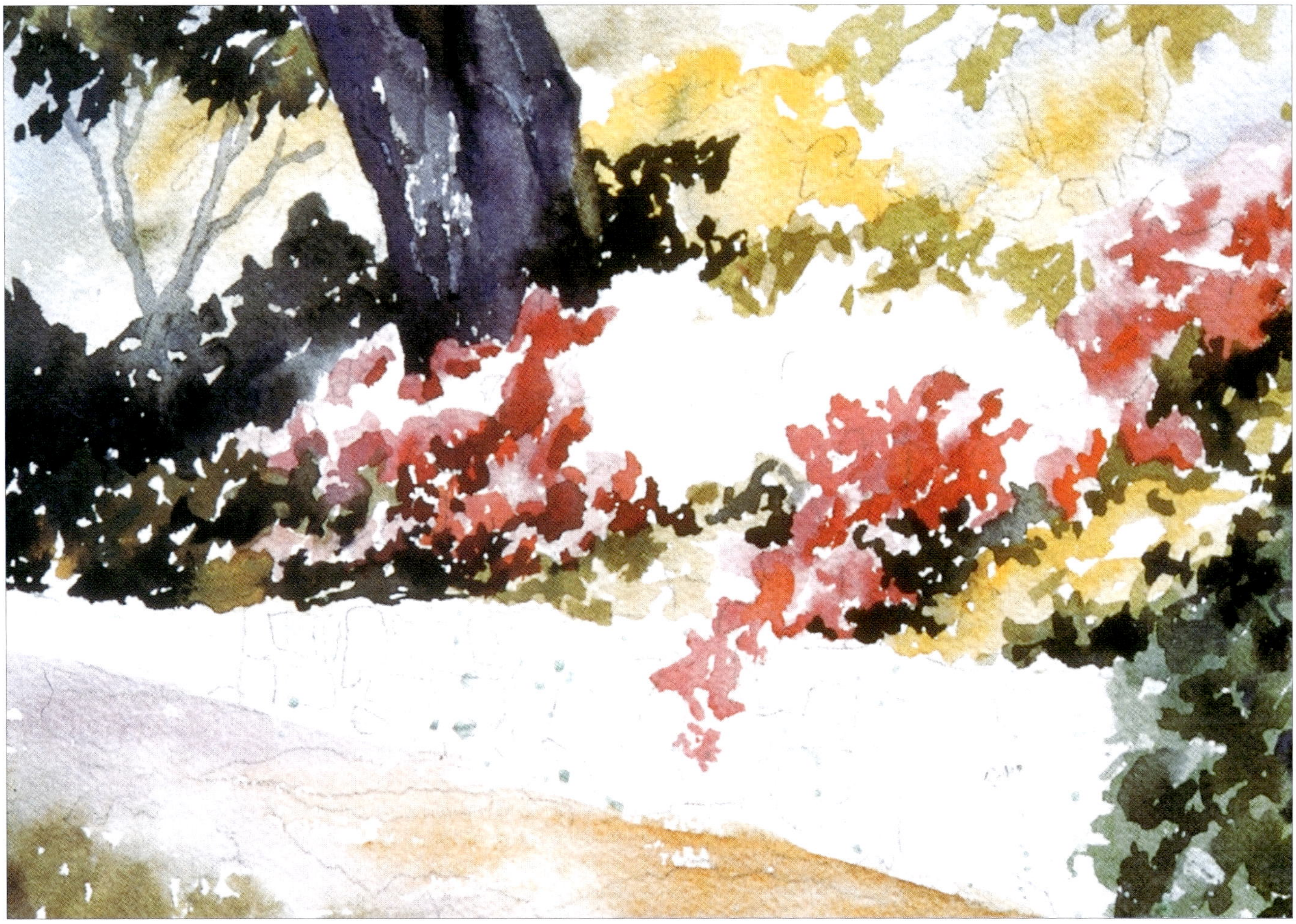

Step 3

Paint the tree trunk, shrubbery and sidewalk

- Create the tree trunk in gray/blue/violet tones — not brown (as many beginning artists assume). When applying your grays use Ultramarine Blue, for its sedimentary qualities as well as for its color, and Burnt Sienna. Or you could try several combinations of your three primaries, blue, red and yellow, because all will lead to a variety of lively grays — as long as you don't choose two opaque colors in that formula, which would muddy your resulting gray.
- For dominant tree trunks, occasionally drop in some pure blue (Cobalt); and at the base where the trunk meets the red/pink flowers, use Carmine as the dark to act as reflected light. The rough trunk is also an opportunity to create texture with both dry brush and palette knife scraping (or a corner of a credit card, or even your own fingernail!). Scraping is best done when the sheen has left the paper but the paper is still DAMP. Then you will create a lighter line in the surrounding darker color. If you scrape too soon, the wet color will slowly creep back into the scraped line and the result will be a darker line.
- Using a variety of medium to dark greens (Phthalo Blue and New Gamboge, or Phthalo Green and Burnt Sienna) will give form and dimension to the shrubbery. Some of the most distant greens will be cooler (Viridian and Cobalt Blue). When placing these greens, keep in mind the importance of saving white shapes to act as sparkles of sunlight. This is especially important in a painting with dense foliage.
- At this point we'll introduce the sidewalk with Raw Sienna and a touch of Permanent Rose as its base color. Although in reality sidewalks are a cool cement color, we want a little warmth with all the greens so we'll use the sidewalk as an opportunity to add some warm color.

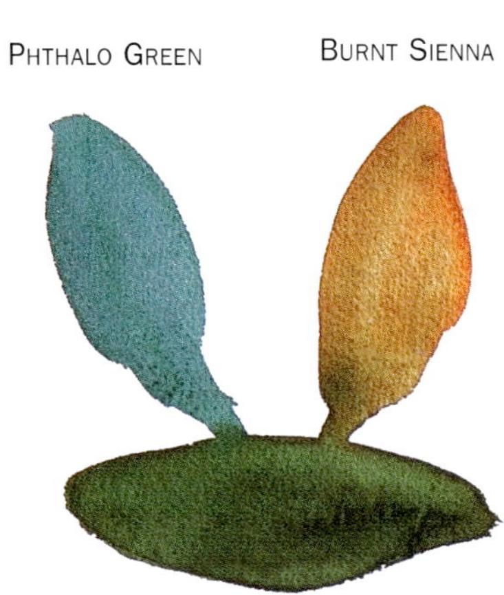

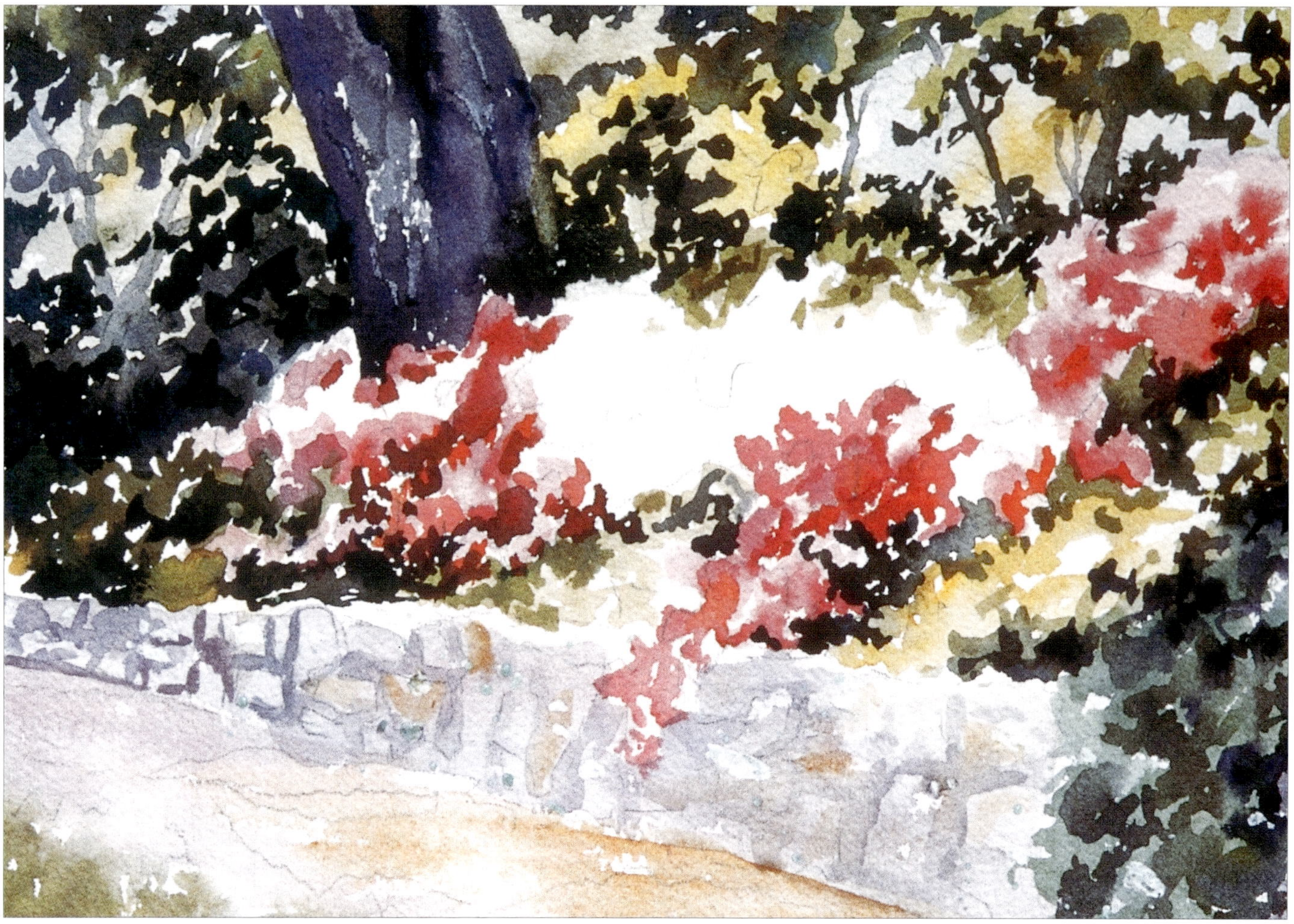

Step 4

Unifying with gray and painting the stones

- The cool blue/violet grays of the stonework will repeat the grays of the tree trunk. Remember that repetition of a color helps to unify a painting.
- After splattering the stonework with dots of masking fluid to save dots of white paper, use a pale mixture of Cobalt Blue or Ultramarine Blue with Burnt Sienna, applied in a dry-brush technique for added texture.
- **It's important to save the top edge of the stone wall as white**. Note that this edge is not a stiff straight line but dips in places and changes from thinner then thicker as it follows the irregular stone shapes.
- When that's DRY, add some pale lines delineating the individual stones in the distance. Occasionally blot these lines while they're still DAMP in order to make some distant ones recede and to reduce the obvious outline of each and every stone.

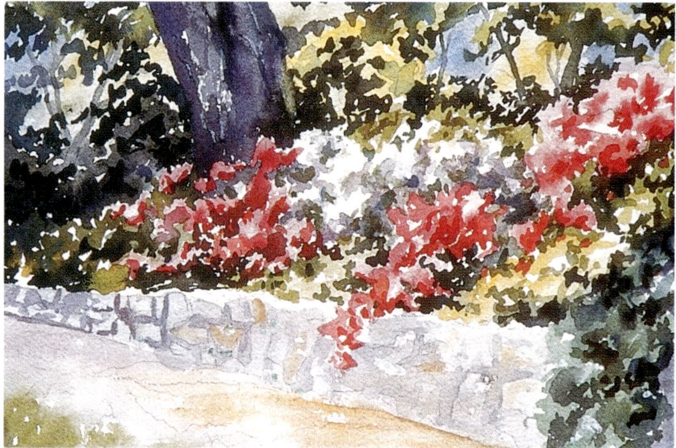

- When all of the greens are completed it's time to shade our white azaleas. Drop in a very pale violet mixture of Permanent Rose and Cobalt Blue — sometimes more rose, sometimes more blue — onto a pre-moistened area of shade in the white bush. The pre-moistening will assure a softer look. Don't overdo the violet.
- Step back frequently and view your progress from a distance. It's easy to go too far and obliterate all your whites. Note that the gray/violet color also ties in with the tree trunk and the stone wall, so it's now repeated several times throughout the painting, which is excellent.
- When that's DRY, add a few pale green leaves.

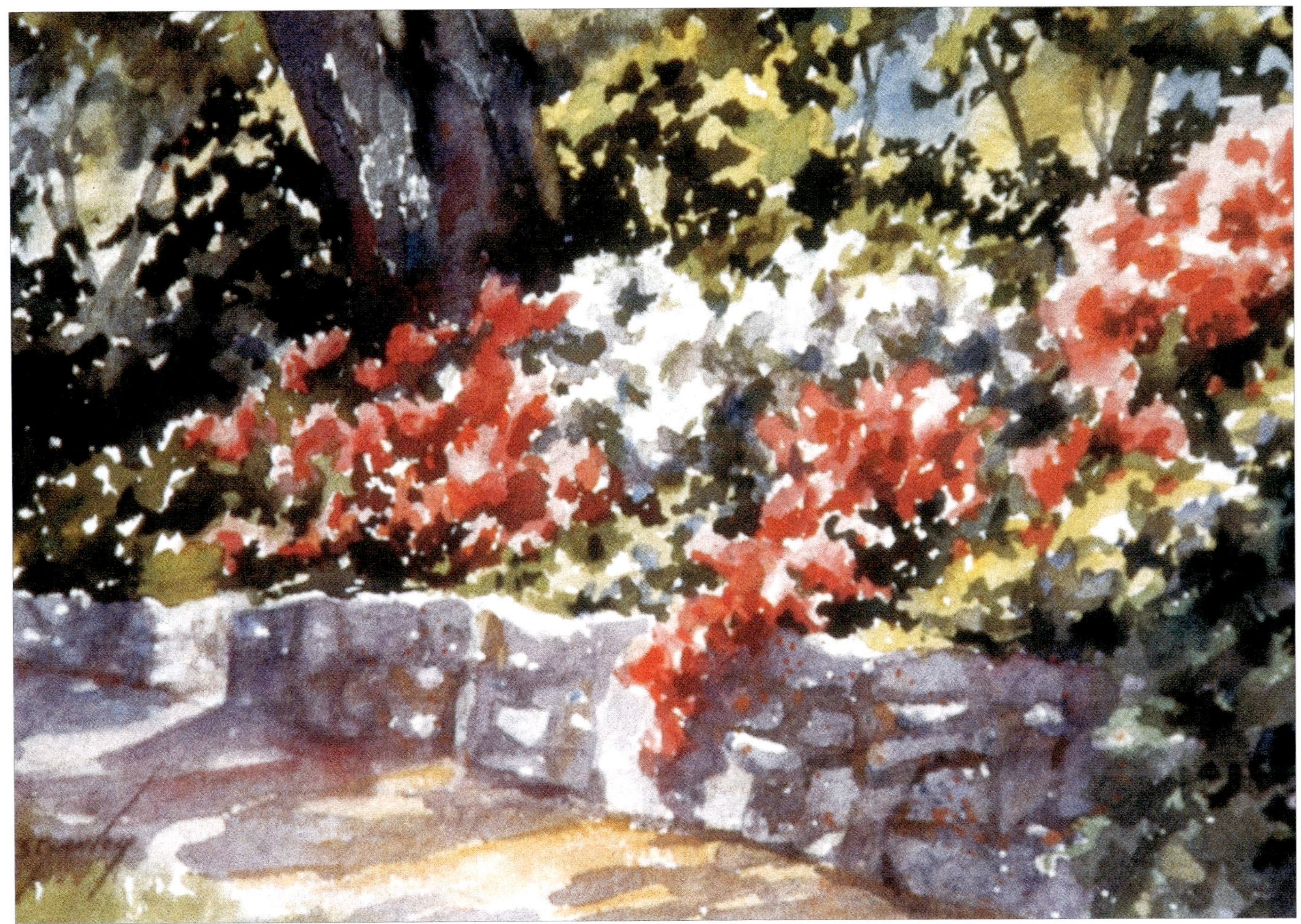

Step 5

Finally: the all-important shadows!

- Now we'll create that dappled light that makes the scene so attractive. Do this quickly using Cobalt Blue and Permanent Rose, following the contours of the stone wall and the uneven pathway and up and over the clump of grass in the lower left.
- When the painting's DRY we'll finish the remaining texture on the stones and add all the cracks and fissures, and the splattering that I love so much on stone textures.
- You can use your darker grays for splattering and use some pure blues and a few of the pinks that are in those azaleas. Again, don't outline each and every stone in the foreground, that becomes boring. Instead, just make an occasional outline. In places, while the outline is still DAMP, take a very damp brush and drag it along the stone into the damp crack. That will cause an interruption in the outline and help to soften an occasional edge.
- All that's now left to do is remove the mask on the wall.

Repeating a main color combination

By repeating a main color or a color combination, throughout a painting we go a long way towards unifying the whole painting.

Walking along the streets of Cape May, New Jersey, in July is akin to an overdose of eye candy. Flowers burst through white picket fences on every street and the hydrangeas have no comparison (except possibly in Cornwall, England). They range from blues to pinks, violets, whites and pale greens. We will use hot press watercolor paper this time.

The challenges

- To make a long sidewalk appear to recede into the distance.
- To ensure that that long sidewalk doesn't "walk" the viewer's eye right out of the picture.
- To keep round flowers from looking like balloons.

What you'll learn

- How to exaggerate important whites by painting darker colors around them.
- The use of natural greens versus unnatural greens.
- How to cluster shapes.
- How to isolate the center of interest.
- How to mix violets.
- How to keep a diagonal line from cutting a painting in two.
- Why most artists make their own color charts.

Techniques you'll use

- Wet-on-dry.
- Dropping color onto pre-wet areas.
- Glazing.
- Applying a graded wash.

Before you begin, read the entire project through so you know what's going to happen in each stage.

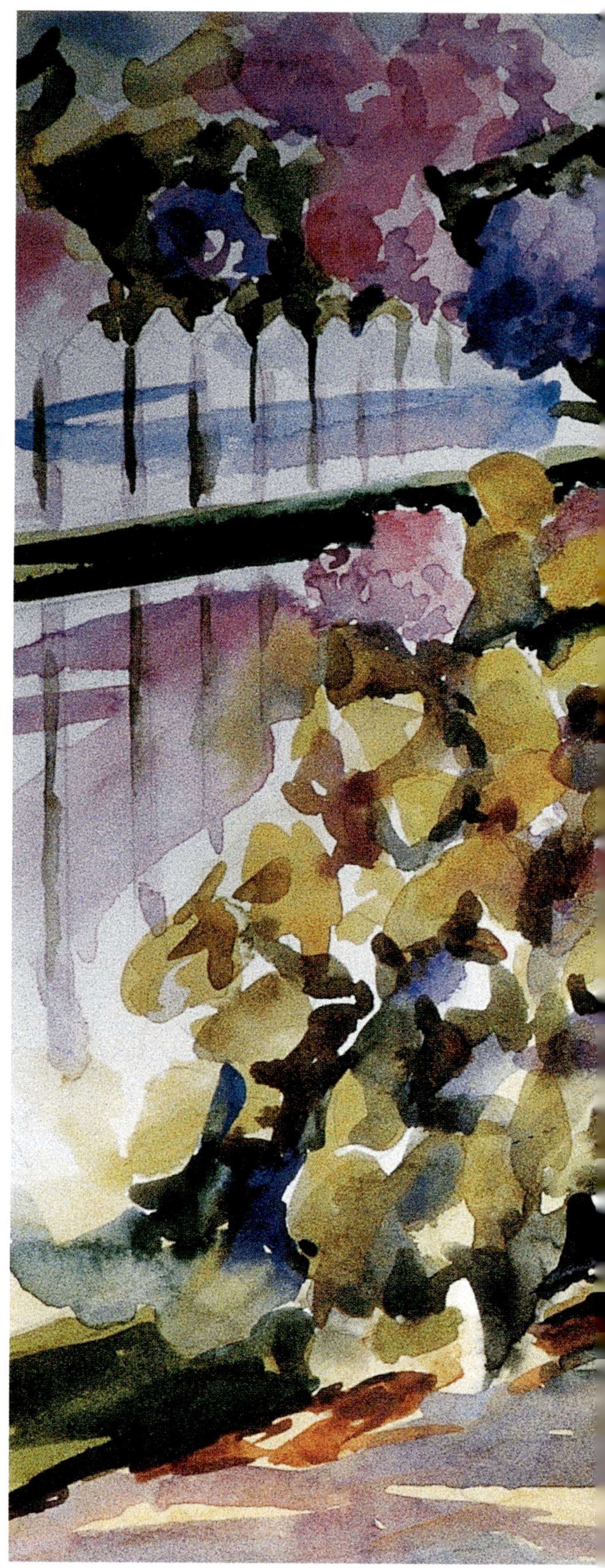

Bursting Out All Over
watercolor, 10½ x 14½" (27 X 39cm)

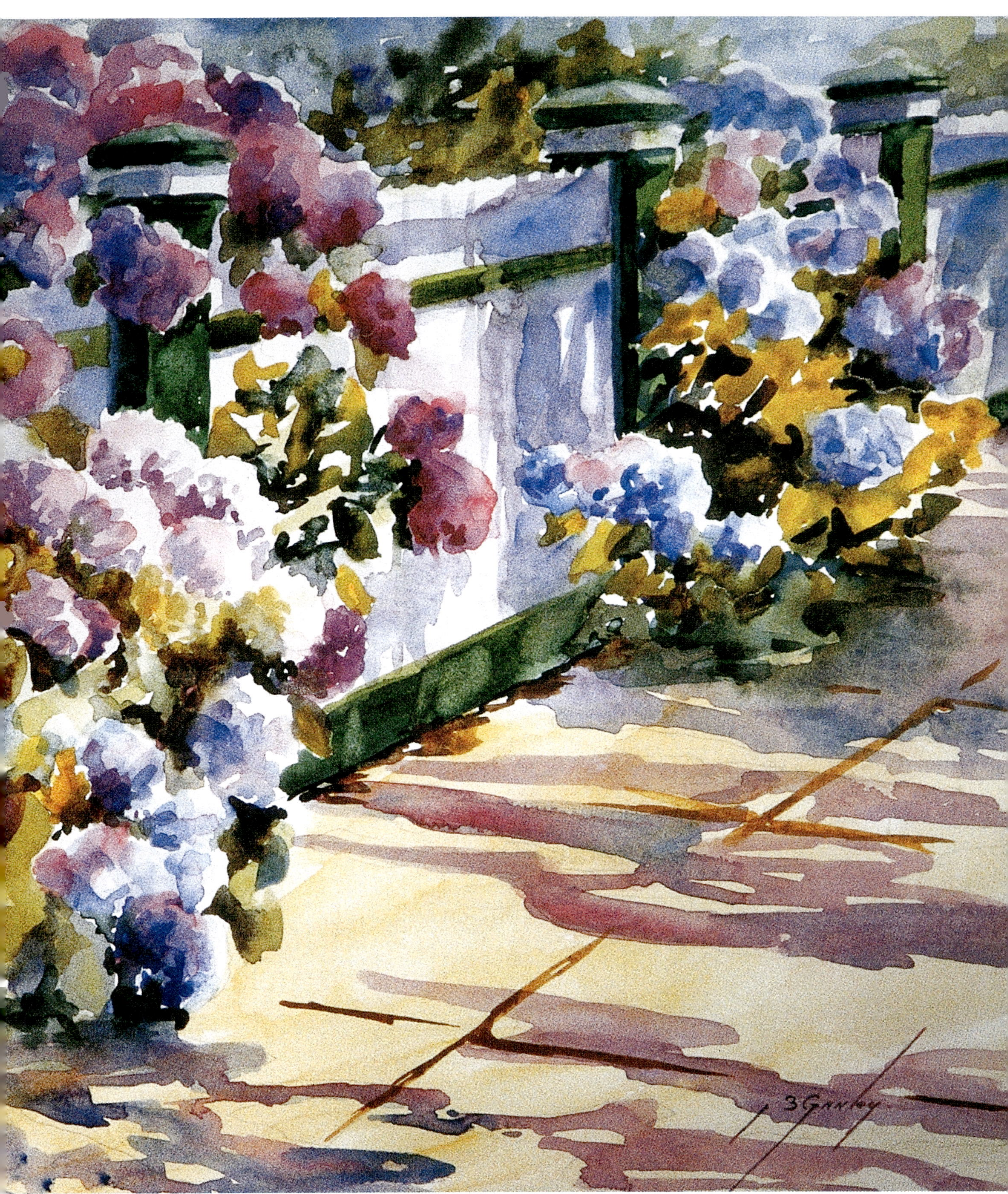

The materials you'll need for this project

Paper and board

- Gator board as a support for the paper
- 140lb (300 gsm) hot press watercolor paper

Brushes

- Daniel Smith 22-50 Series, Size #8 and #10
- Pro Arte Series 100, Size #12
- Fritch Scrubber (a stiff white nylon bristle brush with very short bristles, sold through Cheap Joe's catalog)
- Stiff round brush for mask application
- ¼", ½" and 1" flat brushes
- 2" hake

Odds and ends

- No. 2 pencil for the initial drawing
- 2" masking tape

Artist quality watercolors

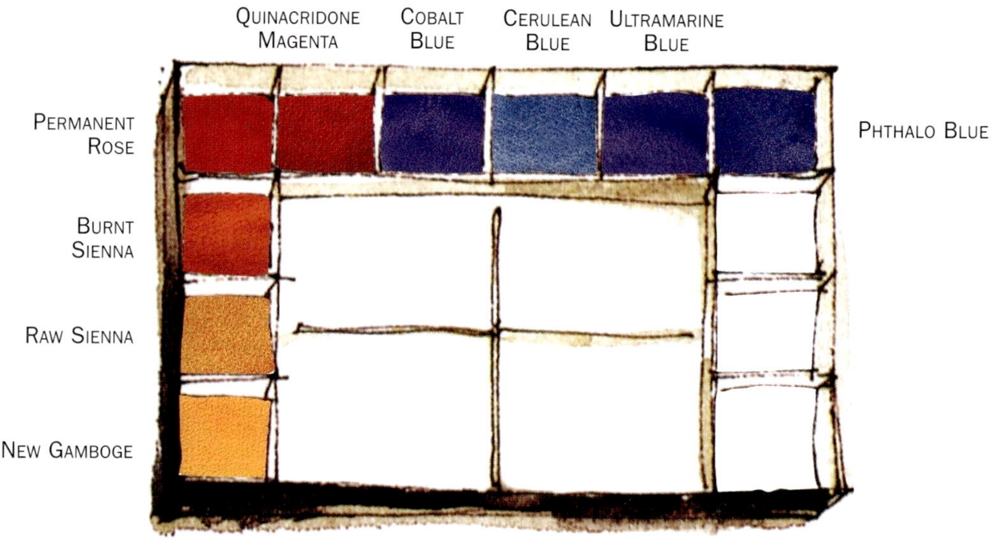

What's so hot about hot press paper?

For this project we will be working on hot press paper, which presents another challenge. Paper is fed through giant rollers that compress the paper. The surface becomes smooth, almost slick, and loses most of its absorbency. Thus any paint applied will set on the surface rather than be absorbed, which is the case with cold press or rough papers. I have had many lovely results with hot press papers, and trying new papers and techniques is an exciting side trip in the watercolor adventure that can lead to many wonderful discoveries.

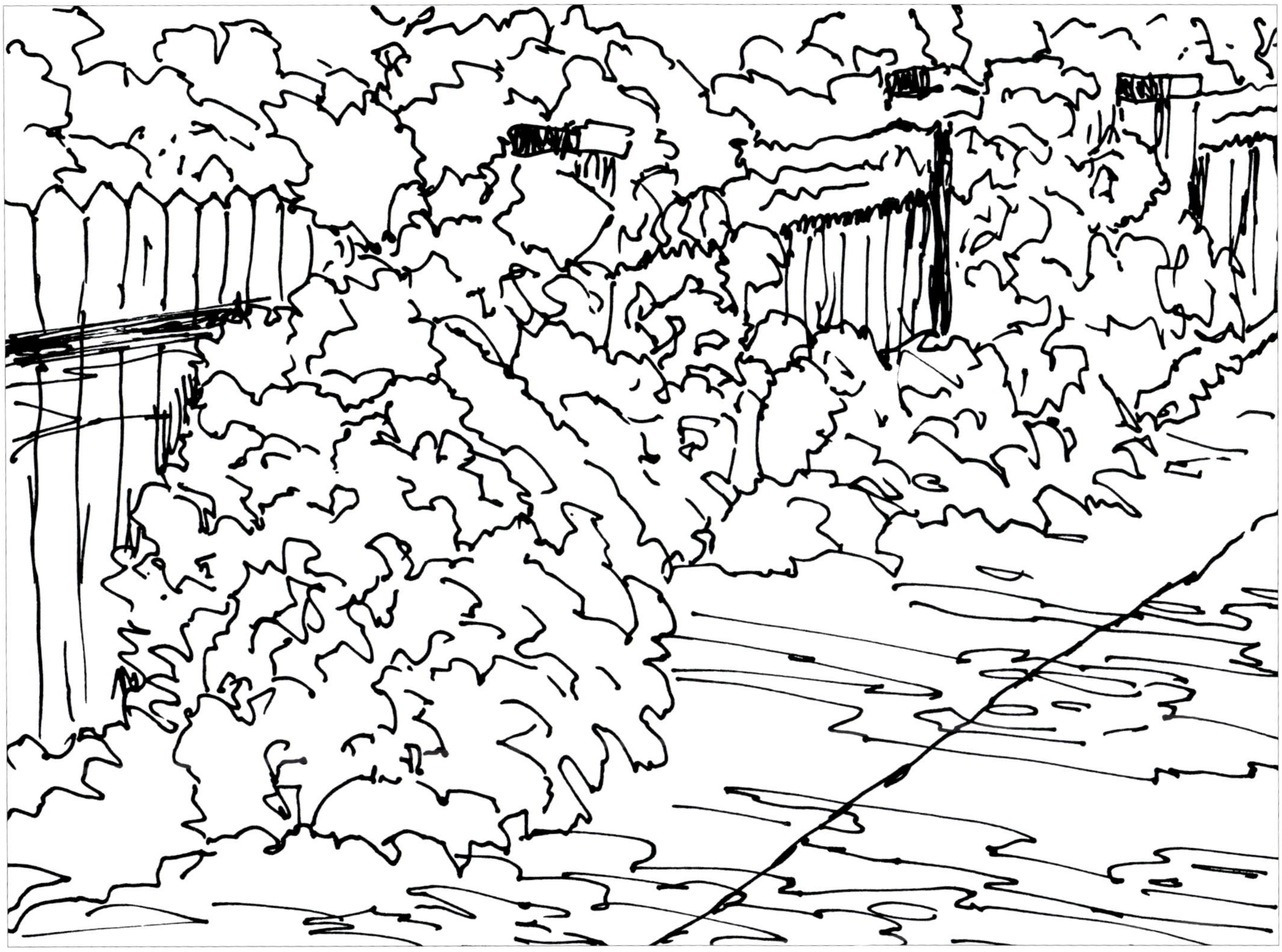

Step 1

Sketch or trace this design onto your paper using pencil

Many artists have trouble with the round shapes of hydrangeas, which presents the first challenge. The secret will be in the initial drawing where we will overlap many of the round shapes until they become large clusters. These clusters form their own shapes, which will be elongated, almost rectangular.

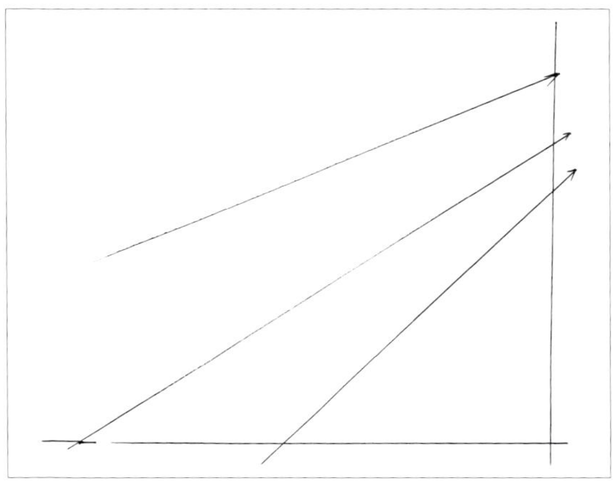

CAUTION: Vanishing Point Ahead

In any painting it's important to keep the viewer's eye from wandering off toward the vanishing point. There are three strong lines in this painting that all threaten to lead the viewer's eye up and off the right edge of this picture: the top of the fence; the bottom of the fence; and the primary sidewalk crack. What prevents that happening, and keeps the viewer's eye in the picture, are the interruptions to those three lines: the clumps of flowering bushes that break up the fence lines and the intriguing shadows splayed across the sidewalk.

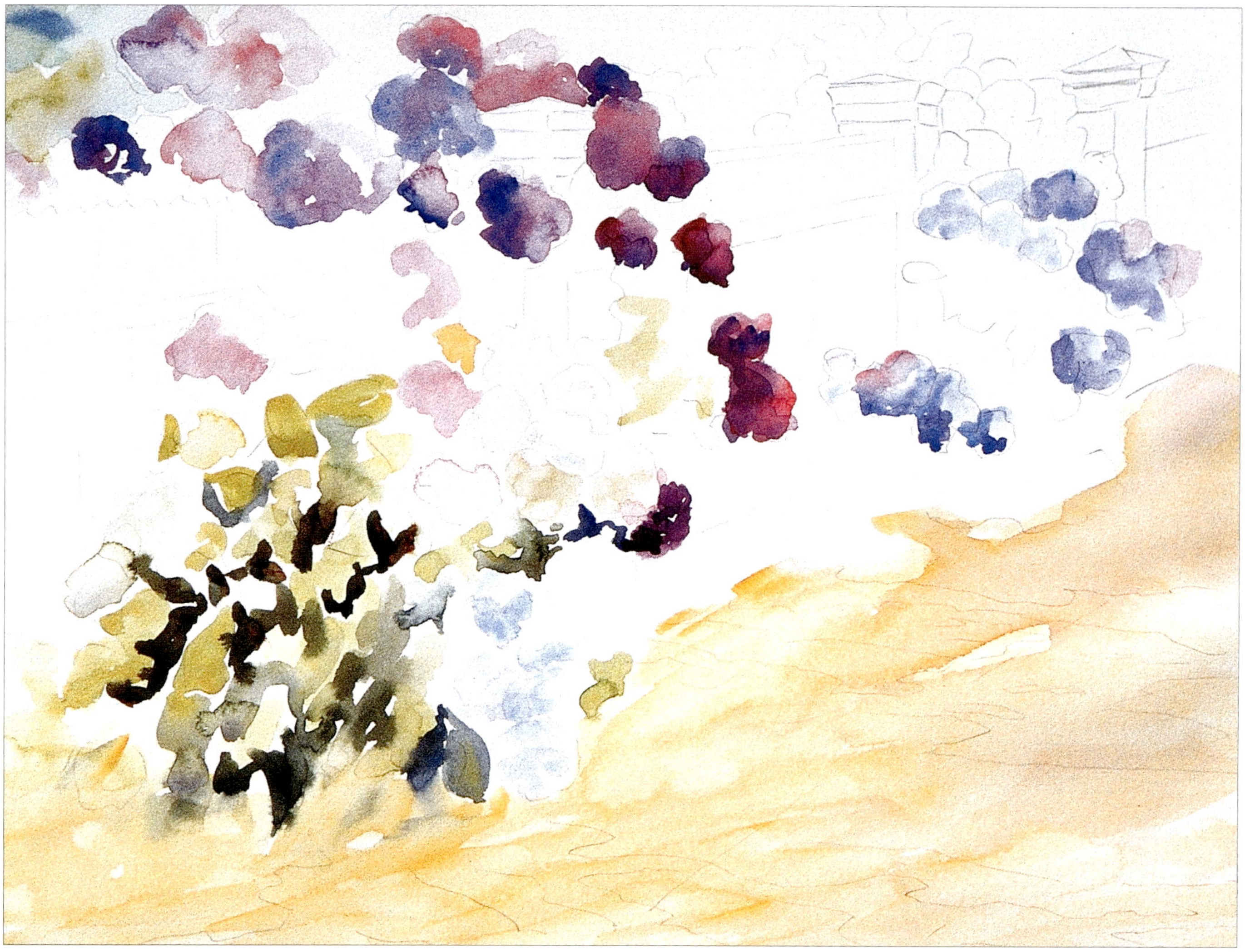

Step 2

Lay in the violet flowers

- The center of interest will be the foreground cluster of hydrangeas, so the plan is to keep those as light in color as possible, as if the sun is spotlighting them. To do this we will make the areas around them dark, and that is a great place for one of the darker fence posts. The clusters in the distance will have less white and will appear to be in shadow.
- Starting with the pale spotlight area, just lay in pale violets where one flower casts its shadow onto another, and avoid putting any color on the top portion of the individual flowers.
- As you paint the flowers, vary the amount of Permanent Rose, Quinacridone Magenta and Ultramarine Blue to achieve a nice variety of violets. Apply the violet wash to several of the flowers in the foreground cluster. At times use wet paint on DRY paper and at other times WET an area of the flower and drop in the paint, letting it travel on its own throughout the wet area. If you use that technique, make sure that you wet an area larger than you will need. That way the paint won't stop abruptly at the edge of the puddle and produce a hard edge.

Vibrant violets

Once-upon-a-time I found it difficult to achieve vibrant violets. I tried every violet on the market and finally did find one I liked, but then it was discontinued. So I was determined to make my own. I made numerous color charts using every blue and pink and violet combination I could think of. One of my winning combinations is Permanent Rose, Quinacridone Magenta, and a touch of Ultramarine Blue. Another winner is Cobalt Blue and Permanent Rose. The moral of the story is — it's possible to find your own special colors by making color charts.

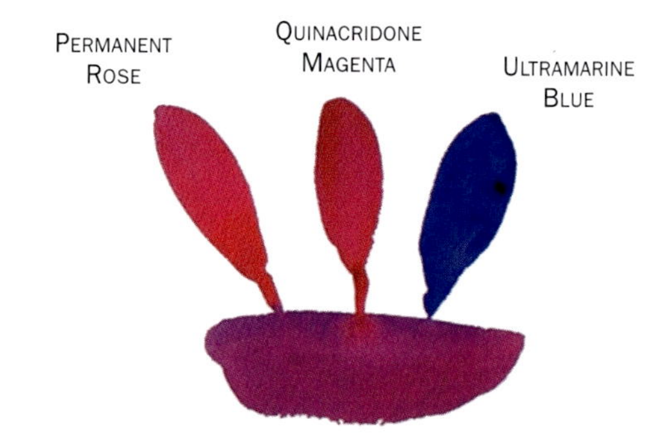

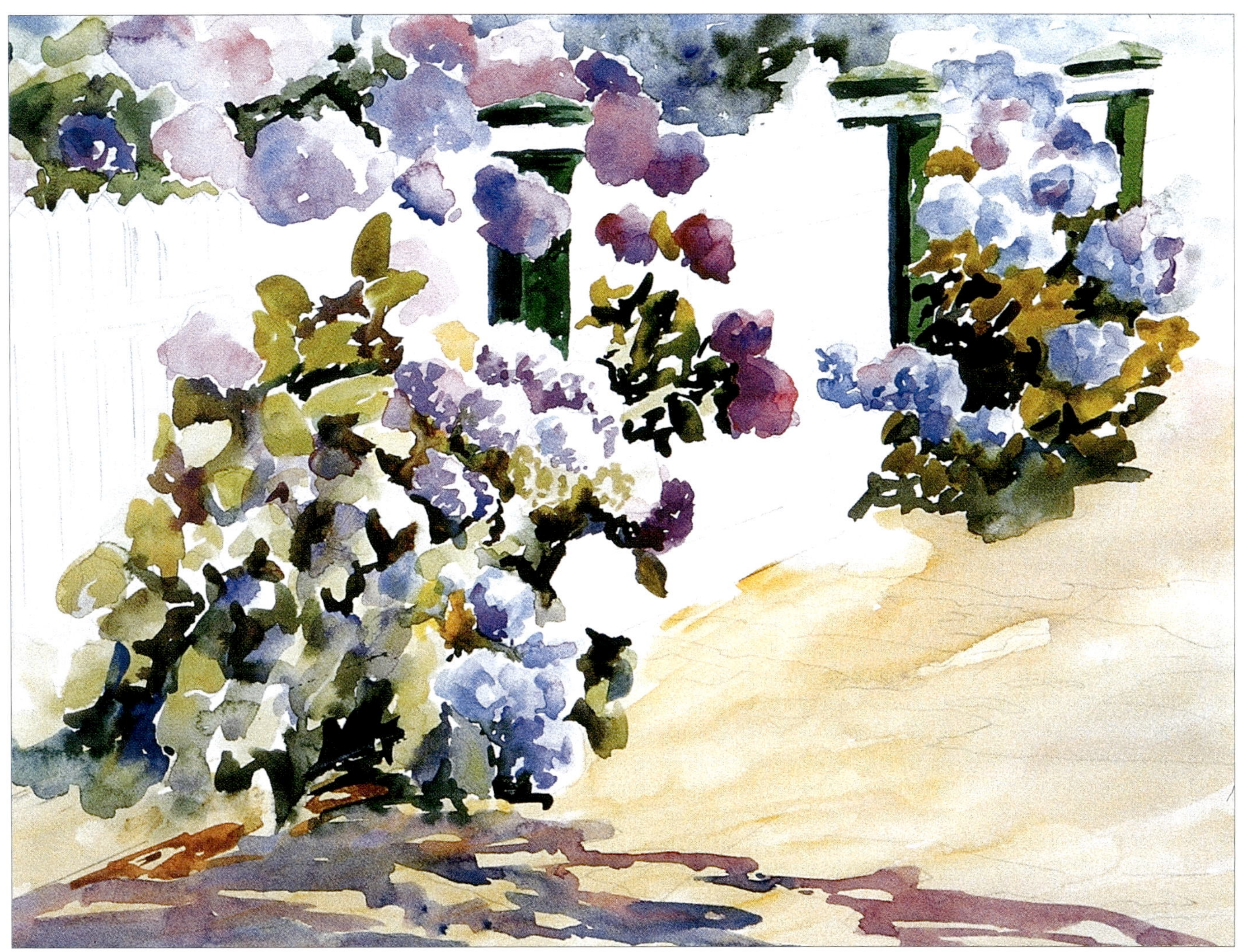

Step 3

Lay in the blue flowers and green leaves

- For the blue hydrangeas try Cobalt Blue and Cerulean Blue, either mixed or side-by-side.
- To create a variety of pale, spring-like leaves, try Phthalo Blue and New Gamboge, sometimes with a touch of Permanent Rose. Personally, I can't help but add a touch of a dark green to begin to establish the dark values.
- The flowers fall on the cool side, so we will establish some contrasting warmth on the sidewalk. Add a wash of Raw Sienna with a touch of violet at the furthest part of the sidewalk in order to gray it and create the illusion of distance or depth. Let this DRY.

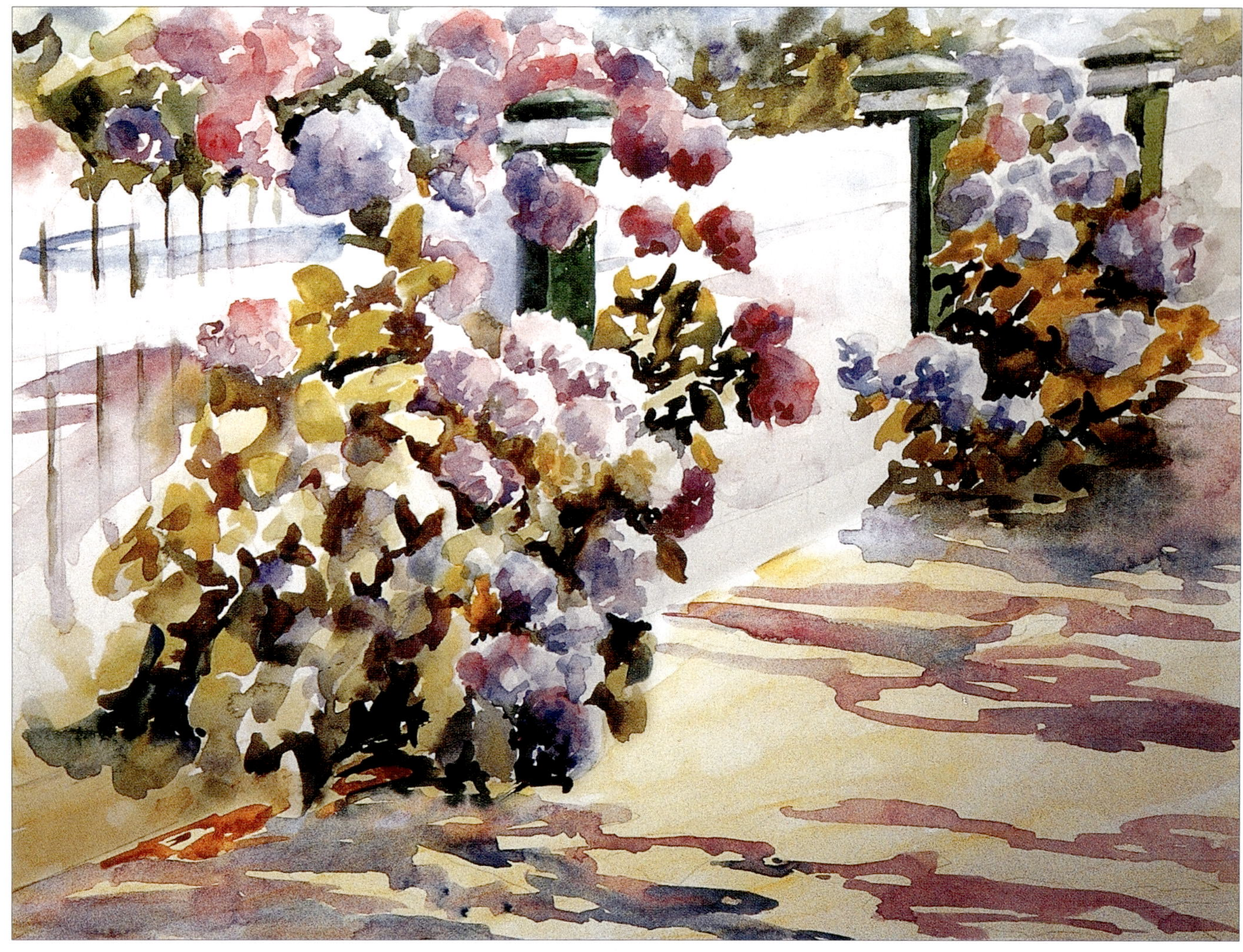

Step 4

Painting the fence posts

- Because there are so many natural greens in this painting I think the hue of the fence posts should be an unnatural green, meaning one that does not occur in Nature. So the fence posts will be predominantly the aggressive Phthalo Green with a little Cobalt Blue or Burnt Sienna to tame it.
- Backgrounds frequently cause trouble, whether in a still life or a landscape. In this instance where the flowers end at the top of the paper, just a simple plain blue/green wash will suffice to create distance and a finished look. (In reality, at the end of the fence was a very large house with a multitude of windows and porch pillars. Remember that the artist chooses what to eliminate!)

Step 5

Getting the background, and glazing

- Continue to add glazes to the violets, pinks and blues of the flowers. Only a few flowers in the foreground should receive some petal shapes, done with negative painting. In other words, add a darker-value paint around the lighter petals.
- With a swish of your 1" flat brush and some bright colors, quickly paint in some shadow shapes on the white picket fence. Be careful about using blues and pinks separately — they can start to look like a baby shower! Combining them can be quite effective, and Permanent Rose and Cobalt Blue work well together. You can delineate a few of the foreground pickets in the fence. The viewer's eye will know that the rest of the fence has individual pickets.

Incidentally, it's a perfectly acceptable practice in painting to allow the viewer's eye to fill in some areas. Doing this actually helps to bring viewers into the painting, and that makes of it more interesting to them.

- Notice that by breaking up the long expanse of the picket fence with flower clusters placed at irregular distances we have effectively eliminated the problem of a long white fence visually cutting the painting in half.

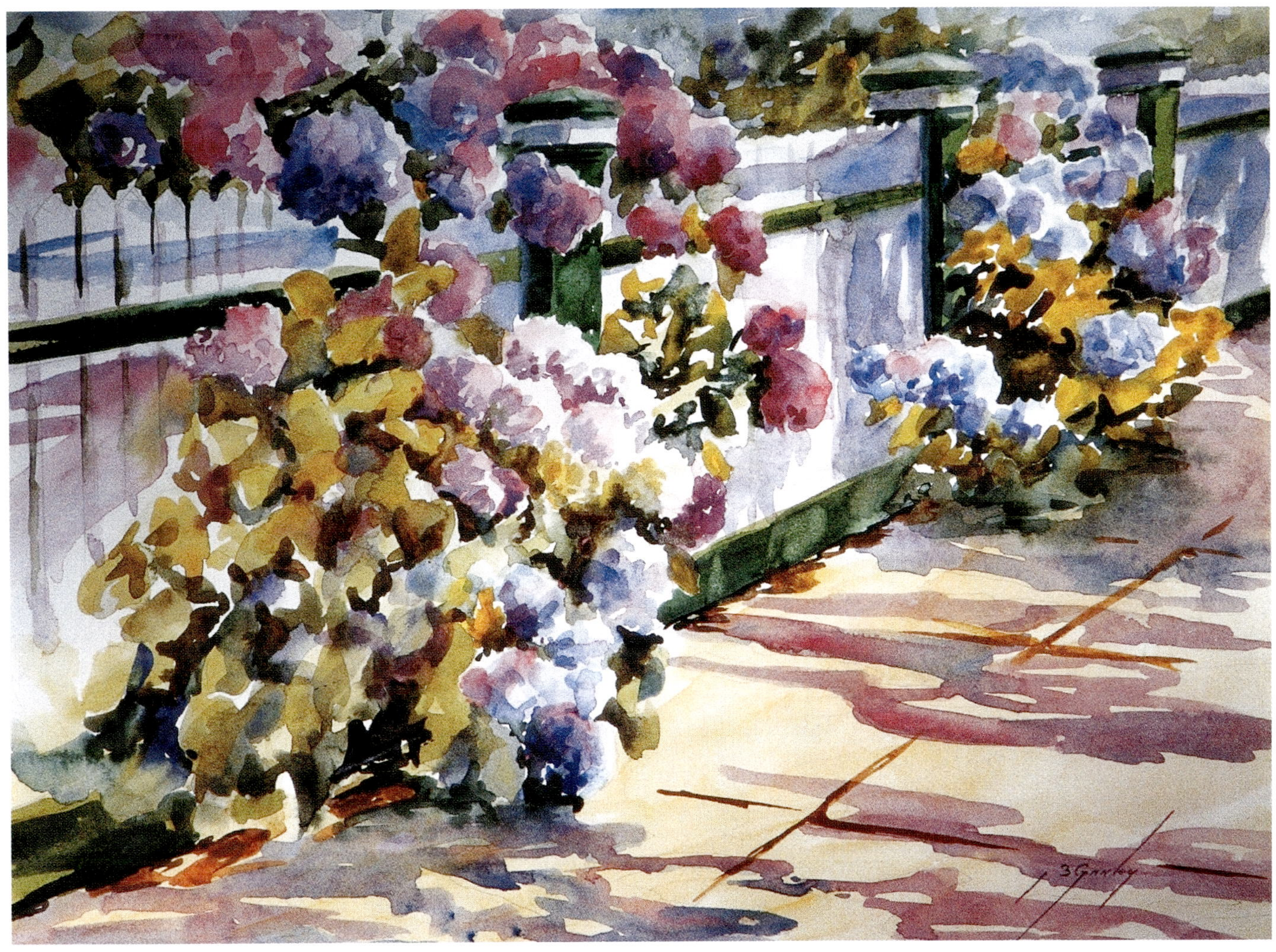

Step 6

Strengthen the flowers and greenery

- Continue to strengthen some of the flowers with further glazes of violet or blue. At this point add darks to the greenery and glaze over many of the pale green leaves in order to throw them into shadow.
- Especially at this stage, frequently walk away from your work to view it from different distances.
- Now that all the paper around the foreground flowers has received color, what previously seemed like saving too much white in the foreground flowers suddenly makes sense.
- Finish up with violet shadow shapes on the sidewalk cracks.
- We have now repeated the use of our main violet color combination throughout the picture, and in doing so we have effectively created a unified painting.

PROJECT 9 BURST OF SPRING

How to use tonal value to achieve depth

By carefully composing interesting and interconnecting designs in the flower masses these will appear far more realistic than if we painted each individual plant. Introducing a neutral shadow color throughout the picture will unite the whole painting.

We will be using cold-press paper for this project.

The challenges

- To consider perspective in our drawing skills, since the structure has so many bisecting angles.
- To make distant flowers recede.
- To avoid the pasted-on look of too many isolated individual shapes.

What you'll learn

- How to keep flowers looking loose.
- How to soften hard edges.
- How to correctly place eye-catching items.
- How to make corrections by rewetting and blotting.
- How to maintain continuity by weaving a neutral color throughout the painting.
- The importance of having your camera or sketching materials with you at all times.

Techniques you'll use

- Dropping paint into a trail of water.
- Wet-in-wet.
- Glazing.
- Lifting out color.
- Dry-brush and splattering.

Before you begin, read the entire project through so you know what's going to happen in each stage.

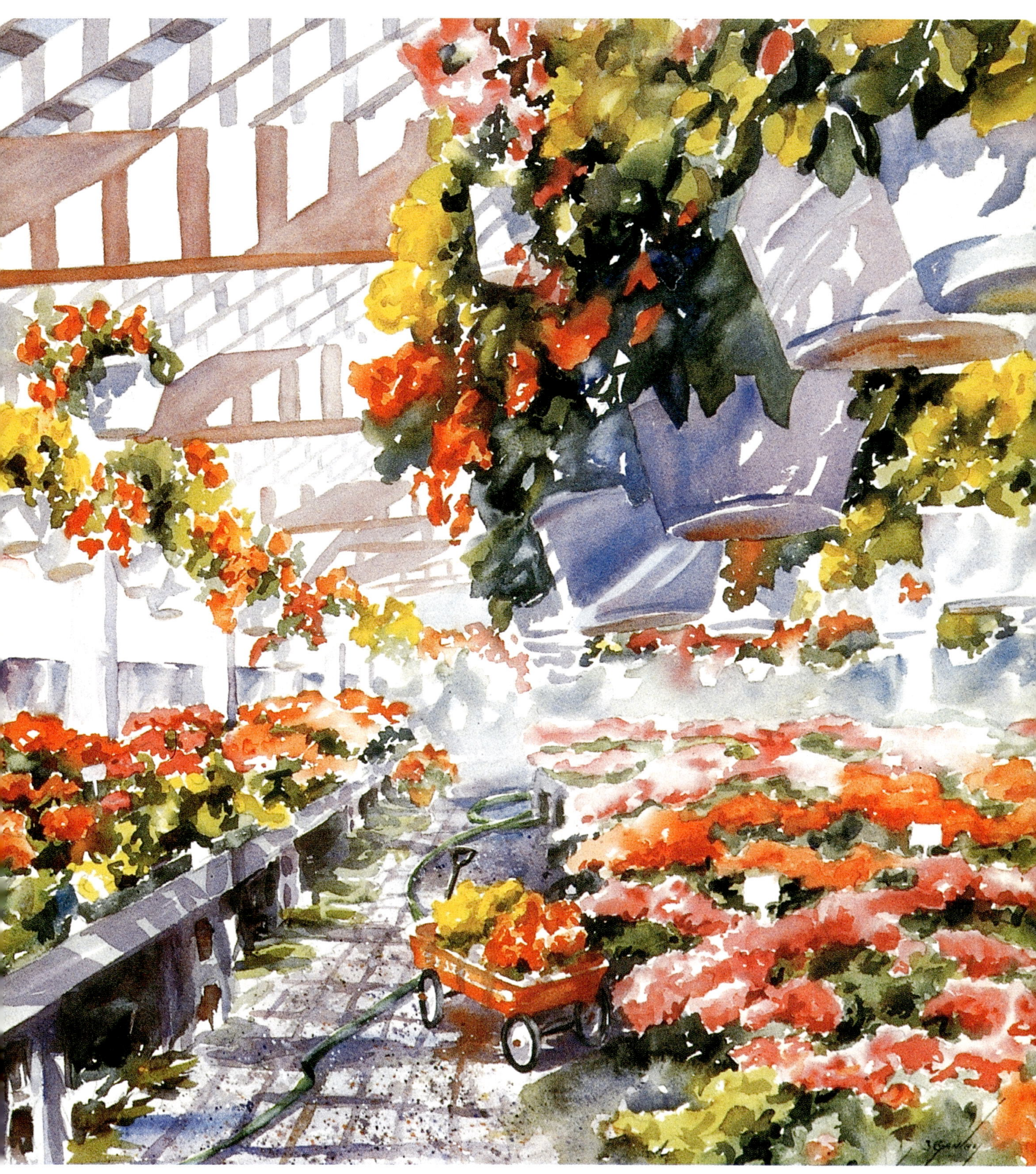

Burst of Spring, watercolor, 19¾ x 25" (50 x 64cm)

The materials you'll need for this project

Support

- Gator board as a support for the paper
- 140lb (300 gsm) cold-press watercolor paper

Brushes

- Daniel Smith 22-50 Series, Size #8 and #10
- Pro Arte Series 100, Size #12
- Fritch Scrubber (a stiff white nylon bristle brush with very short bristles, sold through Cheap Joe's catalog)
- Stiff round brush for mask application
- ¼", ½" and 1" flat brushes
- 2" hake

Odds and ends

- No. 2 pencil for the initial drawing
- Stapler and staples
- Waxed paper
- Permanent white gouache

Artist quality watercolors

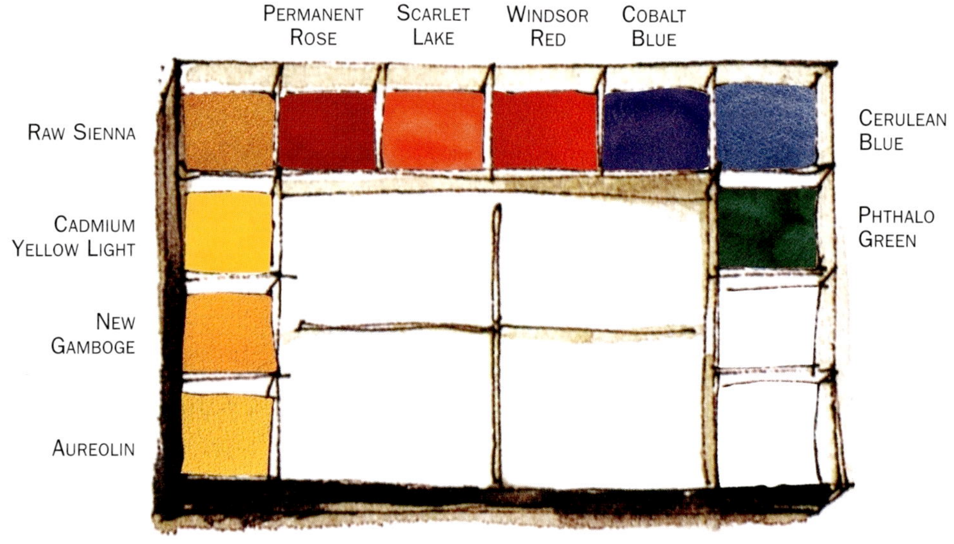

Thank goodness I had my camera

This greenhouse garden is one of my favorite haunts in the Spring — a time of year when I always have my camera with me. I am drawn to the explosion of color but the magical shadows on the ground and the cast shadows from the overhead beams can be mesmerizing. Over the years I have taken hundreds of photos , thank goodness, because subsequent owners roofed over the beams and that was the end of the magical shadows. So the lesson is: Keep a camera or sketchbook with you whenever you take even a short drive. You never know when you'll screech to a halt because the sun is hitting an otherwise ordinary scene, turning it into a truly magical subject.

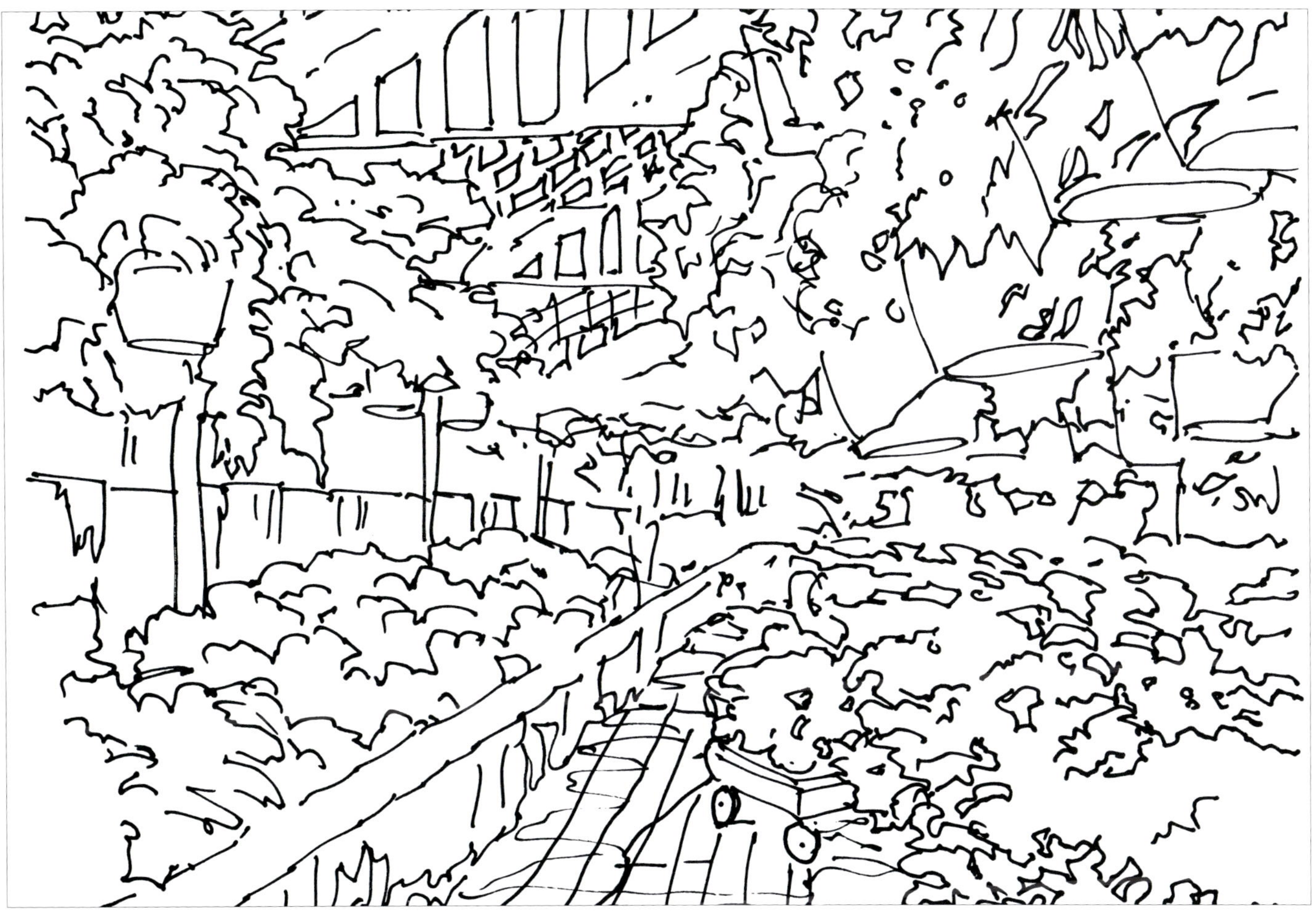

Step 1

Sketch or trace the initial drawing in pencil

The rules of perspective are imperative to make these beams look correct and you have to pull out all the stops, so to speak, to make them recede. The boards and their shadows become smaller and narrower with distance. In your initial drawing take the time to get the perspective absolutely right.

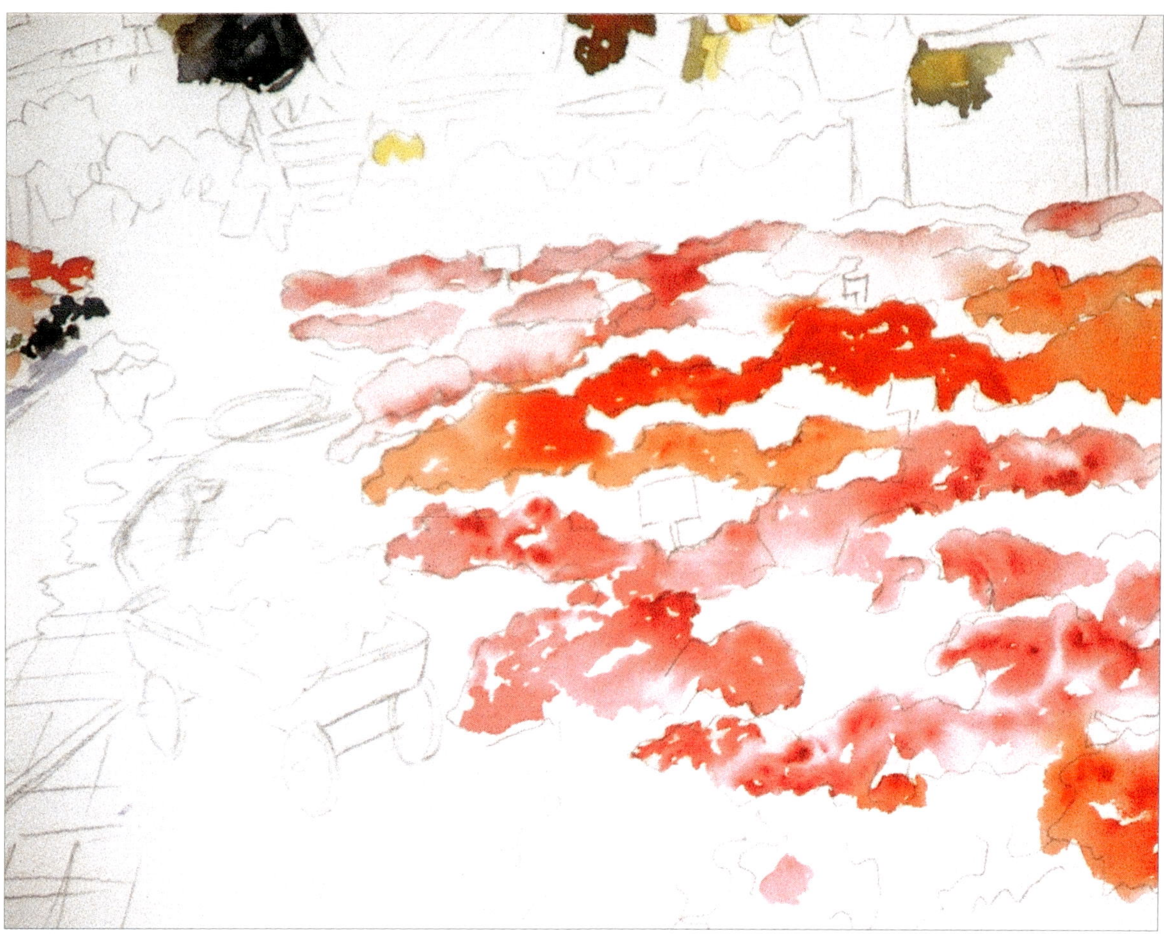

Step 2

Place the bright flowers and add the greens

- Start by placing the bright flowers at the top of the painting. A nice way to paint a mass of flowers and to keep them looking loose is to WET the area arbitrarily.
- Then drop in some Permanent Rose. The water will suck up the paint and swirl it around in lovely configurations. In some areas you can go back in with a loaded brush creating darker values in those areas. On the right start with yellows and work your way up to darker greens, using Phthalo Green and Cadmium Yellow Light and switching to New Gamboge, with a touch of Permanent Rose. Occasionally drop in some pure blues in some of the darker background foliage. Notice that the flowers are just barely outlined, not wet-blended. You'll soften those edges later.
- The greens at the top left are a little farther away from the viewer, so use a wet-in-wet technique to soften them, first drop in yellows (Aureolin and New Gamboge) and while still WET add greens. Soften items in the distance. Items closer to the viewer can have sharper edges.

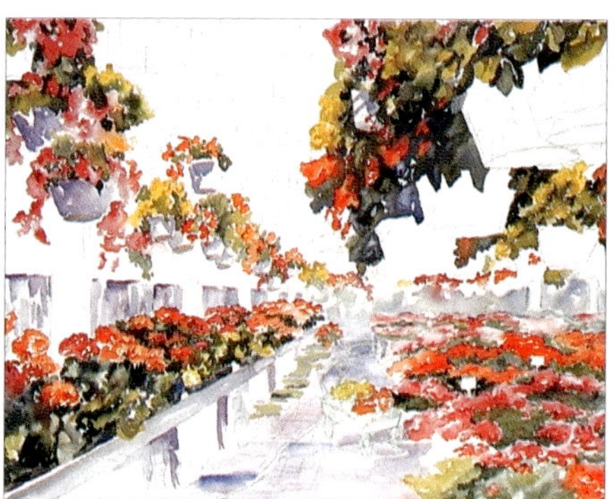

Step 3

Making realistic flower masses and adding greens

- For the flower mass on the bottom, work in small sections at a time, brushing in a trail of water, and in various spots along the water trail drop in pink (Permanent Rose) or red (Scarlet Lake) in various degrees of intensity. You want to have masses of color rather than dots of individual flowers. In the distance the pattern is long and skinny, becoming wider as it nears the viewer.
- Now add more greens to the lower left, and drop in Carmine in some darker areas of leaves. Also on the lower left, add deeper values to a few of the single flowers in the foreground. Then add greens to the lower right, and add some form to the flower masses using deeper Permanent Rose and Windsor Red. Don't overdo it. You don't want to turn your lovely soft washes in the distance into dots of color. Of course, if you do, then you can always rewet the offending darker colors and lift some of the color off with a damp brush, or blot it with a tissue.

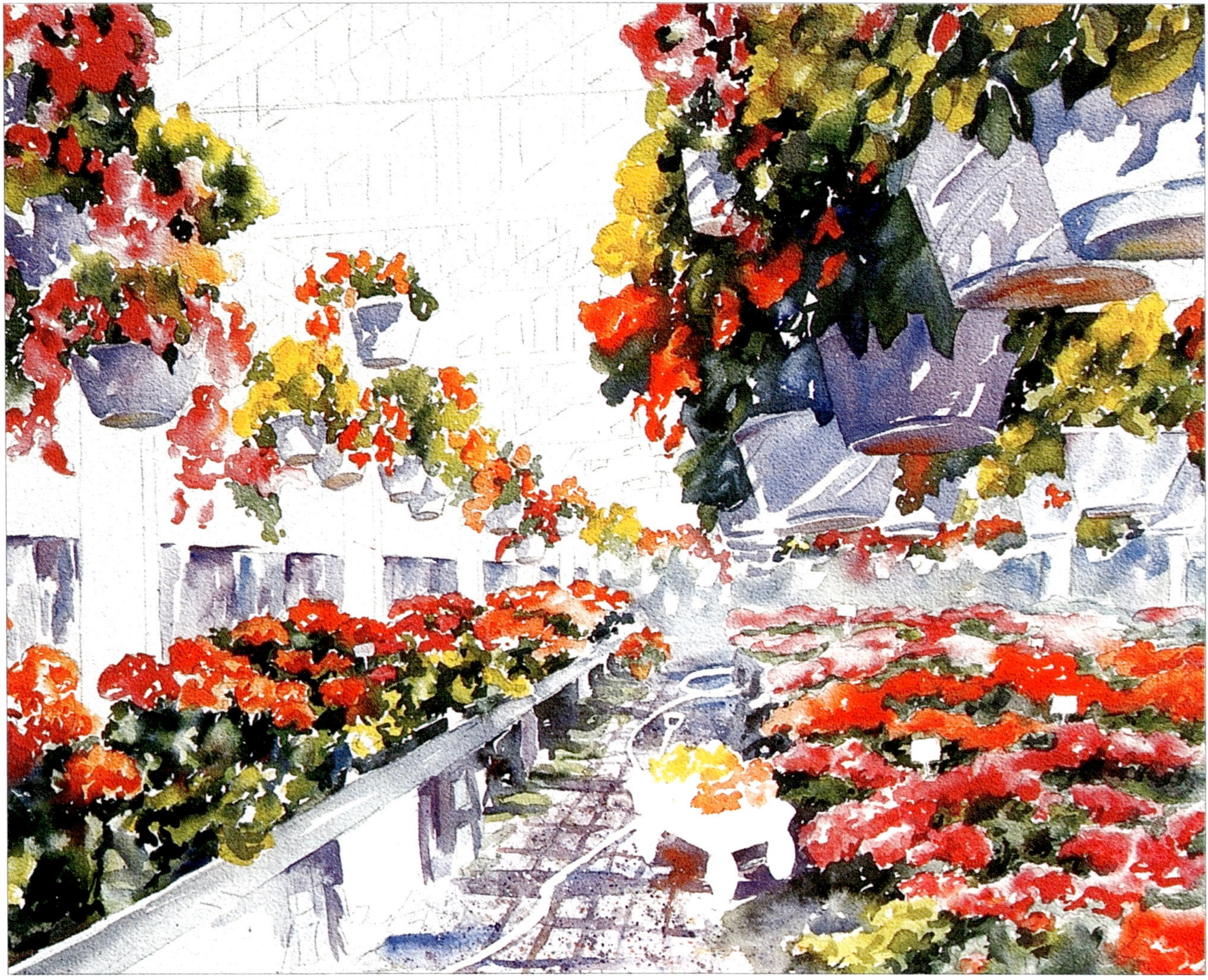

Step 4

Paint the windows

- Paint the greenhouse windows very loosely with a ½" flat brush. Use Cobalt Blue, Cerulean Blue and Permanent Rose in various combinations. Leave plenty of white shapes, especially near the front. Because blue-violet shadows will be added later, repeat these colors to maintain some continuity.
- Mask the hose and the wagon and its flowers and then paint the far background. Paint it by wetting that area and applying soft blue-grays, letting some of the pinks and greens from the distant hanging baskets meld into the soft wash. Continue this right down the pebbled pathway and over the masked areas. Keep this first wash light. When DRY, add texture and shadows.

Step 5

Soften edges to meld the flowers

- Up to this point you have a single dimension layer with mostly hard edges. For the red flowers, glaze over a portion of the flowers with Cobalt Blue and then without lifting the brush continue the stroke onto the surrounding leaves. This will soften the edges and meld the flowers into the plant. For some of the very dark leafy areas wet a small section and gently blot, establishing a lighter value within the leaf mass.
- In areas of flat leaves, glaze a wet wash of translucent Cobalt Blue or even Permanent Rose over a portion of the leaves, going right into the background. Now you have added another dimension to that area and, voilà, the flat appearance is gone!

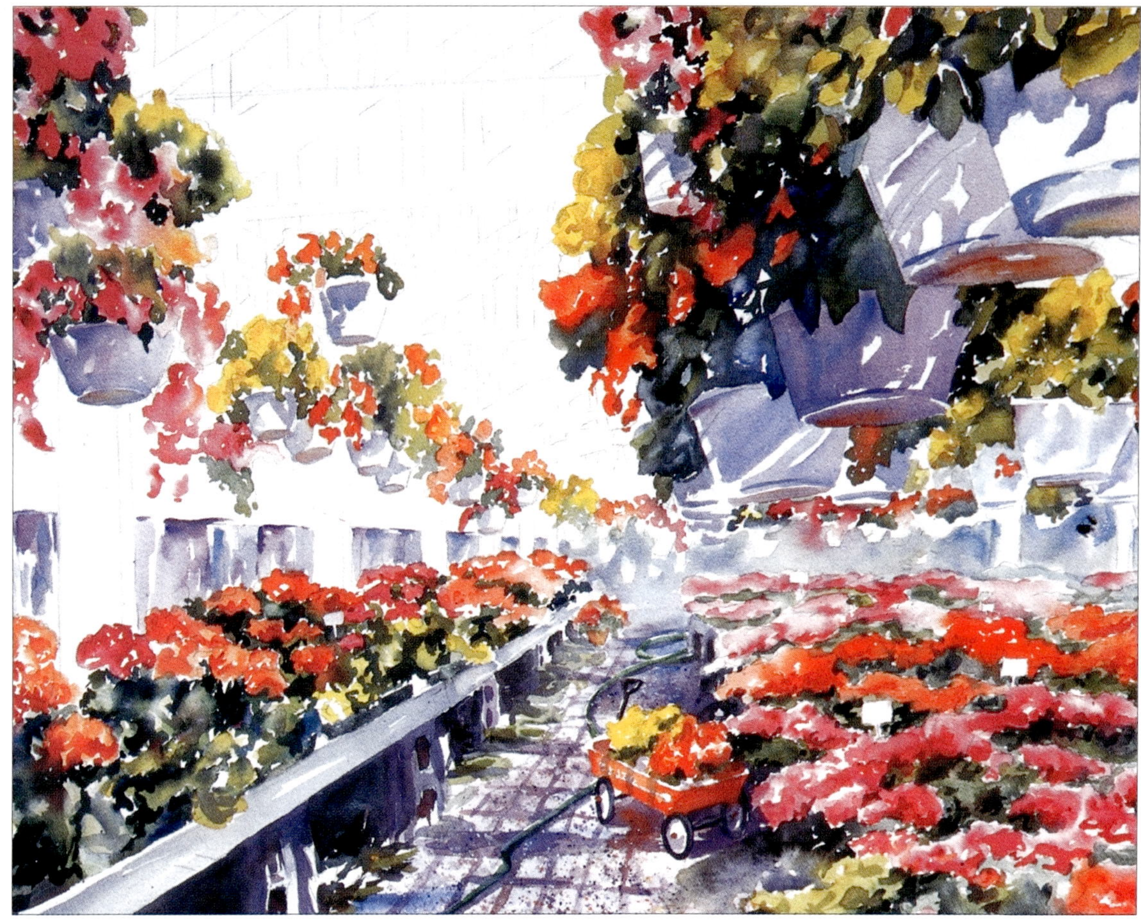

Step 6

Work on the flowerpots

- Using a gray mixture (Cobalt Blue, Permanent Rose and Aureolin, at times with more rose and at times with more blue), work on the shadowed areas of the hanging white flowerpots, being mindful of interesting edges. For the bottoms of the pots drop in a warm color while the wash is still wet — Scarlet Lake to Raw Sienna — to show the light being "bounced" from the warm flowers below; and add some of the same to the crossbeam shadows on the pathway.
- Texture the pathway with some dry-brush techniques. Use the side of a round brush that's slightly damp with paint on it, and gently drag it over the paper, just hitting the hills of the paper. Don't overdo this. After protecting the surrounding areawith waxed paper, splatter with darker grays, pure blues, and a few reds. When it's DRY, splatter with Permanent White gouache.

The wagon is still masked out.

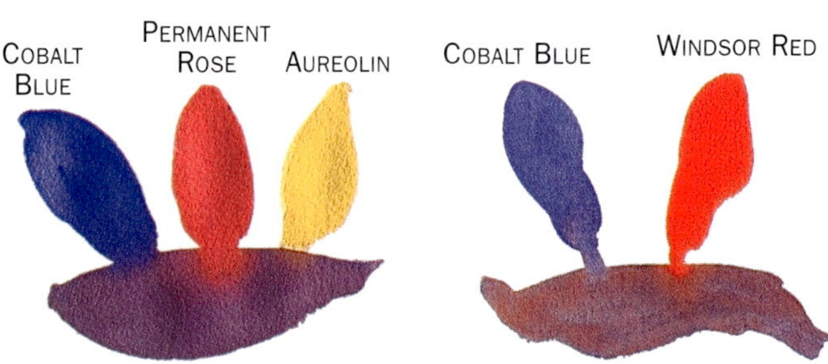

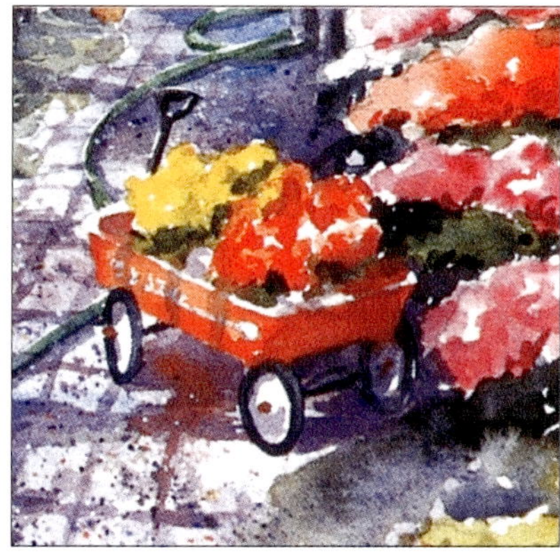

Step 7

Paint your wagon

- Peel the mask from the wagon.
- Paint the wagon with a variety of warm and cool reds. Note the lettering: It's there but is unreadable, which is as it should be. A few Cobalt-Blue glazes over portions of the wagon, going right into the pathway, will create a shadowed area, suggesting the wagon is part of the scene and not just pasted on.
- Loosely add warm darks to the underside of the left table, for added interest and sparkle saving some small bits of interestingly shaped white designs. Note that the red underside of the wagon is reflecting red into the wagon's shadow.

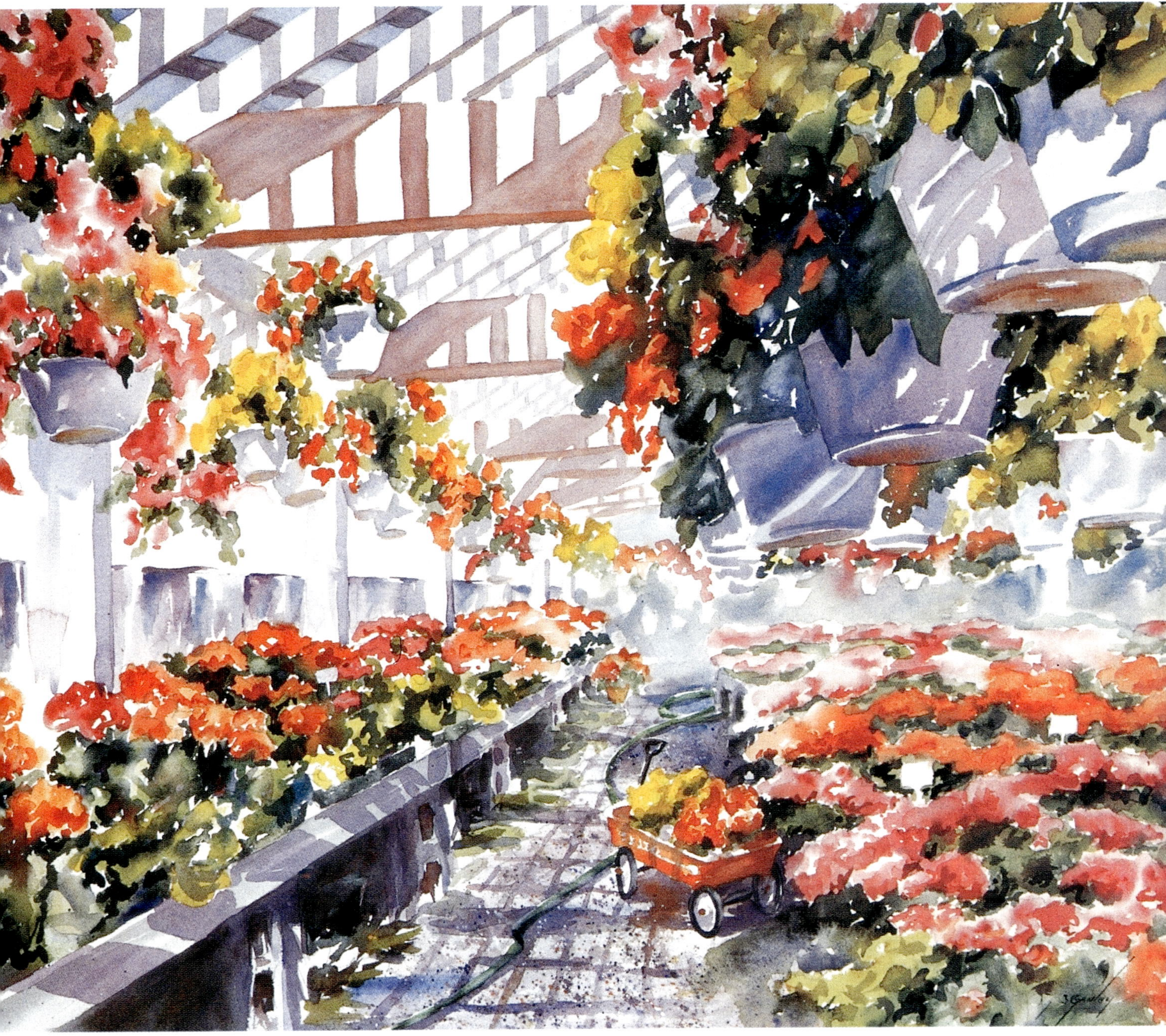

Step 8

Finish the beams, and the painting

- Finish off with the shadows on the beams, which obey the rules of perspective because of the care you took to get them right in the beginning. On the diagonal beams use our "base" color of Cobalt Blue, Permanent Rose and Aureolin, moving toward violet in the foreground and for distance changing to a softer and paler blue-gray. For the horizontal beams use a warmer mixture of Cobalt Blue and Winsor Red (a cool transparent red), again reducing the intensity as the boards recede. As a final touch add just a bit of a warm red (Scarlet Lake) in a glaze to show how the undersides of the large beams are reflecting all the warm color below.

PROJECT 10 DIPPED IN COLOR

How to use strong color and tonal values to add drama

By strengthening the color and value of shadows, and by carefully planning their positions and shapes throughout the painting, your painting achieves a sense of balance.
We will be working on cold-press paper.

The challenges

- To paint large washes of color in areas with intricate edges.
- To give a unified look to an area of large masses of flowers and greenery.

What you'll learn

- How to plan the flower placements in a large mass of flowers.
- How to choose the correct time of day for the optimal shadow effect.
- How to give flowers dimension by using added values.
- Why you should plan ahead to save pathways of white paper.
- How to use color changes in areas of shadow on different surfaces.
- How to use reflected light.
- How to lighten a large wash.
- The importance of using an area of a large wash as a place for the viewer's eye to rest in a busy composition.
- And more tips on using maskoid.

Techniques you'll use

- Glazing.
- Wet-in-wet washes.
- Masking large areas.
- Wet painting on dry paper.

Checklist

When painting a mass of flowers it's important to keep these aspects in mind:

- Balancing colors.
- Balancing shapes.
- Introduce a variety of shapes.
- Overlap and/or interconnect shapes.
- Place individual flowers facing different directions.

Here, I began this painting by locating my source of light. Since I wanted the main shadow to be almost directly beneath the flowerbox rather than angled off to either side, I picked close to midday to paint. Notice that the shadow, a major part of the composition, is nicely balanced within the composition.

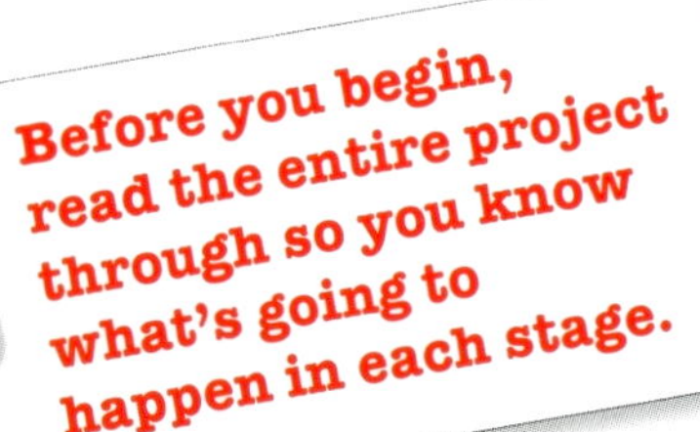

***Dipped in Color*, watercolor, 25 x 19¾" (64 x 50cm)**

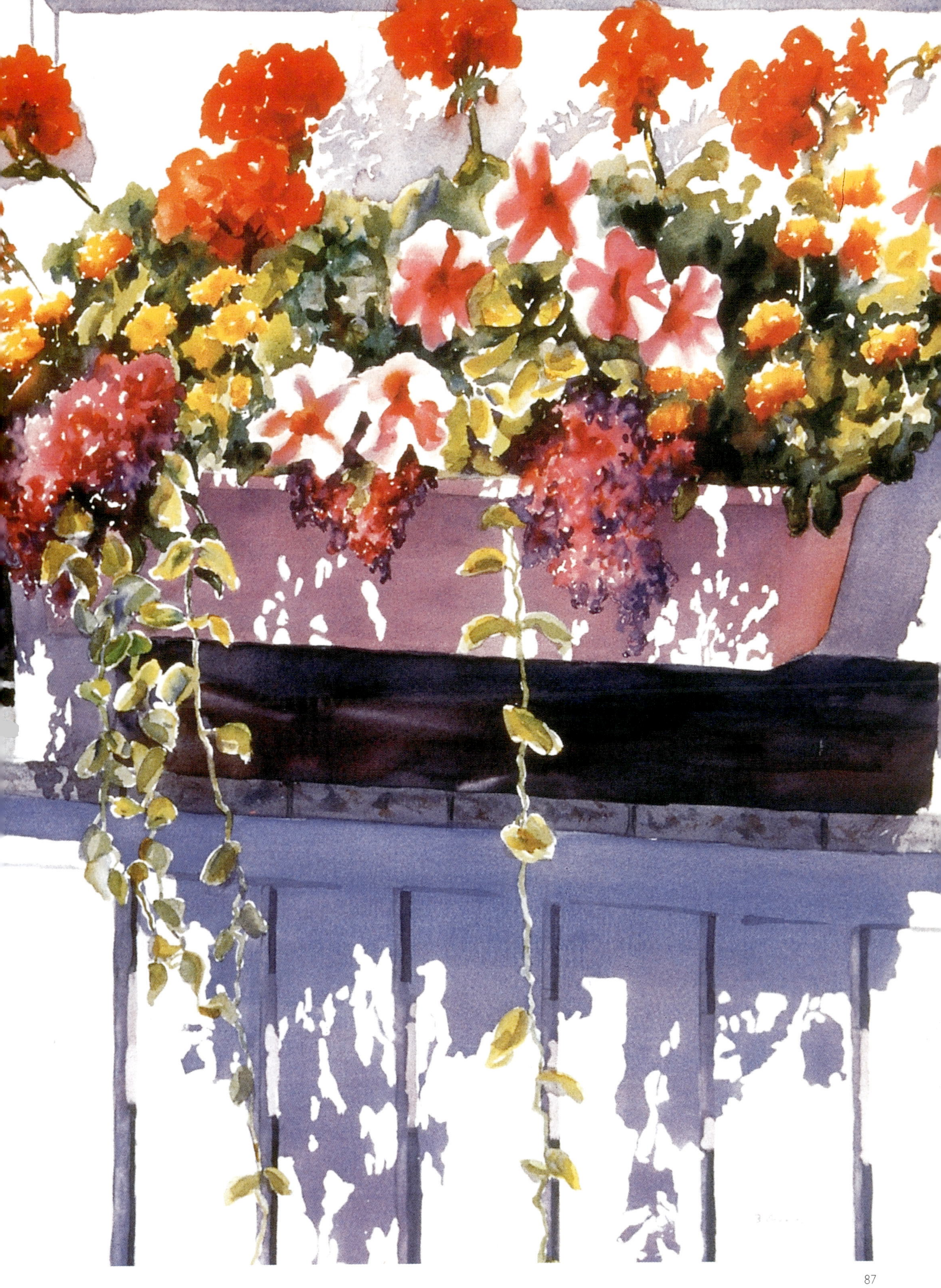

The materials you'll need for this project

Support

- Gator board as a support for the paper
- 140lb (300gsm) cold-press watercolor paper

Brushes

- Daniel Smith 22-50 Series, Size #8 and #10
- Pro Arte Series 100, Size #12
- Fritch Scrubber (a stiff white nylon bristle brush with very short bristles, sold through Cheap Joe's catalog)
- Stiff round brush for mask application
- ¼", ½" and 1" flat brushes
- 2" hake

Odds and ends

- No. 2 pencil for the initial drawing
- Stapler and staples
- Mild shampoo
- Tinted masking fluid

Artist quality watercolors

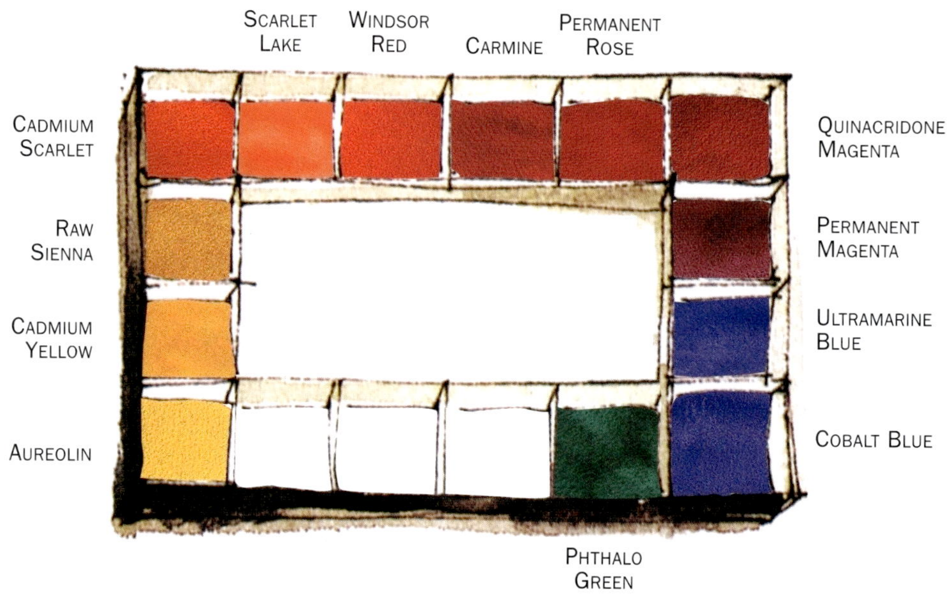

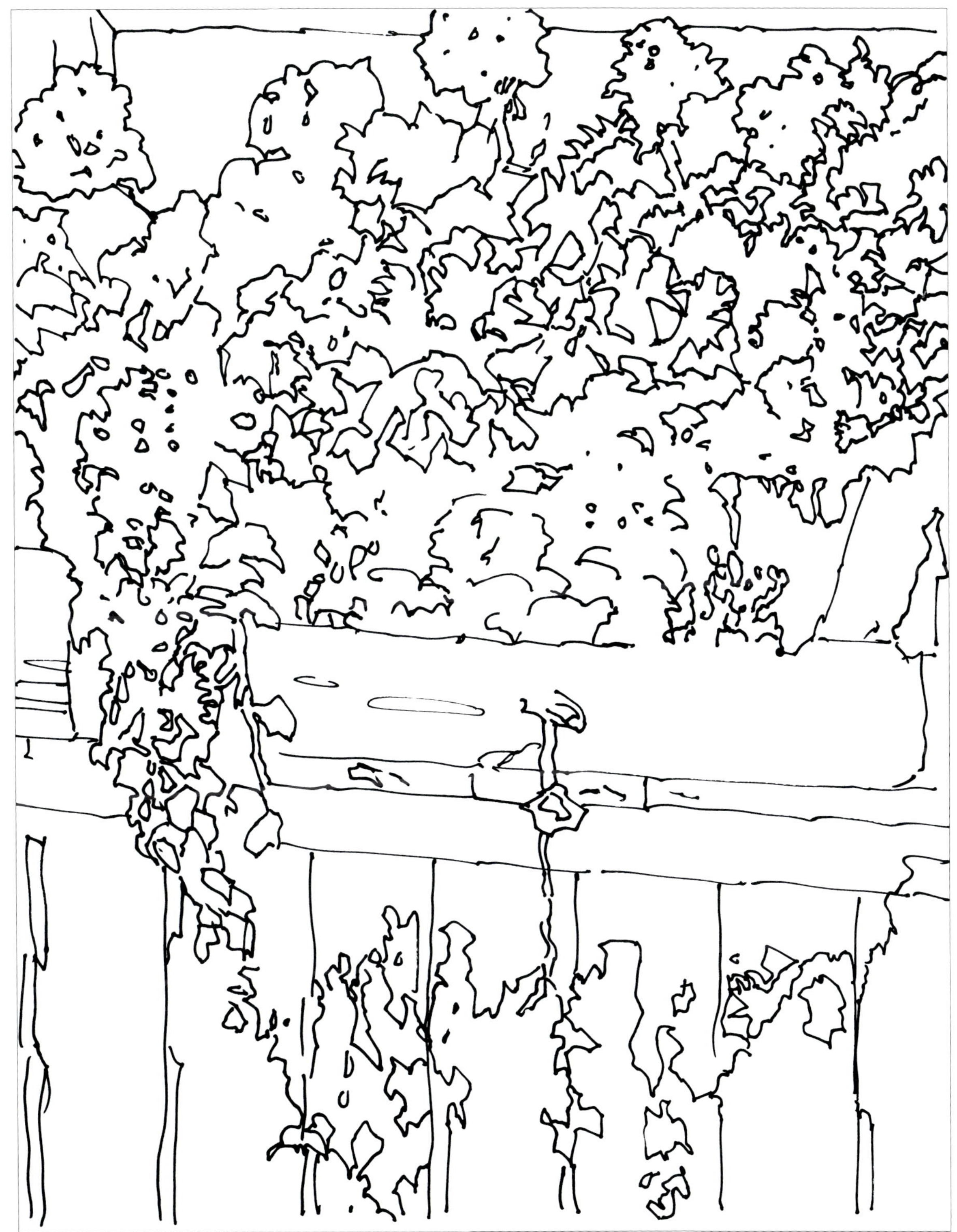

Step 1

Sketch, photocopy or trace this drawing in pencil

In this step, all we can see is a somewhat confusing mass of lines. It will be our task to turn the lines into flowers and make this flat drawing look three-dimensional.

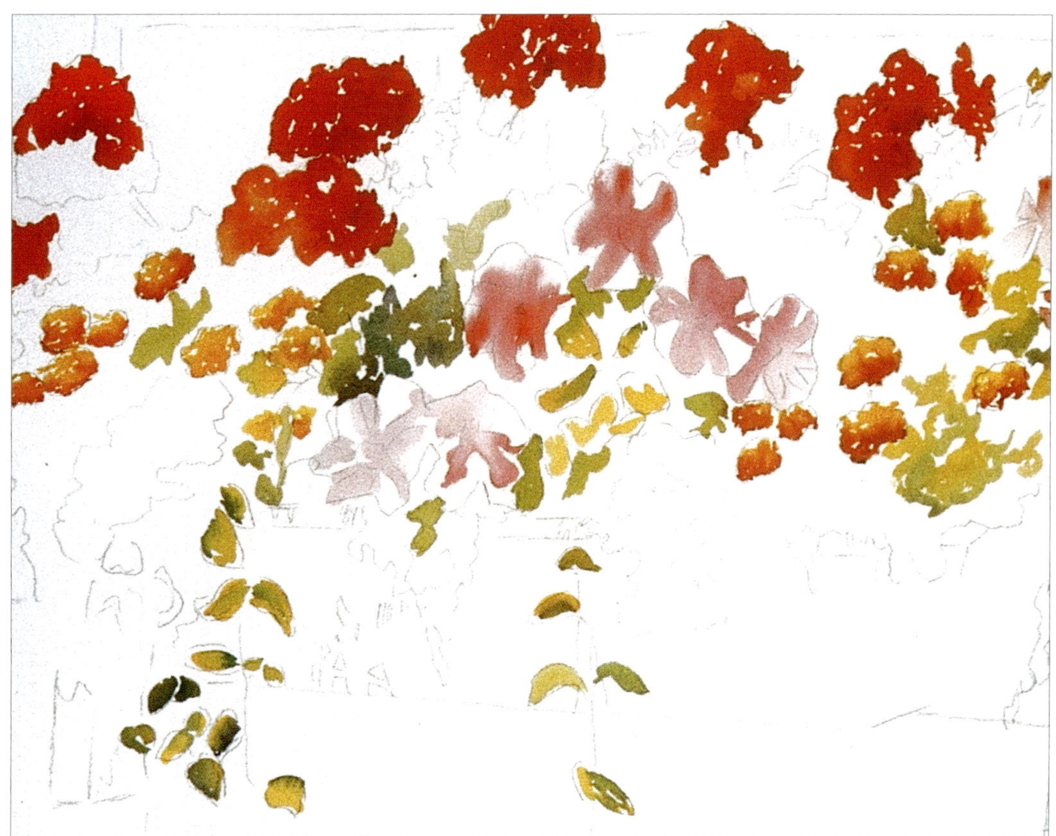

Step 2

Get started with your reds

For the most part in this project you'll be applying paint to DRY paper, wetting edges as needed. Occasionally you'll WET just one small area and then drop in color and let it swirl around, forming its own pattern within the wet area.

- Start with the red geraniums. Use a very warm orangey-red (Cadmium Scarlet) on the light side, gradually switching to Scarlet Lake then to cooler Windsor Red on the shadowed side. Then drop in a little Carmine or Permanent Alizarin where you want deeper shadows on the undersides of the flowers. Use a variety of pale pinks/violets for the center petunias, being careful to save the white areas, which will add sparkle to the center of interest. They will also be a pathway through the painting since they will connect the whites of the upper and lower portions of the painting, creating balance of the white areas.

Step 3

Paint the leaves

- Now start to spot in the yellows and pale greens for the lighter leaves, shading some leaves with a slightly deeper green. Start with Phthalo Green and Cadmium Yellow Light, at times adding just a touch of Permanent Rose to tone down the bright color.
- Paint around these lighter leaves with a medium-value green, varying the mixture of Phthalo Green with Raw Sienna to Phthalo Blue with Raw Sienna.
- Finally, to keep the colors varied, add the darkest greens with just a touch here and there of Carmine or Ultramarine Blue.

Painting the purple clustered flowers

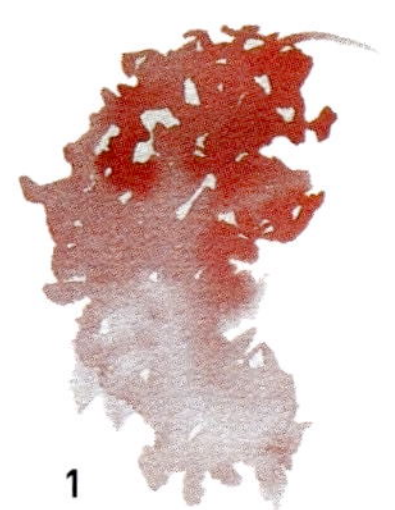
1

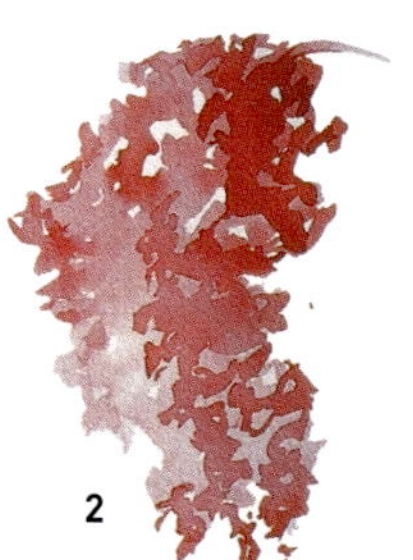
2

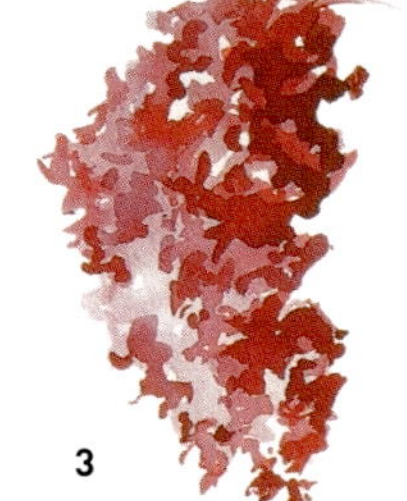
3

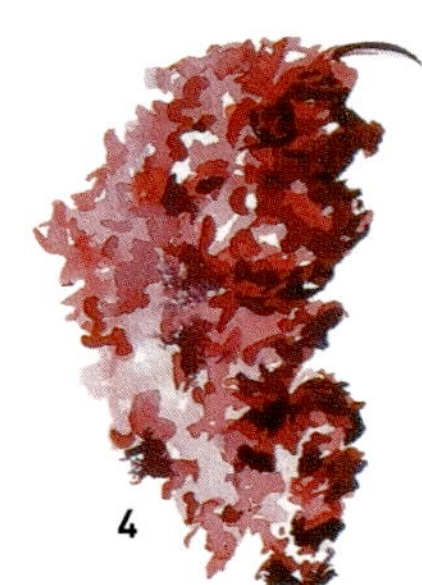
4

Note that there are three clusters rather than two or four — always an odd number — and that they vary in size and are not equidistant from each other.

Working from light to dark and paying attention to the wispy edges, apply four layers of color in various areas of the flowers.

1. Use your nicely pointed No. 8 round paint for this sequence. Start with Quinacridone Magenta applied in a pale wash, saving little areas of white. **2.** When that's dry apply Quinacridone Magenta darker and wet-in-wet in some areas and dry in others. **3.** Then use Permanent Magenta. **4.** Finally, use Permanent Magenta with Cobalt Blue.

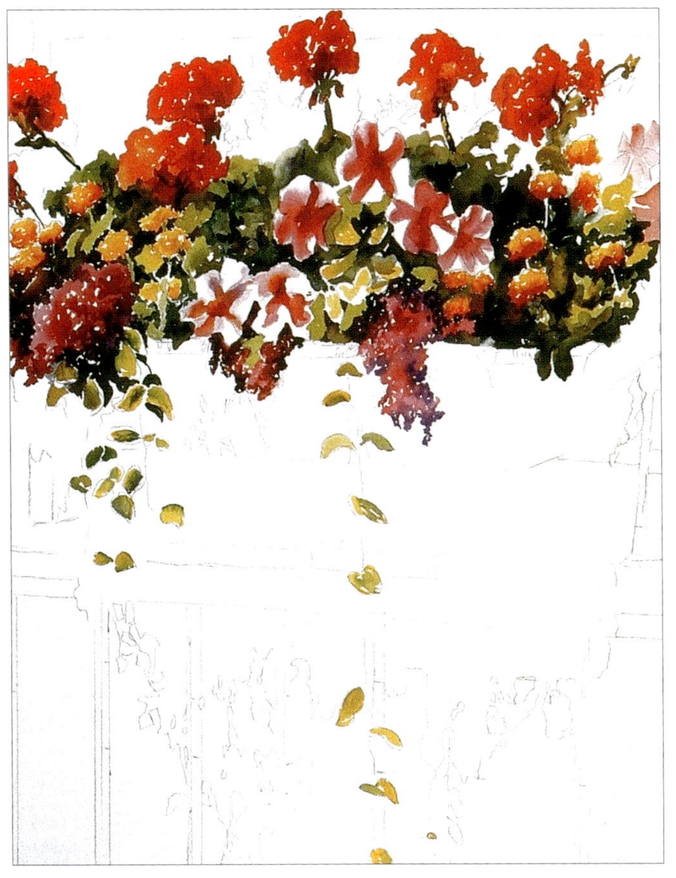

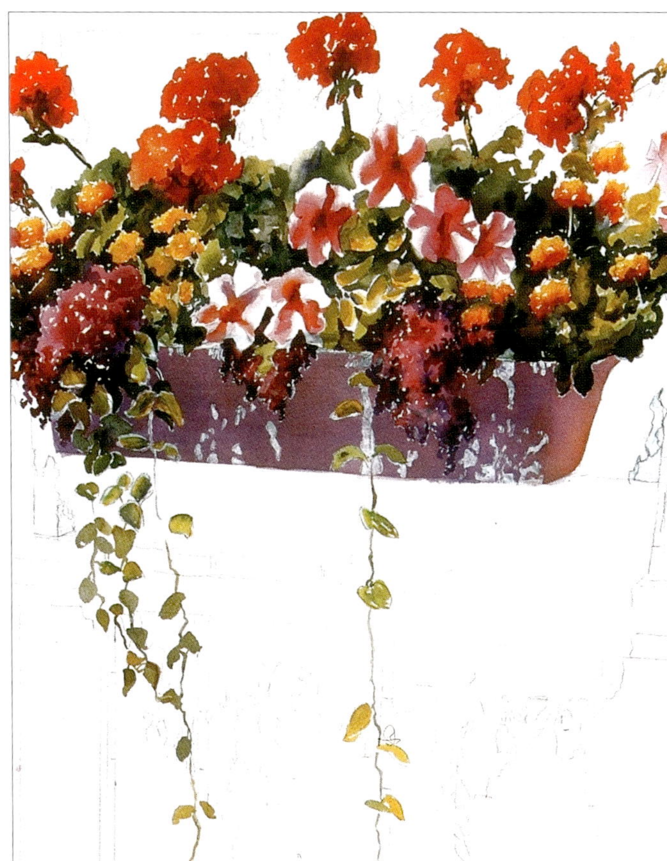

Step 4

Unify the greens

- Your next step is to unify the greens, which you do by glazing over some sections of the paler leaves with a pale to medium wash of Cobalt Blue. As you are applying this wash go right over the portion of the leaf that's in shadow as well as into the background of darker greens. This will loosen the crisp edge and cause some of the darker background color to flow into the newly applied wash, resulting in a more unified look.
- For the pale leaves under the violet flower mass, glaze with Quinacridone Magenta, a pale violet color. This will read as reflected light bouncing off the violet flowers.
- Refine some of the flowers, add the rest of the hanging vine, and let everything dry.

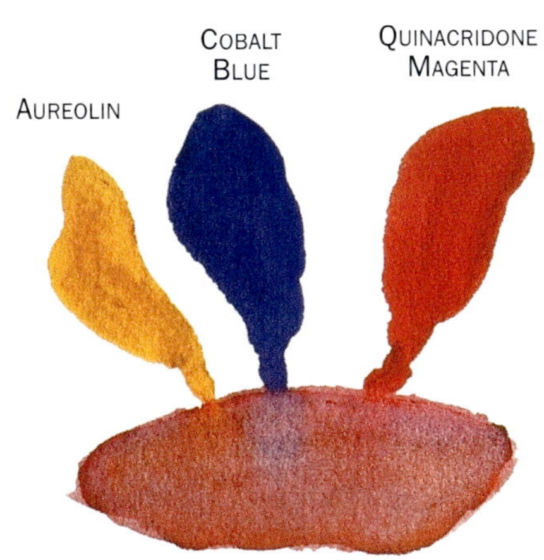

Step 5

Mask, paint and mop up puddles

- Using a stiff round or an old round brush first dipped in mild shampoo, add tinted mask to the flowers hanging over the flowerbox and to all the areas of the flowerbox that are to remain white. Then, you can quickly apply a single wash to the flowerbox without having to go around leaves and so on. For the wash, mix up a violet/blue/gray using Quinacridone Magenta, Cobalt Blue, and a touch of Aureolin — more towards the Magenta color. Use much less blue on the right side of the box, making that area brighter to show it has turned a corner and is receiving a different source of light.
- Because you're applying a wash over masked areas, note that the raised areas of mask create little dams that cause the wash to pool in those areas. It's important to pick these pools up or they will cause backruns as the area dries at different intervals. To do this, use a round brush with a good point that is barely damp. Just touch the point to the accumulated pool of color and it will mop the puddle right up.

HINT

Some artists don't realize that you can mask over already-painted areas. I've never had trouble with color lifting off when I remove mask from painted areas. But the same caution goes for mask no matter where you put it: Don't leave it on for more than two or three days or it will start to meld into the paper.

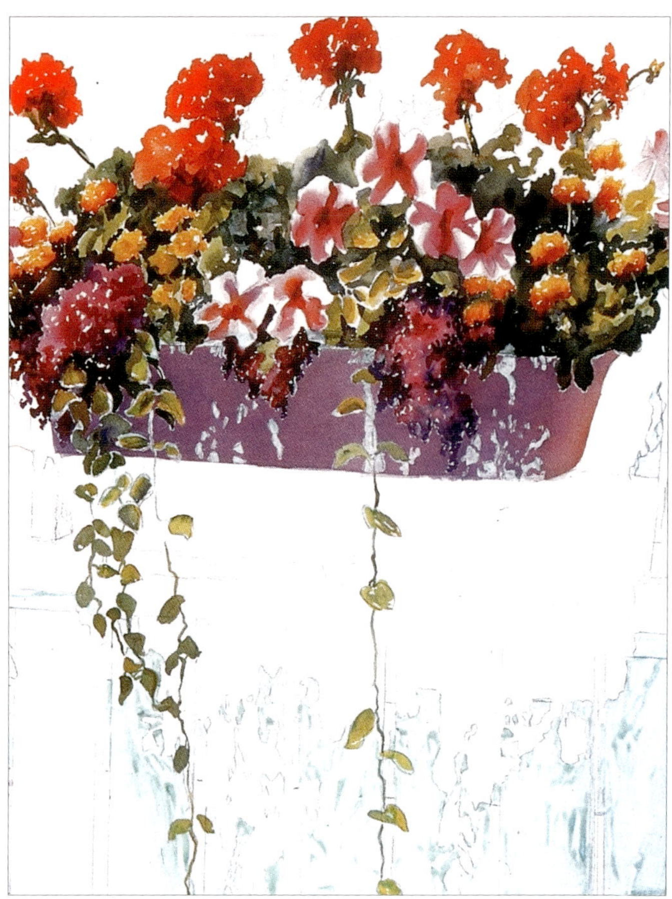

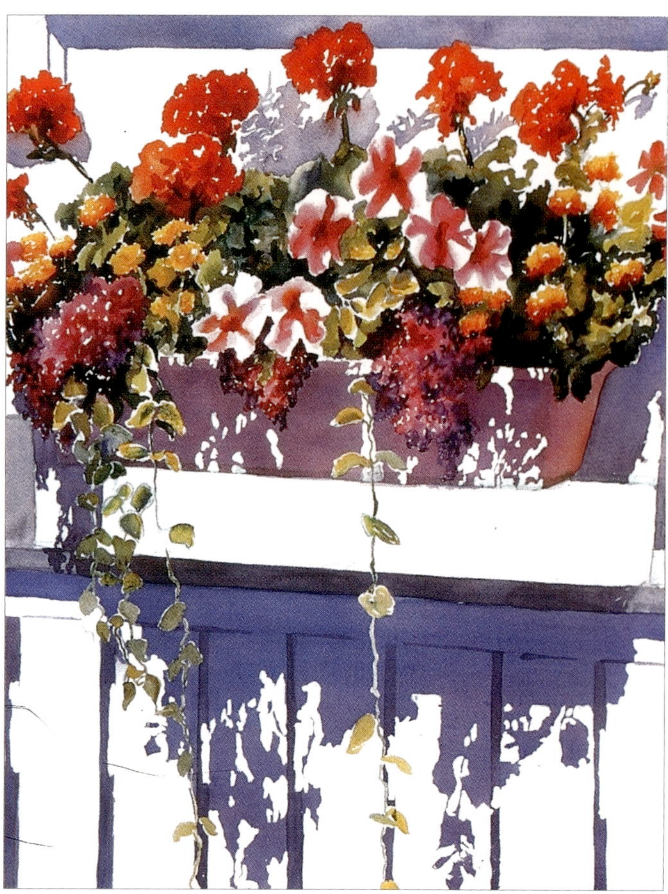

Step 6

Mask and paint the hanging leaves

- Follow the same masking procedure for all the hanging leaves and all the areas to be left white on the bottom portion of the painting.
- When the mask is DRY, quickly paint in the large mass of shadow using a 2" hake brush. Then with the brush still damp apply the color in left-to-right even sweeps across the paper, this time leaning more towards blue at the top and violet at the bottom.
- Use the same colors for the shadow on the flowerbox (Cobalt Blue, Quinacridone Magenta and Aueolin), but in different proportions, leaning more towards the blue than the Magenta.

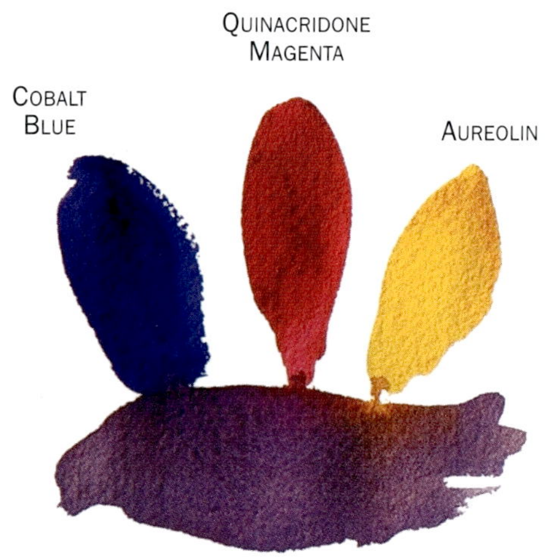

Step 7

Add details

- Once the painting is thoroughly DRY, remove the mask. Then add the finishing touches for the cracks in the lower boards.
- With the same colors add the flowerbox and the linear shadows on the upper part of the painting, which will serve to balance the completed work.

HINT

If a color turns out too dark, here's how to correct it. Wait until it's bone-dry, since the color is lighter when dry than when freshly applied and therefore you can more accurately judge just how dark it is. Then apply a wash of water with a 2" hake brush. When the whole area is very wet, go over it again with the still damp hake applying very slight uniform pressure and wiping the brush of excess color after each sweep across the paper.

This procedure can smooth out an unevenly applied wash — and sometimes even remove nasty blossoms!

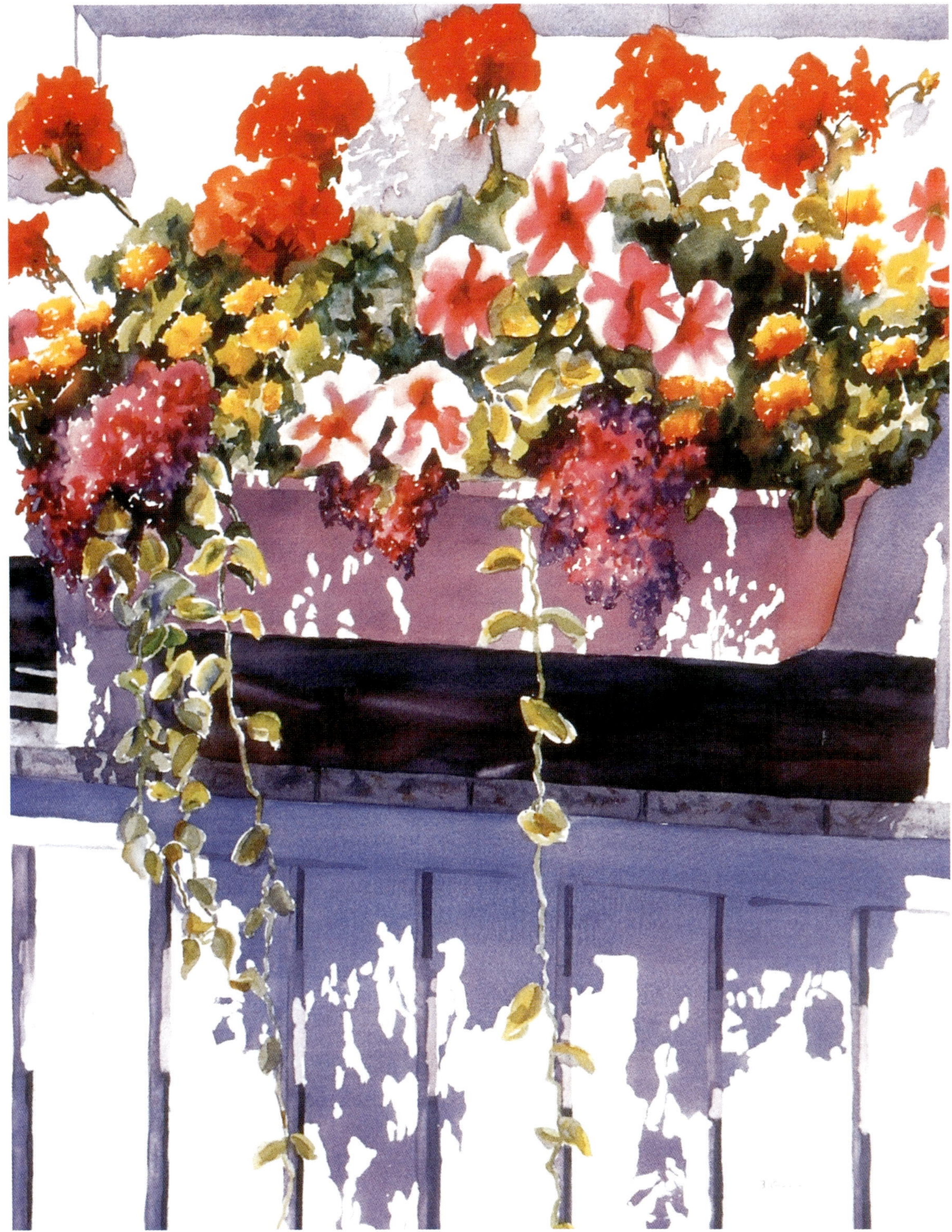

Step 8

Finish up

- Finish up with the darkest area beneath the flowerbox. Use Phthalo Green, Ultramarine Blue and Carmine, leaning more toward the warmer Carmine. Paint areas of deep recess in warmer tones to give a more inviting look, as opposed to a cooler, more formidable look.

- While that's still WET, lift out a barely visible floorboard with a thirsty, very slightly damp brush. This will signify that there is something happening within all that darkness.

By adding this intense area of dark you have gone from the very lightest end of the value range to the very darkest, in one painting. My own feeling is that this use of extreme values adds drama and acts as a magnet for the viewer's eyes. I call it pushing the values, and I do it frequently.

LEARNING POINTS

✓ Design

Without a good design you can't create a good painting, no matter how well you have mastered the techniques. Before you put pigment to paper, take time to plan.

- Define your center of interest — the area of the painting with the most detail and the most contrast.
- Evaluate possible eye-paths to lead your viewer into and around your painting.
- Plan the values in your painting to strengthen the eye-path and center of interest.

Even when you can't wait to get painting, take a few minutes to plan; it's well worth the investment.

✓ Glazes (layers)

Layering — or glazing — is the application of additional washes of color over DRY ones. Glaze when you want to:

- intensify color or value,
- change or create a color,
- combine colors that would turn into mud if mixed on your palette.

✓ Hard and soft edges

Painting gardens and flowers presents many challenges in painting contours, shape and undulations in the petals and leaves? Then there's the concept of space and depth in the garden. Mastery of hard and soft edges is the key to giving a three-dimensional look.

- An area of color with a very distinct and crisp edge is said to have a hard edge. Hard edges attract the eye and are often used at the center of interest and to separate the subject from the background.
- Soft edges are often called "lost." They are subtle transitions of color and can be used to represent curves and gentle shadow.

✓ Shadows

A good design incorporates dramatic shadows. Shadows lead the eye to the center of interest and provide the contrast that makes a painting interesting. When painting shadows, remember to:

- establish a consistent light source,
- use cooler colors when you want the shadows to recede, and
- include colors in your shadows.

If you're painting outdoors or are using field sketches, make sure to take into account those constantly moving shadows. It's best to take backup photos to capture light and shadow patterns.

✓ Primary colors

Have you ever wanted to mix a special color, but had no idea how? Understanding how your pigments interact makes it easier to mix the colors you want. Start with just the primaries to learn what your pigments can do.

- Create a simplified palette from six colors — the warm primaries and the cool primaries.
- Learn which of your pigments are biased toward warm and cool colors.

✓ Color temperatures

Each color on the color wheel is considered either warm or cool. You can use color temperature in combination with value to give your painting depth. Watercolor pigments, however, are never pure colors from the color wheel. Learn the color bias of your pigments so you can more effectively give your two-dimensional painting a three-dimensional look.

- Warm colors — red, yellow, orange — seem to come forward in a painting.
- Cool colors — blue, violet, some greens — seem to recede.
- Individual pigments, themselves primarily either warm or cool, may also contain a secondary warm or cool component.

✓ Complementary colors

You can create dramatic paintings using a complementary color scheme. Complementary colors, when used together, have unique visual properties. Use complementary colors to:

- Create interest and "vibration".
- Complementary colors also brighten each other when placed side by side.
- Gray down a color by adding its complement.

✓ Value contrast

Value is the lightness or darkness of a color. Your paintings will have more depth if you use the full range of values.

- Squint at your painting to reduce it down to its basic values.
- A value scale can help you incorporate the full range of values in your painting.
- Although you don't have to use every value on a value scale, use at least a light, a medium and a dark.

✓ Translucence

Flowers are often at their most beautiful when bright light shines onto and through their translucent petals. To achieve this effect, you must preserve the white of your paper. Wait to tone the lightest areas of the painting until you can determine how all the values of the painting relate as a whole. Be patient and wait. If you need to tone down a white, it's best to do it later in the process than too early — you can't retrieve it once it's gone.

✓ White flowers

Painting white flowers gives you the opportunity to create intriguing, colorful shadows. Shadows are more interesting if you paint them with color instead of a gray. As long as you leave the main part of the petal white, most colors will read as shadow. Do remember to keep the colors cool to give the illusion of depth.

✓ Yellow flowers

There are so many yellow flowers that it's important to know how to manipulate this delicate color. It's the lightest color on the color wheel, so creating dark values of yellow is a challenge.

- Add deeper yellow pigments to darken pale yellows.
- Use diluted yellow for light areas, less diluted pigment for dark areas.
- Add Raw or Burnt Sienna to yellow to create a warm deep value.
- Add Manganese or Cobalt Blue to create a cool deep value.

✓ Learning from mistakes

The most important thing you need to remember is: Don't be afraid of making a mistake. Most of them are fixable. Watercolor is a vibrant, flowing medium that allows us to do things we can't do with any other medium. We may never fully master it, but we can sure have a lot of fun learning all its possibilities.

ABOUT THE ARTIST

Betty Ganley began as an oil painter but more than 25 years ago switched to watercolor. Getting the best of both worlds of preparation, she was initially self-taught but subsequently attended more than 15 years of formal classes and workshops, many conducted by nationally recognized instructors. Betty is now an enthusiastic proponent of continuous education for artists through classes and workshops, as well as through "self-teaching with the aid of the amazing assortment of wonderful books now available." A member of 11 art societies, Betty is recognized as an inspiring speaker to art groups large and small.

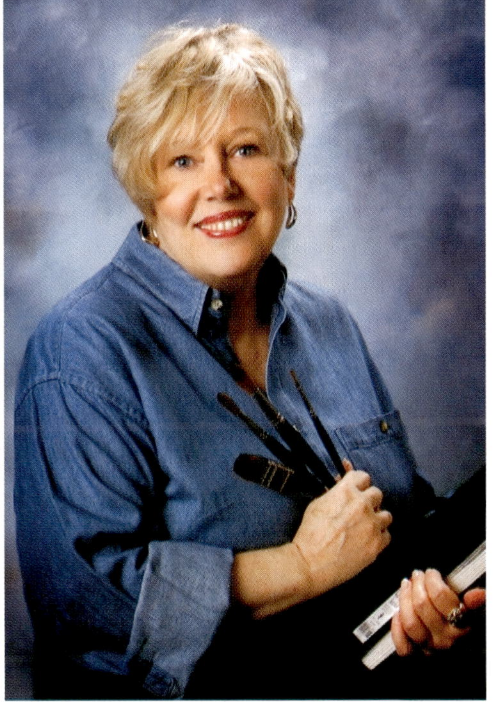

Betty's watercolors have received local, regional, national and international recognition in more than 75 juried shows. They have won more than 50 awards, many of them "Best of Show," and one of her paintings was selected among the top 100 in the prestigious *Arts for the Parks* competition in 2001. Her paintings have also been featured in magazines including *Australian Artist* and *International Artist* magazines and in compilation books. Her prizewinning watercolors are also to be found in private and corporate collections in her home state of Virginia and throughout the United States. Excellent examples of her work may also be seen on her website, www.bettyganley.com.

What artists want!

If you liked this book you'll love these other titles written specially for you.

Artist's Projects You Can Paint

Each of the 10 thrilling step-by-step projects in these books gives you a list of materials needed, and initial drawing so you can get started straightaway. Dozens of individual color swatches will show you how to achieve each special mix. Clear captions for every stage in the painting process make each project a fun-filled painting adventure.

- **10 Artist's Projects**
  FLORAL WATERCOLORS
  By Kathy Dunham
  ISBN: 1-929834-50-0
  Publication date: August 04
- **10 Artist's Projects**
  FAVORITE SUBJECTS IN WATERCOLORS
  By Barbara Jeffery Clay
  ISBN: 1-929834-51-9
  Publication date: October 04
- **10 Artist's Projects**
  WATERCOLOR TABLESCAPES LOOSE & LIGHT
  By Barbara Maiser
  Publication date: Spring 2005
- **10 Artist's Projects**
  LANDSCAPE STYLES IN MIXED MEDIA
  By Robert Jennings
  Publication date: Spring 2005
- **10 Artist's Projects**
  EXPERIMENTS WITH IMPRESSIONISM EN PLEIN AIR
  By Betty J. Billups
  Publication date: Spring 2005

Art Maps

Use the15 Art Maps in each book to get you started now!

Art Maps take the guesswork out of getting the initial drawing right. There's a color and materials list and plenty of tit-bits of supporting information on the classic principles of art so you get a real art lesson with each project.

- **15 Art Maps**
  HOW TO PAINT WATERCOLORS THAT SHINE!
  By William C. Wright
  ISBN: 1-929834-47-0
  Publication date: November 04
- **15 Art Maps**
  HOW TO PAINT WATERCOLORS FILLED WITH BRIGHT COLOR
  By Dona Abbott
  ISBN: 1-929834-48-9
  Publication date: October 04
- **15 Art Maps**
  HOW TO PAINT EXPRESSIVE LANDSCAPES IN ACRYLIC
  By Jerry Smith
  ISBN: 1-929834-49-7
  Publication date: December 04

How Did You Paint That?

Take the cure for stale painting with 100 inspirational paintings in each theme-based book. Each artist tells how they painted all these different subjects. 100 fascinating insights in every book will give you new motivation and ideas and open your eyes to the variety of styles and effects possible in all mediums.

- **100 ways to paint**
  STILL LIFE & FLORALS
  VOLUME 1
  ISBN: 1-929834-39-x
  Publication date: February 04
- **100 ways to paint**
  PEOPLE & FIGURES
  VOLUME 1
  ISBN: 1-929834-40-3
  Publication date: April 04
- **100 ways to paint**
  LANDSCAPES
  VOLUME 1
  ISBN: 1-929834-41-1
  Publication date: June 04
- **100 ways to paint**
  FLOWERS & GARDENS
  VOLUME 1
  ISBN: 1-929834-44-6
  Publication date: August 04
- **100 ways to paint**
  SEASCAPES, RIVERS & LAKES
  VOLUME 1
  ISBN: 1-929834-45-4
  Publication date: October 04
- **100 ways to paint**
  FAVORITE SUBJECTS
  VOLUME 1
  ISBN: 1-929834-46-2
  Publication date: December 04

How to order these books

Available through major art stores and leading bookstores.

Or visit: www.internationalartist.com

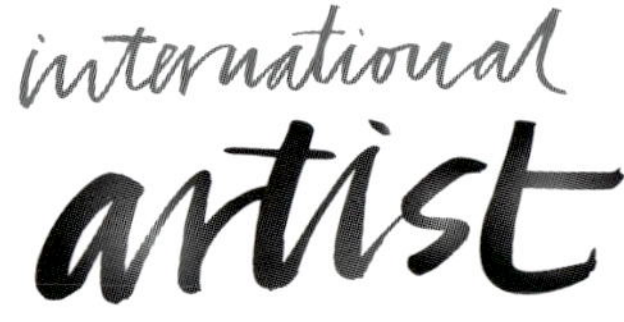